To Charlie
from
Keith

about a famous Australian engineer.

# SIR JOHN MONASH

*Also by A. J. Smithers*

THE MAN WHO DISOBEYED
Sir Horace Smith-Dorrien and his enemies

# Sir John Monash

*by*
A. J. SMITHERS

LEO COOPER · LONDON

*First published in Great Britain, 1973, by*
LEO COOPER LTD
*196 Shaftesbury Avenue, London WC2H 8JL*

*Copyright © 1973 A. J. Smithers*

*ISBN* **0 85052 095 9**

*Printed in Great Britain
by Ebenezer Baylis and Son Ltd
The Trinity Press, Worcester, and London*

## CONTENTS

| CHAPTER | 1 | The Colonial | page | 15 |
|---|---|---|---|---|
| | 2 | An Army of a New Model | | 29 |
| | 3 | The Mustering of the AIF | | 37 |
| | 4 | Australia was There | | 62 |
| | 5 | Gallipoli Summer | | 86 |
| | 6 | Sari Bair and Evacuation | | 114 |
| | 7 | The Western Front and Salisbury Plain | | 133 |
| | 8 | The Third Division goes to War | | 149 |
| | 9 | Interlude | | 184 |
| | 10 | The Corps Commander | | 191 |
| | 11 | A New Doctrine of Warfare | | 222 |
| | 12 | Australia Victrix | | 241 |
| | 13 | The Last Battle | | 262 |
| | 14 | Australia Goes Home | | 276 |
| | 15 | Back to Concrete | | 285 |
| | 16 | Envoi | | 290 |
| | | Notes on Sources | | 294 |
| | | Index | | 297 |

## ILLUSTRATIONS

*facing page*

1 John Monash with his wife, 1891     80
2 Colonel Monash in Egypt, 1915     80
3 General Sir William Bridges     81
4 General Sir Cyril White     81
5 General Sir William Birdwood     81
6 Lieutenant-General Monash presents a V.C.     96
7 King George V confers a knighthood on Monash     96
8 'Billy' Hughes and Keith Murdoch     97
9 The AIF entertain the Prince of Wales     97

*Nos 4, 5 and 8 are reproduced by kind permission of the Imperial War Museum and No 3 by kind permission of the Mansell Collection.*

# AUTHOR'S NOTE

Nobody is more conscious than I of the imperfection of this account of the life and work of Sir John Monash. There are reasons additional to my own shortcomings. His private papers, which are voluminous, are deposited in the National Museum at Canberra but they are not available to researchers. The Australian Jewish *Herald* on 16 May, 1958, published a letter from the General's grandson deprecating the fact that somebody was reputed to be writing a biography and expressing the hope that nobody would attempt the task without reference to the family papers. These, the writer explained, were being used as the basis of a book then in course of composition. So far as I am aware, it has not yet been published.

One would, naturally, wish to respect the expressed wishes of Sir John's posterity but to observe them would mean the complete abandonment of any attempt to tell the story of this illustrious man. That would, in my view, be a great pity for time passes and memories grow dim. In Australia a generation is growing up to whom Monash is simply a name from history along with Governor Philip, Burke and Wills. In England he is almost forgotten. These things should not be.

I cannot sufficiently acknowledge my debt to those who have had the kindness to supply me with information or to direct my attention to the places in which it can be found. Sir Robert Menzies, who as a rising young statesman was acquainted with the General, has been good enough to read the typescript and to furnish me with a copy of his speech made at the unveiling of the statue of Sir John with permission to quote from it. Mr Rupert Murdoch has also helped very materially with information about his father, Sir Keith Murdoch, whose influence on the fortunes of the First AIF was considerable. The Vice-Chancellor of Monash University, Dr J. A. L. Mathieson, and Dr A. G. Serle, Reader in History at the same foundation, have been generous with their time and without their unstinted help I should have abandoned the task in despair. Lieut-Colonel A. G. Hollings of the Australian Military Staff in London has been another tower of strength. As always, I owe much to the people in charge of the great libraries at Australia House, Canada House, the Royal Commonwealth Society, the U.S. Embassy, the Imperial War Museum and the Royal United Service Institution. Various elderly French gentlemen, all of whose names I never ascertained, gave me the benefit of their personal recollections of events in the Somme valley during the summer of 1918.

Fortunately there is a fair amount of material available regarding Sir John's early life and his activities during the First World War are well documented. A selection of his letters was published in 1936 by his former Intelligence officer and, while they cannot tell of all his thoughts and actions, they are sufficiently comprehensive to give a fairly good picture of the man. Many works by other people who came into contact with the General in one way or another have given glimpses of him but the gaps remain. It would be pleasant to think that some day, before it is too late, they will be filled in.

# INTRODUCTION

'THE only General of creative originality produced by the First World War.' That was Mr A. J. P. Taylor's assessment of Sir John Monash. It does scant justice to men such as Sir Ernest Swinton, Sir Hugh Elles and Sir Hugh Trenchard but, taking the words as applying to those who held high commands in the Army, it is true. Mr Lloyd George, in his unrelenting efforts to denigrate Sir Douglas Haig, takes it even further. 'Since the war I have been told by men whose judgment I value,' he wrote, 'that the only soldier thrown up by the war on the British side who possessed the necessary qualities for [the chief command] was a dominion general. Competent professional soldiers whom I have consulted have all agreed that this man might and probably would have risen to the heights of the great occasion. But I knew nothing of this at the time. No report ever reached me either as War Secretary or Prime Minister which attributed any special merit to this distinguished soldier. The fact that he was a civilian when the war broke out may have had something to do with the tardiness in recognizing his exceptional abilities and achievements.' Mr Lloyd George was being disingenuous. He had been in Paris in July, 1918, when the news of the welcome victory of Hamel first came in to hearten the dispirited statesmen and he had sent the Australian general a message of congratulation. After that his interest in him seems to have fallen off; it was also only true in the narrowest sense that Monash had been a civilian when the war started. He had then been a colonel in the militia of his country and the inference that he had instantly changed bowler for bush-hat and begun to learn the soldier's art from scratch is colourful rather than true.

John Monash was a man of many talents. His parents had come from Prussian Poland and were devout Jews. They had been far from well off and his boyhood had been passed in the Australian outback, a world of billabongs and boomerangs, bunyips, bull-roarers and Cobb's Coaches. At the price of great sacrifices by them he had been educated at a public school and university where he graduated in engineering. In addition to these credentials he qualified in law, had more than a nodding acquaintance with medicine, spoke fluent German and passable French, was a pianist of near-professional competence, sketched to a standard higher than that of most amateurs and was well versed in archaeology. Like Cromwell, he came late to war and was nearly 50 when he first experienced battle. In some ways this was an advantage to him, for the duties of men of his age and seniority are not those of the young men who lead the charge sword in hand. Monash's great talents were for planning and, by means of lucid and careful exposition, for the communication of every detail of his plans to those who would have to execute them.

Dr C. E. W. Bean, appointed Official Australian Historian by the acclamation of his fellow journalists, noted at an early stage that Monash would be a better commander of a division than of a brigade and a better corps commander than either. Events proved the shrewdness of his judgment. As a brigadier at Gallipoli, Monash had been unremarkable; as commander of the 3rd Australian Division, which he trained and took to France, he acquired a high reputation under Plumer at Messines and Third Ypres. It was the victorious summer of 1918, however, that saw him at the height of his career, when, in less than a hundred days, the Australian Corps passed from the defence of Amiens to the breaking of their section of the Hindenburg Line.

In many ways he was a lucky general. His predecessor, Sir William Birdwood, and his splendid Chief-of-Staff, Brudenell White, had made a nearly perfect instrument which they handed to him to wield. These wider horizons gave Monash the chance to expand that he needed. Almost alone of Australian generals, having been untouched by the experience of Bullecourt, he understood the tank and employed it to the full extent of the capacity it possessed in 1918. To him it was a tool, a power tool; there were some things it could do and others that were still beyond its powers. There can be no doubt that, had technical progress been fast enough, the tank in Monash's hands would have ceased to be the hand-maiden of the infantry and blossomed into the armoured force that it later became. Perhaps it is not without significance that two of the best Australian divisional commanders, Rosenthal and Hobbs, were architects. The disciplines of engineering and architecture were by no means irrelevant to war as it was fought in France then.

It is misleading to use of Monash the adjective 'creative', for he created nothing new. The measure of his genius was that he learnt how to wring the greatest possible usefulness from every tool he was given and this at times meant a departure from accepted practices. He did not invent the smokescreen or the machine-gun barrage but, under him, they achieved a perfection not seen elsewhere. He did not initiate the conference, but the conferences of the Australian Corps became a legend. Nor, Mr Lloyd George would have been saddened to hear, had he any eccentric schemes for winning the war in obscure places far away. Monash was a dedicated Westerner.

His personal relations with the other generals were invariably excellent. Plumer he admired and he must have learnt much from the thoroughness of Second Army. His immediate chief, Rawlinson, was exactly the man with whom Monash would get on. Rawlinson's father had been a famous archaeologist in the Near East and Sir Henry, the least hidebound of generals, had shared his interest. War apart, there was much common ground between the two men and they greatly liked and respected each other. With Currie, the Canadian, Monash's relations were 'most cordial'. But the oddest of all was the friendship he enjoyed with Sir Douglas Haig. The Chief had some taste for exotics, as his choice of Sir Philip Sassoon, scion of a rich Parsee family, for his private secretary proclaims. Monash he found to be a man who, for all the difference in their backgrounds, was entirely congenial to him and he took him into his confidence to an extent which seems unprecedented. The August conference at Villers Bretonneux produced an odd selection of Christian soldiers with Clemenceau the agnostic, Foch the rigid Catholic, Haig the Presbyterian and Monash the Jew.

Jewish generals were something almost unknown to the army, but, if heredity counts for anything, there is no reason why a descendant of Joshua, Gideon and the Zealots who fought against the Emperor Trajan should not march with the successors of Marlborough and Wellington. Monash never tried to play down his Jewishness; he was an important member of the Jewish community at home and, naturally enough, he selected as officers of his personal staff members of his own faith. Those with eyes to see could readily descry that here was a kind of Jew different from the South African millionaires and the old clothes dealers of Petticoat Lane. Monash undoubtedly was interested in the Jewish national home but it does not seem that he was ever an active Zionist.

He was a single-minded man. Dominant amongst his emotions was a fervent patriotism and a love for Australia and Australians. So long as the war lasted he had no thought for anything but his duty towards the winning of it; when it ended, despite the fact that he had not seen his wife and daughter for four years, he readily agreed to remain in England for a further year in order to make sure that his men had every possible chance to prepare themselves for the kind of life they wanted when they returned home. Such absolute dedication is rare.

In the last ten years of his life, he 'went back to concrete', as he put it. In addition to the chief part in building the great electricity supply industry for his native Victoria, he became one of those indispensable men dear to all governments. He had never been active in politics and was consequently trusted by everybody. His enormous prestige was useful, whether it was a matter of settling a police strike, advising about the size of the navy or going to India to unveil a pillar at New Delhi. The history of Australia has been such that she never needed to produce a Washington or a Thomas Jefferson, still less a Lincoln. It was at the Peace Conference that Australia suddenly realized that she was no more a group of half a dozen colonies in a remote corner of the earth but a nation, and a nation whose future could be unbounded. Amongst the names of the men who brought about this consummation none stands higher than John Monash.

CHAPTER ONE

## The Colonial

THE year 1831 was one of anxiety throughout divided Poland. In that part of the country which owed grudging allegiance to Imperial Russia, an insurrection, inspired by the events in Paris the previous summer, had been suppressed with all the cruelty and expertise that the Czar disposed. In the Prussian part of the land things were not as fearful, for the Prussia of von Bonin was very different from the Prussia of Bismarck still to come. Nevertheless, Krotoschin was not the most comfortable of towns in which to live: it was near enough to the frontier with Russia to be accessible to the Poles whom the Partitions had sundered from families and friends. In particular, it was the cultural centre of those of the Jewish faith throughout the whole of Poland.

Amongst the most respected figures in the Jewish community of Krotoschin was Bar Lobel Monasch, the publisher of religious books. He could trace his ancestors with certainty to that Rabbi Alexander who had lived in Breslau nearly a century earlier and all his family had been firm adherents to and teachers of their ancient beliefs. Bar Lobel and his wife Mathilde had ten children; his third, the boy Louis, who was born in that year, came early to the conclusion that the life of an under-privileged, even sometimes a persecuted, European was capable of improvement and, not surprisingly, he interested himself in the fashionable quest for gold. The gold craze in California was past its booming peak, South Africa was in the middle of a native war and was, so far as anybody knew, innocent of the metal. It was to the fields of Ballarat that men directed their attention in the 1850's, and to Australia Louis Monasch decided to go as soon as he reached his majority. He sailed, with the blessing of his father, in 1853, as an emigrant in the ship *Julius Caesar* out of Stettin.

Once in the colony, Louis soon found that his business acumen would make him a living by methods less crude than wielding a pick and shovel. The country was a market ready and waiting for manufactured goods of every description and, in the year of his arrival, Louis became junior partner in the firm of Martin & Monasch, Soft Goods Importers, 19 Little Collins St, Melbourne. The firm proved reasonably profitable but it was apparent to the junior partner that goods far cheaper than those of Manchester or Bradford were to be had from Poland if somebody would take the trouble to organize their supply. It is possible that this was not his only reason for wanting to return home, for Louis Monasch had become a naturalized subject of Queen Victoria at the earliest moment the law allowed and, at 31, he was still a bachelor. In 1862, he went back to Stettin to buy stock and there he married Bertha Manasse, sister to the wife of his elder brother. They did not linger in Europe — Prussia was on the point of starting the war with Denmark over the Duchies — and by June, 1864, they were installed in a small house in Melbourne. On 23 June, 1865, Bertha was delivered of their first child, a son, at 1 Richhill Terrace, Melbourne.[1] They named him John. For all its biblical origin, it was a fitting name for a boy born under the flag of the Union, but when his two sisters arrived they were named after the older branch of the family, Mathilde and Louise.

Unlike many of his kinsmen, Louis Monash (he had dropped the 'c' on naturalization) made no fortune. There was little money in the home but Mrs Monash did much to compensate her children for the lack of things that mere wealth can supply. She was a woman of culture, if of no great education, and John from his earliest beginnings learnt to appreciate the beautiful; from his mother he also acquired much knowledge of music, for she was a pianist of talent and he proved an apt and willing pupil. Music

---

[1] Here begin the contradictions and lacunae that bedevil his biographer. The date of birth is that shown in his birth certificate. Everywhere else, including his tombstone, it appears as the 27th. The same certificate shows the address by the good Jewish name of Rachel Terrace. But the nameplate in the street spells it as above.

remained throughout his life one of his great loves and his competence was such that he might, had other matters not intervened, have made his living as a concert pianist. The family was bilingual and the boy equally at home in English or German. His intellectual capacity, it soon became plain, was something out of the ordinary. In the ancestral fashion, the Monashes stinted themselves of many things to ensure that he had the best education the colony could furnish and it began at a school called St Stephen's on Dockers Hill. Here he attracted the attention of the headmaster by reason of an unusual capacity for all English literary subjects and also by his skill at making amusing drawings, an art that never deserted him.

In 1874, when John was 9, Louis, for business reasons, moved to the little township of Jerilderie in New South Wales accompanied by the family. There John became the pupil of an expatriate Englishman named William Elliott, who discovered in him a natural bent for higher mathematics. His time at Jerilderie, however, was not one of unabated schooling, for the outback life made a strong appeal to him. He became an excellent horseman and spent much of his time amongst the aboriginal inhabitants whom he came to know well.

One day he made the acquaintance of Australia's most famous, if not most laudable, citizen. The rumour went about that Ned Kelly himself was in the hotel at Jerilderie. John, fascinated, crept through the bush in order to observe the great man taking his ease on the verandah. In spite of his precautions, Kelly spotted the small figure and called him over. 'He gave me much sound advice,' Monash later recorded, though he did not say what it was.[1]

In time, Elliott had to admit that he could teach young Monash no more and strongly advised that such gifts should not be wasted. Louis could not leave Jerilderie but both he and his wife were determined that John must continue his studies, cost what it might. They therefore decided that Louis must stay and attend to his business while John and his mother went back to Melbourne, a considerable self-sacrifice by both parents. So in

[1] This story persists though there appears to be no evidence to support it.

1877, Bertha Monash returned with her son to Melbourne where he was enrolled in the Scotch College, the best school in the town. There was, inevitably, little money to spare — but they managed; John played his part by becoming a model pupil and eventually rose to be 'Dux'.

Though the family remained entirely orthodox, John Monash was the complete young Englishman when he went up to Melbourne University in 1881. He found himself disappointed by the academic standard; many of the lectures he was obliged to attend were dull, prolix and repetitive. Since he had the facility of learning easily and possessed a retentive memory, he fell into the habit of cutting some of them. This was not a symptom of idleness, for no undergraduate ever worked himself harder. To help out with the housekeeping he sometimes assisted, for modest fees, other students; he devoured every book imaginable and did not permit an hour to pass without it being turned to some useful purpose. He attended the sittings of the Law Courts, haunted the Public Library and spent hours watching the builders and engineers at work making a fine, modern city. He played no games, but never missed a concert and, indeed, is said to have been an occasional performer in the symphony orchestra.

Too wide a variety of interests was his undoing; in November, 1882, he failed his first-year examinations and, after receiving the condolences of his friends, 'I returned home, there was great mourning and I felt fit to drown myself.' It was a miscalculation never to be repeated; it had all been too easy so far. He had entered the university in March and by May he was writing in his diary; 'Went at 10 o'clock to Melbourne Public Library where I read part of Hallam's *Middle Ages*, the *Encyclopaedia Britannica* article on Haroun-al-Raschid and finished Congreve's *Love for Love*. In the evening, went to Archibald Forbes's lecture on "The Armies of Europe".' For the next few months he attended the lectures as well and next time he experienced no difficulty. Indeed, he obtained an Exhibition to the value of £25 which not only paid all his university fees but also provided him with a haul of books. They included Gibbon and Josephus's *Wars of the Jews*.

Though his interest in military affairs was developing, he

# THE COLONIAL

continued also to expand his eclectic interests. He took lessons in painting, kept up his music, became a skilful wood carver and kept himself fit by walking and mountain climbing. His only failure was as a conjuror, at which he rather fancied himself; but, by all accounts, he was not a very good performer.

Shortage of money still dominated the life of the little household and in 1884, he had to leave the university without taking a degree in order to earn his living. The available accounts of the next three years of his life do not exactly tally, but the differences are not of importance. Two events are certain, events which shaped the course of his future. At the age of 19 he obtained a position with the firm of David Munro & Co, the engineers who were building the new Princes Bridge. He also joined the newly raised Militia as a private soldier. The reasons for the former need no explanation but it is less certain why he should have wished to become a part-time soldier. Probably there was no short and simple answer; his interest in soldiering was entirely unforced, such small sums of pay as might go with it would be welcome and it has also been suggested that it was a stepping-stone towards the *entrée* into Melbourne society. The causes are not mutually incompatible.

In his engineering work he was entirely successful, despite his lack of a professional qualification. Within two years, at an absurdly early age, the firm entrusted him with everything connected with the earth works both on the banks of the river and in its bed, together with responsibility for all the masonry. In the University Company of the Victorian Rifles he progressed also, acquiring the singular nickname of 'Corporal Potash'.

This cannot have been an easy time for him, for, many years later, one of his family described him as 'the gentlest soul I have ever known'. His photograph shows a young man of rather under middle height, slightly built and with a brave attempt at a military moustache. Gentleness is not a quality that always succeeds in getting men to work and the labouring classes in Australia in the 1880's were not, as a rule, persons of refinement. Nevertheless, John Monash seems to have acquired the art of managing men at an early age, for the work was well done and no strikes or fights seem to have come his way. When the Princes Bridge had been completed, the company set him to work on others; at the same time, his thoughts about the future began to crystallize.

The Militia, Australia's only military force, had been constituted in 1884 after the old Volunteers had been ridiculed out of existence. The company to which Monash belonged was stationed in the university buildings and, as most of its men were undergraduates, it was commanded by the Professor of Natural Philosophy. He does not seem to have been a Stonewall Jackson, for attendance at parades became so irregular that eventually the company was disbanded. This caused some chagrin to Colour-Sergeant Monash (as he had become by 1886) and, on its final disappearance, he applied for and was granted a commission in the Militia Garrison Artillery. The entry in his diary for 6 March, 1887, shows the way his mind was working. 'The undercurrent of my thoughts has been running strongly on military matters. I have been attached to Major Goldstein's battery with the prospect of appointment before Easter; a combination of military and engineering professions is a possibility that is before me.'

That, in fact, is very much what was happening to him, though the precedence of the professions was reversed. The year found him with plenty of scope for the employment of all his prodigious energy and he must have blessed the fact that he was one of those happy men who can manage quite well with very little sleep. In rapid succession he was appointed to take charge of the construction works of the Outer Circle Railway from Fairfield Park to Oakleigh and to the command of the North Melbourne Battery of Garrison Artillery (his first commission being dated 7 April, 1887); between the two, he somehow found time to finish his studies and gain the degree of Bachelor of Civil Engineering.

Between the ages of 19 and 22, probably as the result of hard work in the open air, he had filled out considerably and photographs of this date show a stocky young man, good-looking in a way that promises heavy, slightly semitic features before very long. To his omnivorous studies he now began to add that of the law, not because it was a profession he ever intended regularly to practise but because he had not failed to discern that it could provide a useful adjunct to his other interests. In a fast-growing country, with much building and engineering work going on, disputes were bound to occur. The commonest form of these was — and is — of a particularly irksome kind: the builder (or engineer) demands payment of his account. The customer refuses, averring that work has not been properly done, that it does not conform to specification, that the materials used are not those stipulated, that there has been delay, that the prices charged are excessive or some combination of one or more of them. Judges are not trained to answer such highly technical questions and the usual method of disposing of them was to order a reference to some person possessing the skill and experience to give authoritative answers. Once this had been done, the referee's decision had to be brought back to the Judge so that he might pronounce a formal order that could be enforced against the unsuccessful litigant. All this is, obviously, slow, expensive and in every way unsatisfactory. The Judge does not pretend to understand what it is all about, the expert witnesses called on either side speak a language that is incomprehensible to him and, for some time past, people had been looking for a better way to settle such issues. In England, the Arbitration Act 1889 gave regular status to a common usage. The disputants would agree, either by contract before the dispute arose or by subsequent arrangement, that they would not go to law at all but would submit their quarrel to an arbitrator acceptable to them both. Such a man would need not merely a comprehensive knowledge of engineering principles and practice but he must also have a working acquaintance with the law. Given these qualities, it could be a lucrative occupation, especially once the arbitrator had won the confidence of professional firms for accurate assessment and a judicial attitude of mind. Monash had all these qualities in generous measure and therefore he set himself to add a new skill to those he already enjoyed.

In 1891 he was in a position to think of marriage. For a conscientious Jew the choice was inevitably restricted in a country where the number of families with eligible daughters was not great. At a German club in Melbourne he had met Victoria Moss, the daughter of an early settler named Morton Moss, who had recently arrived from England. With the approval of both families, the rising young engineer and the handsome, highly intelligent girl married and set up house in Toorak. Their only child, Bertha (in the family always called Bert), was born there two years later. Then the prospects for their future, so bright in 1891, suddenly fell apart. The land boom, that had caused the great amount of construction work both public and private, suddenly deflated, and John Monash found himself out of work. He had obtained his Master's degree in engineering in 1893 but it did not create any demand for his services. After a short but extremely worrying period, Monash thought himself fortunate to find employment as Assistant Engineer and Chief Draftsman to the Melbourne Harbour Trust. There he was engaged in design work, bridges, transit sheds, roads and drainage systems. But the appointment was of short duration for in 1894 the Trust had to practise economies and dispensed with his services. In the same year Louis Monash died, bequeathing to his son nothing but his debts.

Monash now decided to take a considerable risk. He had always wished to be his own master, but with a family to maintain it was a decision that demanded courage. On leaving the Harbour Trust, he put up his plate as a Civil Engineer in private practice, with the additional qualification of Patent Attorney. Sir Robert Menzies recalled a dictum of Sir Leo Cussen—'perhaps the greatest judicial lawyer we ever had on our own Supreme Court'— to the effect that any solicitor who failed to retain John Monash as an expert in any patent matter was *prima facie* guilty of negligence. He had never been a gambling man and the scope of his new enterprise would allow him to employ in full measure the skills he had acquired. There were, inevitably, moments of anxiety when the absence of a monthly pay cheque was a serious matter but, in spite of the recession, work in plenty came to him.

His military life during the 1890's was unspectacular but his insatiable curiosity about every aspect of the soldier's business was satisfied by reading. It was a period during which many magazines devoted themselves entirely to army or navy matters;

the United Service Gazette, the Naval and Military Magazine and several others are now only seen in neatly bound rows in the more comprehensive libraries but during the last decades of the nineteenth century and the first of the twentieth they enjoyed large circulations. In 1894, the same year as he became his own master, Lieutenant Monash delivered a lecture to the United Service Institution of Victoria, 'illustrated with lime-light views', on 'The Evolution of Modern Weapons'. His special study in this field had been the American Civil War for, in addition to the brilliancy of generalship displayed by Lee and Jackson on the one side and the painstaking, though less colourful, campaigns of Sherman, Sheridan and Grant on the other, there was more to be learnt here than in all the wars in history put together. A war that had begun with clashes of armed mobs equipped in a style little better than had been the armies of Napoleon had developed into a highly sophisticated business. Railways and bridges, the Spencer repeating carbine, the Gatling machine-gun and barbed wire had transformed war in four short years. For the first time (excepting during the siege of Sebastopol) the pick and shovel had won themselves a place as primary weapons and the value of quickly constructed field fortifications was apparent to those with eyes to see. The raising, training and maintenance of great civilian armies had its lessons also, far more relevant to an unmilitary and undefended continent than Moltke's quintessence of professional staff work a few years later.

For Monash it had all to remain in the realms of theory, together with his studies of medicine and other non-essential subjects but he was as well-read a soldier as most British generals. His militia promotions were fairly routine; Captain in 1895, followed by field rank two years later. Fortunately for him, command of the North Melbourne Battery did not make too exacting demands on his time for the firm of 'Monash & Anderson' was now thriving. His work took him all over the continent, by railroad or horse and buggy, to design and supervise the building of railways and bridges.

His services, too, were much in demand for arbitrations and, in a more partisan role, as an expert witness in the tedious but moderately lucrative building disputes. In one of these actions a disgruntled litigant felt it worth his while to appeal to the Judicial Committee of the Privy Council in London, the ultimate Court of Appeal from a colony. A book of notes prepared by Monash during the trial in the court below seems to have been the most lucid and authoritative exegesis of the matter when it came before their Lordships and was more important to his client's cause than all the cliché-ridden speeches of counsel. Though the fees were handsome, Monash did not enjoy this aspect of his work. To devote much time and talent to the purpose of nothing but destructive criticism is not an ennobling occupation and his inclination was always more towards the constructive aspects of life.

His mind was always restless to discover better ways of achieving what he was set to do. Bridges of masonry were still built in very much the same fashion as had been used by the Romans; surely it was possible to procure better materials and techniques than those that had been available to Augustus Caesar? There was one commodity that Rome had not known (and perhaps might have rejected, for Rome built not for centuries but for millennia) and articles had been appearing in British and American papers about it for some time. Ferroconcrete, unused and so far unknown in the Antipodes, might be the technique of the future. Monash and Anderson, in 1896, decided to become specialists in the subject. They had a head start over their rivals for most of the technical publications were written in German. This was the year of the achievement that was to make the reputation of John Monash. The Anderson Street Bridge across the River Yarra at Melbourne was his design; it comprised three spans each a hundred feet long and introduced reinforced concrete to Australia. This showed the way to the future projects that Australia would demand and it needed a commercial organization to develop it. In 1900 Monash managed to communicate some of his enthusiasm to David Mitchell (whose daughter is better known as Dame Nellie Melba); he arranged the financing and the Monier Pipe Company was formed.

## THE COLONIAL

The period of his greatest professional activity happened to coincide with the early stages of the South African War. Once the shock of 'Black Week' had brought it home to the British Government that this was not to be a small police operation lasting a few weeks, the appeal went out to the colonies for men who could shoot and ride. Monash had enjoyed more military training than most people in the country and he was no more than 35; yet he did not join the Australian contingent that sailed for Table Bay. Until his private papers are made available, his reasons can only be the subject of conjecture. He certainly could not afford to go at a time when his name was just becoming known; he had a duty to his young family, to his partner Anderson, to Mitchell and to his clients. In any event, the war was not expected to last for long and it would only be an adventure. There was no reason to suppose that he would ever have the chance or need to smell powder again and there was no shortage of volunteers. It seems reasonable to suppose that Monash thought on some such lines as these, though he may well have regretted it later.

During the first ten years of the new century, Australia became an independent nation and the affairs of John Monash prospered. The old North Melbourne Battery became the 3rd Victorian Company of the Australian Garrison Artillery in June, 1903, and Major Monash remained in command. He was now becoming a prosperous citizen (although Sir George Pearce, a relative of Mrs Monash, said in his funeral oration that he was not a wealthy man), and added to his interests the cultivation of the garden of his new house. Characteristically, he set himself to learn everything that was to be known about flowers, fruit, and how to care for them; it developed into an intense love for the whole subject.

In March, 1908, there came into existence the Australian Intelligence Corps, founded by the Hon J. W. M'Cay, also an alumnus of Scotch College and the Victorian Rifles. For all its name, it was intended to become the corps that would provide the staff officers of the future and it was a mark of distinction for the command of that part of it in the Victoria Military District to be conferred on Monash after a dozen years in his military backwater. The appointment carried the rank of lieutenant-colonel. Pearce spoke of this part of Monash's life; '[He] was one of a small band which organized what was then called the Australian Intelligence Corps and was the beginning of the General Staff of the Australian Army. Composed of scientific and professional men like himself, it devoted all its spare time to the most essential part of army organization and was the brains of the Army.' The commander kept up his own studies, for Col Henderson's monumental work, *Stonewall Jackson*, was now in circulation and constantly accompanied him as reading matter on journeys. In 1911 he won a gold medal with his essay *Lessons of the Wilderness Campaign, 1864.*

His forty-fifth year, 1910, marked the summit of John Monash's personal happiness; he had worked hard, amassed a noticeable private fortune and felt that he needed a holiday. His partners took the same view and they agreed that a sabbatical year to be spent in touring Europe would be for the greatest good of the greatest number. Accordingly, Monash, accompanied by his wife and seventeen-year-old daughter set out for the old world. First they visited London. The available documents tell little or nothing about his feelings, and one must therefore draw such inferences as the few known facts admit. The Monashes were present at the Ritz on the occasion of the reception given by ex-President Theodore Roosevelt who was in London for the funeral of King Edward VII. Clearly, money was no object now and the tour was to be done *en prince.*

One would much like to know what impression Monash obtained of the capital. Of a certainty he would have been in touch with the leaders of the Jewish faith, for the family were strict in their attendance to matters of religion. The Jews in England at that time fell into two sharply contrasting groups; at one end of the social scale were the miserable, poverty-stricken refugees from Eastern Europe who worked like horses in the sweat-shops of the East End, turning out the products of the cheap tailors for wages that just kept body and soul together. For them, it was the time of the Sydney Street siege and the culturally named anarchist Peter the Painter. At the other end were the very rich, the raffish friends of the late monarch who had made vast fortunes by the genial process of 'salting' gold mines in South Africa and cognate enterprises. Their manner of life was faithfully reflected by *Punch* in the hilarious weekly cartoons depicting the doings and sayings of the unspeakable 'Oofy' Goldberg and his equally odious family. Neither branch of the Semitic race was popular, though the tolerant English were far less uncompromising in their unpleasantness to the poor Jews than were 'Oofy' and his friends.

They went to visit the battlefield of Waterloo, and to Switzerland where John could do some climbing. They stayed in Lucerne and passed several months in Germany. It would be fair to assume that Stettin and Krotoschin were visited, for the publishing business of Bar Lobel Monasch was still in existence though its founder was long dead. As a sentimental journey it seems to have been something of a failure, for John Monash returned home quite convinced that the Kaiser's Germany was determined on war.

In 1912, he reached the top rung of one of his professions: the Victoria Institute of Engineers elected him President. He was also made a member of the Institute of Civil Engineers in London. His speech in Melbourne on the occasion of his installation took as its text the virtues of private practice and the speaker's abhorrence of being a paid servant of the State. Any of those who heard it and were still in places of authority in 1920 had the charity not to remind him of it.

He was no less assiduous in his other profession. In 1913 he was taken from the Intelligence Corps to be given command of an infantry brigade, the newly formed 13th, with the rank of full colonel. To show that the translation back from staff work and heavy artillery to the original arm of 'Corporal Potash' held no mysteries for him, he published a little book called *A Hundred Hints for Company Commanders*. It contains no revolutionary aphorisms, but one is worth quoting for in it the author mirrors himself. 'Be natural. The assumption of mannerisms is easily detected by men, personality is lost and, in most cases, respect suffers.'

His photograph of 1913 in blue undress uniform shows a well-fed but thoughtful and manly face. He might very easily pass as a regular colonel in the British service but for the paucity of ribbon on his left breast: only the green of the Colonial Auxiliary Forces Officers Decoration (infelicitously abbreviated to VD) so far enriches it. In military education, or in some aspects of it, he was as well equipped as many of his regular peers, but the misfortune of the colonial irregular officer, in time of peace, was not to have professional regiments at hand to whom he could be attached and from whom he could learn something of the mystique and traditions. Monash could lecture on Jackson's stroke at Chancellorsville or exercise his brigade with any man, but he had never lived the half-family, half-monastic life of a good Mess. He was a good horseman, but he had never played a single chukka of polo, ridden in a point-to-point or stuck a pig. He was an adequate shot, but, as he wrote years later from Kent, he hated to reduce a beautiful bird to a tangle of bloody feathers. Though on parade he demanded the deference due to his rank, for to fail in this would mean the end of all discipline, he was a humble, modest and courteous person. If his forecast of the Kaiser's intentions were to turn out correct, it would be interesting to see how he would get on with opposite numbers who had been trained in a different school. If he was not on Christian name terms with the greater part of the Army List, at any rate he knew far more about engineering of every description than any other colonel, not excluding the professional sappers. And all his reading went to show that on the modern battlefield, the engineer would be king.

CHAPTER TWO

## An Army of a New Model

AUSTRALIA was fortunate in that, alone amongst the great colonies, she had suffered no internal warfare. Canada had had the unhappy experience of domestic rebellion, South Africa had been occupied for a century with wars against the Kaffirs, the Basuto and the Zulu, and New Zealand had undergone a series of wars with the equally redoubtable Maoris. In Australia the only armed conflict going beyond the scope of ordinary police action had been the few minutes of battle at the Eureka Stockade in 1854. In consequence of this and with the knowledge that the Royal Navy would always be at hand if any foreign power entertained designs on her shores, Australia had never had occasion to occupy herself greatly with military problems. This did not mean that no army existed, for there had been for many years past the separate State militias, which were probably neither more nor less efficient than their counterparts in the home country, and the universities each had their own Rifle Corps. When the Commonwealth came into existence in 1900, these were taken over on a federal basis.

Though there was no army in the sense in which the word was understood at Aldershot, a martial and patriotic people would not be denied the right to make their presence felt when the necessity arose to remind outsiders that the British family of nations included others beside those who dwelt in Great Britain. A small contingent was raised for service in the Sudan and also for service in South Africa. These men, drawn largely from the 'bushmen', won golden opinions from all with whom their duty brought them into contact. Even before they signed their attestation papers they were half-trained as soldiers, for no Australian of the 1890's would walk a yard, from earliest youth, if he could go on horseback; rifle shooting was a major national sport and the way of life in the outback inculcated a habit of self-reliance and decision-making unknown in urban societies. Even the Australian townsman spent all his available free time camping in the wilds. More than one British officer, subsequently to rise to high rank, made a mental note on the veldt that these would be good men with whom to go tiger shooting. When the war was over, however, they returned to civilian life and no progress was made towards the creation of a standing army, save for the small cadres needed to keep the militia in existence.

In the years between federation and 1914 two men changed all this. One was the Australian William Morris Hughes, then Attorney-General, who had for long past been convinced that one day his country would have to fight for her life; the other was Lord Kitchener. Kitchener, of course, had observed the mettle of the Australian soldier already and it is not surprising that he wished to see the military potential of the country expanded to the utmost. Hughes, however, was a Minister in a Labour government and it seems odd to English eyes to read that a party bearing this name should have been the foremost in demanding a greatly increased expenditure on guns rather than on butter. He was not even a lone voice within his party, for Andrew Fisher, the Prime Minister, and George Foster Pearce, Minister for Defence from 1910 to 1913, were firmly with him.

A start was made at the Imperial Conference of 1907 when R. B. Haldane, the greatest War Minister Britain has ever known and himself a member of the pacific Liberal party, first mooted the question of joint defence. He did not achieve all he had hoped for but from this meeting came the creation of the Imperial General Staff, charged with the duty of ensuring that whatever forces the colonies might choose to raise (a decision which was theirs alone) they should at least have all things common in the way of armament and doctrine. This was not wholly successful, for when Canada went to war in 1914 her soldiers carried the excellent but not very robust Ross rifle. Nevertheless, it was a great improvement on anything that had gone before.

Soon after federation the Commonwealth decided upon a form of compulsory service for the newly formed citizen force. This experiment had hardly got under way when Lord Kitchener paid a visit to the country and was invited by the government to inspect its new creation and to advise upon any method by which it could be improved. Kitchener, whose distaste for irregular troops dated from his experiences in France in 1870, found little to admire and said so. The new Prime Minister, Alfred Deakin, whatever may have been his mental reservations, announced that having appealed to Caesar he would defer to Caesar's judgment.

Caesar knew exactly what he wanted: the country was to be divided into 224 'areas' each under an area-officer; in each of these, boys were to be entered for compulsory training at the age of 12 and there they would remain until, at 18, they passed into the 'active' battalions and regiments of the Commonwealth Army. Thus organized, they would undergo a short annual training for a further seven years. The old militia would cease to exist but men whose three-year engagements in that force still had time to run could join the Commonwealth Army. None but officers and NCOs of the militia could otherwise transfer to the new force. There were the inevitable delays of a political nature and the new order of things did not begin until 1911 with the result that the Commonwealth Army would not put out its full strength until 1919. Though the paper strength rose from 23,000 militia to 45,000 of the new model, its average age was no more than 20.

The militia officers were only intended to play out time until a new generation of men, infinitely better trained than ever the militia officers had had the chance to become, was ready.

Kitchener had, as a young man, been a cadet at The Shop at Woolwich. He does not appear to have retained any great enthusiasm for his old academy, for part of his advice to Fisher had been that a military college be established on the lines of West Point in the United States, where the education was more broadly based than that at either Sandhurst or Woolwich. He was very insistent that cadets should be selected from the whole body of the people of Australia without distinction of class or money and that, after a course of four years, they should be sent abroad to gain experience with the British or a dominion army. This should ensure, in Kitchener's own words, that the future Australian officer (especially the officer of the Staff Corps) should be 'equal, if not superior, in military education, to the officers of any army in the world'. The Australian Government, wholly persuaded, acquired the 'fine old homestead of Duntroon in the beautiful rolling country near the unbuilt capital of Australia . . . Round it, in a series of neat wooden barracks grouped like a village on the hillside, the staff . . . trained the cadets of the first four years. These were chosen from every grade of the population; no one troubled as to their parentage.' Soon the college allotted a number of places to cadets from New Zealand and thus began the brotherhood in arms of the two countries.

The senior officers in the army at its beginning were anything but commonplace and it was thanks to their remarkable, if widely differing, talents and personalities that the new venture was launched with outstanding success. The man who above all others deserves the name of father of the Australian Army was an Englishman by birth, William Thorsby Bridges. The son of a Post Captain in the Royal Navy, he was born in Scotland in 1861, and sent to the Royal Naval School at Greenwich. When his father left the Navy Bridges was taken to live in Canada with the family and entered the Canadian Military College at Kingston with a view to joining the British Army. Before he had completed his course, however, Capt Bridges lost all his money in a bank failure and the family moved on again to Australia. Young Bridges somehow managed to remain at Kingston until he graduated, then followed the others.

Life as a penniless junior officer in the British army of the 1880's would have been an impossibility, so he took a fairly humble job with the Roads and Bridges Department of New South Wales. He volunteered to go with the NSW contingent to the Sudan but was too late. However, he did not have to wait long for the furtherance of his military ambitions; in 1885 he obtained a commission in the NSW Permanent Artillery and found himself in charge of the Middle Head Forts in Sydney. The duties were minimal but before very long a School of Gunnery was established there and Bridges was given command. From that time, his career was one of steady but unsensational progress. As a major he was attached to the Cavalry Division of General French (on whose staff was an officer named Douglas Haig) and saw action at the relief of Kimberley and at Paardeburg. Unfortunately, he contracted typhoid soon afterwards and was invalided home, where he joined the General Staff as Chief of Intelligence and was put to work on the Defence Scheme for Australia. This was a task for which he was in every way suited, for Bridges was a profound thinker with a scholarly turn of mind. Indeed his tall, bony frame and permanent stoop gave him the air more of a don than of a soldier.

As a person Bridges does not appear to have been particularly likeable and the art of man-management was unknown to him. His own utter integrity, which scorned the conventional lobbying for promotions and appointments, seems to have made him cold and indifferent to people around him, but those who knew him best wrote it down to an excessive shyness and a refusal ever to manifest the slightest emotion of any kind. Though some loved him, he was a grim man to serve and when he was appointed the first commandant of the Military College (always spoken of as Duntroon) he made no effort at all to get to know his charges. Not surprisingly, he was loathed by some but, like many another shy man, he was a far more praiseworthy person than he appeared.

Bridges' right hand was Cyril Brudenell Bingham White. With such forenames it seems that he must have been connected with the families of Lords Lucan and Cardigan but there does not appear to be any trace of a relationship. In personality White was the antithesis of his chief. His father was an Ulsterman of some means who had migrated and taken up farming in Queensland where a succession of droughts had ruined him. Cyril, after a state school education followed by a year at a private school run by an expatriate Eton master, got himself a job as a bank clerk at the age of 16 and at once became financially independent. To a young man of a keen but only half-filled mind the mechanical drudgery demanded of him in exchange for the pound a week which spelt freedom from being a burden on his father was odious. The time came when he was moved up country at an enhanced salary of £120 a year. Of this he sent a third home to his mother, set aside another third to pay the modest fees of a school master who continued his education and on the remainder he contrived to stay alive.

After three years his chance came. A competitive examination was held for permanent commissions in the Queensland Artillery and White presented himself for it. Another bank clerk named Thomas Glasgow, a name to be remembered, also attended. White was successful and became an officer in the regiment which, after federation, was known as the Royal Australian Garrison Artillery.

It soon became clear that he had what is sometimes called a 'staff mind' and he was appointed ADC to another remarkable man. In the very early days of the Commonwealth, while military reorganization was still in the air, the government borrowed from the British army an officer to act temporarily as commander-in-chief until the Military Board was ready to take over his functions. This was Major-General Edward Hutton, a soldier of brilliance whose career is not as well known in this country as it should be since he spent much of his military life in the colonies. From him White learnt a great deal, not so much about the individual training of men in a regiment as about the higher direction of an army for war.

Like Bridges, White accompanied the Australian force to South Africa where he served as a subaltern of Light Horse. There he came sufficiently to the notice of people who mattered to be selected for the first vacancy given to an Australian officer at the Staff College. He passed his two years at Camberley during the great days of that institution when the successive commandants were Major-Generals Henry Wilson and 'Wully' Robertson. Amongst his fellow students there were two other Australian officers, both then serving with the British army, named John Gellibrand and Douglas Glasfurd.

When the time came for him to leave, White's reputation stood so high that he was asked to remain in England for a further three years to lecture; he nearly missed seeing Australia again, for he was present on the notorious occasion in 1905 when, in the course of cavalry manœuvres, orders were given with such crassness that a regiment of light cavalry and the Horse Guards were sent charging at each other at full gallop. Two men were killed and several injured but White came through unscathed. When he finally reached home he was appointed Director of Military Operations and put in train all Australia's plan for mobilization.

As a man, White was delightful. He had a talent for clarity of thought and painstaking explanation which few others could equal, allied to an integrity fully matching that of Bridges. No man ever left him in anger. When he was appointed Chief-of-Staff at Duntroon the combination of the two men effected a complete complement each to the other. It was of Cyril White that Monash was to write on 22 April, 1916, that 'He is far and away the ablest soldier Australia has ever turned out.'

Thus it happened that the events of 1914 caught Australia at the most awkward moment possible from the point of view of military preparation. She had in the making a splendid army but it was years away from being a force ready to take the field. Nevertheless, the framework was there and so, within limits, were the means of supplying and arming it. Britain had supplied Australia with an adequacy of the new 18-pdr field gun, though shortages at home had made it impossible to do the same with the 4·5 howitzer; machine-guns (still the heavy Maxim) were provided on the same scale as for the British regulars and any deficiencies there might be in rifles were made good by Australia herself, for the factory at Lithgow turned out the SMLE in quantity, and every bit as well as at Enfield. The Australian ammunition boot was, by common consent, so much better than the Northampton brand that years afterwards it was found to be the most acceptable article of barter with the British infantryman.

All through these years of evolution John Monash soldiered quietly on. His discerning mind cannot have failed to approve the changes for they were bringing a disparate collection of State units of unequal quality and idiosyncratic tendencies into a homogeneous army. If ever it had to go to war it would at least be spared the terrible weaknesses which his exhaustive reading of *Stonewall Jackson* had taught him to have arisen half a century earlier from causes of the same kind.

In the meantime, there was still work to be done with concrete and bridges. The question was whether when war came, as it must at some time, judging from events in Europe, he would be too old for it.

## CHAPTER THREE

## The Mustering of the AIF

As war drew nearer, men began to wonder how it would affect Australia. On remote sheep stations the boundary riders read the papers as eagerly as did clerks in insurance offices in Melbourne and schoolmasters in Adelaide. The constitutional position was about as obscure as it could be; Britain was under no strict treaty obligation to France if she should be drawn in as the formal ally of Russia. Nevertheless most well-informed people knew something of the staff talks which had been taking place, on and off, since 1906 and no Australian believed that his own home country could be so base as to allow the German High Seas Fleet to batter French sea-coast towns to pieces while the Royal Navy, in which he took such pride, looked idly on. And what about Belgium? Was there not some treaty dating back to the creation of that kingdom which obliged Britain to come to her aid if anyone attacked her? And if that were to happen, what next? If Britain went to war, was Australia, *ipso facto*, at war also? The Prime Minister of the independent Dominion of Canada, Sir Wilfred Laurier, had given it as his opinion that 'the overseas states of the Empire could maintain neutrality in any of Great Britain's wars in which they had no desire to join'. This assertion had never been contradicted and, although it might be pedantically correct to say that a declaration of war by or on Britain comprehended a similar state of affairs for the Commonwealth, the factual state of war could hardly arise without the free consent of the people of Australia.

Australia, then, must decide what she would do if the mother-country became a belligerent. Looked at in cold blood, the first thing to consider was her own interests. She had no sufficient quarrel with Germany, or with any other state, to cause so extreme a step to be taken. Her own navy was big enough and good enough to deal with a small enemy squadron but it could not defend the whole enormous coastline nor prevent a determined attempt at invasion. If Britain and her friends were victorious without the aid of the southern branch of the family, so much the better. If she were defeated, then in time Australia must inevitably become a part of the spoils of the victor. No doubt she would go down in one great and bloody fight, but with a population of less than five millions the fight could have only one end. It seems highly unlikely that such considerations were ever even seriously weighed up. The matter was not one of the interpretation of documents or the calculation of profits and losses, it was one of pure, honourable emotion. It was a long time since the first Britons had come as settlers and Australians were now in many respects a completely distinct people. Their social behaviour was different, in some respects their values were different; but they spoke the same language, read the same books, played the same games and had tribal memories of snow and Norman castles, of Waterloo and Trafalgar, and their national heroes, so far, were all British.

On 31 July, 1914, two men spoke for Australia. Senator Millen was the first: 'If necessity arises, Australia will recognize that she is not merely a fair-weather partner of the Empire but a component member in all circumstances.' Andrew Fisher, leader of the opposition Labour party, in a speech that night at Colac in Victoria, spoke with the authority of those who followed him: 'Should the worst happen, after everything has been done that honour will permit, Australians will stand beside the mother-country to help and defend her, to our last man and our last shilling.'

The following day Joseph Cook, Prime Minister of Australia, delivered the decision of his government: 'If there is to be a war, you and I shall be in it. We must be in it. If the old country is at war, so are we.' Perhaps the most eloquent voice of all was that of Sir John Forrest, former pioneer and explorer, now Treasurer of the Commonwealth: 'In the past Australians were proud to think of the glories of England. We shared her victories and triumphs. Justice and reason now demand that we must be prepared to share her difficulties and, if need be, her disasters. If Britain goes to her Armageddon, we will go with her. Our fate and hers, for good or ill, are as woven threads.'

These noble words of the great men of the land were echoed at a lower level. Just as Rupert Brooke was expressing in verse the feelings of the youth of England, so a young man named John Burns, the son of a Victoria clergyman, was setting out the mood of young Australia:

> The Banners of England, unfurled across the sea,
> Floating out upon the wind, were beckoning to me,
> Storm-rent and battle-torn, smoke-stained and grey,
> The Banners of England, and how could I stay?

Within a few months he lay, in good company, dead upon a nameless Turkish hillside with a bullet through his brain.[1]

When Britain finally went to war on 4 August, 1914, the next decision to be taken was how these intentions should be translated into action. New Zealand had already offered to send her soldiers if the need arose and Canada, speaking with the voice of the ebullient Colonel Sam Hughes, had undertaken to put into the field a force of 30,000 fighting men. Australia, by comparison of populations, could not immediately be expected to match this, but the dignity of the Commonwealth demanded that she should not lag behind. The moment caught her off balance, for a Federal election was in the offing and Bridges, to all intents and purposes the professional head of the army, was away on a tour of inspection in the north. It made no difference. Political antagonisms,

[1] The same sentiments were expressed, less lyrically, in a fragment of deathless verse by 'some low, vulgar person, taking advantage of the fact that the night editor had gone out for a drink', in the *Pioneer*:

> 'Fellers of Australia
> Blokes and coves and coots,
> Move your ....... carcasses
> Shift your ....... boots.
> Git a ....... move on
> Fetch your ....... gun
> Find the ....... enemy
> And make the ....... run.'

deep though they were, disappeared overnight and the burden of the soldier's work fell upon Cyril White, though he was still only a major.

White was in every way equal to the task. First, he ensured that the normal precautions such as the manning of the forts, the guarding of vulnerable points and the surveillance of German shipping in Australian ports, were dealt with by the existing forces. He knew already of plans to raise a complete division jointly with New Zealand, for the possibility had been discussed by him in the previous year with Major-General Alexander Godley, the British officer lent to the sister dominion in 1912 to inaugurate Lord Kitchener's scheme. White was able to assure his Prime Minister that the two dominions could raise without delay a force of this size of which Australia would find two infantry brigades of 6,000 men each and New Zealand would contribute the third. Other arms would be provided in the same proportion.

The Prime Minister and his colleagues at once decided that this was not enough. If Canada was raising 30,000 men, then Australia would be failing in her duty if she mobilized less than half that number. He asked White whether the total could not be raised to 20,000 horse, foot and guns, ready to sail in six weeks. White, nothing loath, said that the army could do it. On the strength of his assurance, the Commonwealth Government dispatched a cable to London: 'In the event of war the government is prepared to place the vessels of the Australian navy under the control of the British Admiralty when desired. It is further prepared to dispatch an expeditionary force of 20,000 men of any suggested composition to any destination desired by the Home Government, the force to be at the complete disposal of the Home Government. The cost of dispatch and maintenance will be borne by this government.' On 6 August the Secretary of State for the Colonies replied that the British Cabinet 'gratefully accepted the offer'.

On one crucial matter White felt obliged to tender his advice. From his knowledge of the British army and its chiefs he was pretty sure that they would not, if consulted, want the dominion contribution to come in the form of a complete division. Separate independent brigades and the usual ancillary arms and services would be more convenient to Britain, for these could then be encadred with British divisions to make good the losses which were bound to be suffered in the first battles of the war. At that time, of course, nobody contemplated the use of Australian troops anywhere other than in France. Quite apart from this, White was well aware that there would exist in Britain a distrust, not unjustified, of the ability of the officers of an untried colonial army to fill the higher commands and senior staff appointments that a force of this size would require. On this point White was inflexible. There was no question of the creation of a fully fledged Australian army —the war could not conceivably go on for long enough to make such a thing possible—but White was determined to see that the Australian soldier should have the chance to build a military tradition of his own and not merely as an auxiliary to an army which already was weighed down with ancient laurels. White had not misjudged the War Office: within a few days the expected cable arrived—'The Army Council suggest that a suitable composition of the expeditionary force would be two infantry brigades, one light horse brigade and one field artillery brigade.' But the Army Council was too late.

Having decided upon the size and shape of the expeditionary force—the extra 8,000 men making it possible for Australia to find a complete division and a Light Horse Brigade without calling upon New Zealand—the next task was to set about raising it. Bridges was back in the saddle within a few days and it was upon him that the duty fell. For a start, he appointed White as his Chief-of-Staff; no better choice could have been made. He suggested that the chief command be given to General Hutton, for all his 66 years, but the government would not hear of it. When there were perfectly competent Australian officers available it would not be seemly for the command of her first army going to war in the name of the Commonwealth to be entrusted to any man who lacked this qualification.

It was plain from the start that the existing army was far too young to be sent into battle as an entity; something quite separate must be created and it must be built upon whatever foundations there might be. There was no shortage of raw material, for

Australians of all kinds and ages were flocking to the recruiting offices and it will not be amiss to ponder upon the kind of material it was.

The Australian, though still basically an Anglo-Saxon, was by now a very different kind of man from his cousin who had stayed at home. It is true that two-thirds of the population inhabited the comparatively urban states of Victoria and NSW but that did not mean that its people had much in common with the Cockney or the lad from Oldham. All their spare time was passed in open air pursuits, the climate and abundance of nourishing food had made them bigger and stronger, and something in the conditions of climate had even altered their faces. Most Australians were tall, lean and loosely built, with a leathery skin that developed deep facial lines at an early age. Their arms and legs were long and wiry with harder muscles than are usually found in England except amongst the heavy manual workers. Their voices had a nasal intonation all their own and they used them freely in marvellous profanity. Over the years there had developed a society in which the word 'class' had no meaning. 'Society', too, in the sense in which the word was current in Mayfair, simply did not exist outside the precincts of Government House. Unlike the former colonists of America, they had no respect at all for a man simply because he was rich. Money, no matter how come by, meant as little to them as birth. A man was judged by what he was and by nothing else; the giving of a direct order unsoftened by a politeness that seemed to turn it into a request was the kind of insult that might be rewarded by a blow from a knobbly fist. The very existence of men called officers was regarded with deep suspicion; the nearest thing to respect paid by an Australian boundary rider was the tacit acknowledgment given to the manager, provided that he was the right sort of man, that he probably knew more about the job than did a fairly new hand. British officers wearing the conventional eyeglass, dressed in well-cut suits and speaking in the accents of Oxford did not as a result find themselves treated with deference. Such characteristics could not possibly be natural to any man and were described as 'putting on dog'. The best that such an officer could hope for was that his appearance and speech did not excite derisive laughter and imitation. The situation, however, was open to change. When the same immaculate man was seen walking through storms of Turkish shrapnel and machine-gun fire with the same nonchalance he manifested during a walk in the park, the Australian soldier took him to his heart and his fists were very ready if any outsider spoke a word against him. The reason is probably just that the soldier took it for granted that the native-born Australian officer would bear himself bravely, for anything else would be unthinkable; the shock of seeing a man whom he expected to run like a rabbit at the first shot behaving in a manner at least as gallant as those he knew swung admiration to the point of worship. But it had to be earned.

Off duty, the Australian could be a formidable companion. His capacity for beer was heroic, he would bet large sums on anything —which of two flies would land first on a knob of sugar, or which raindrop would first reach the bottom of a window pane—and if he should get it into his head that he was being cheated by a barkeeper then an orgy of riot and arson would swiftly follow. Nor was he averse from writing home colourful accounts of events that had never happened and Monash wrote on several occasions to reassure his wife about the bloodcurdling conditions invented by 'our young liars'. He was not unique in this. Anybody who has ever censored soldiers' letters will recognize such lies, which do not seem to have changed since the armies of Alexander left Macedon.

Amongst other troops, particularly in company with the tractable British, the Australian always seemed to become the leader. When he was a good Australian as in the vast majority of cases he was, nothing but good resulted, but it was not always so. One variety of Australian, whom Robert Louis Stevenson had long ago stigmatized as 'the lowest class in the world', was the Sydney Harbour larrikin. Not surprisingly, the larrikin did not usually appear in the queue outside the barracks in the early days but a few must have slipped through later on and somehow survived the attempts made by better men to teach them the error of their way. Sadly, one larrikin could do more harm to the reputation of the Australian away from the front line than whole battalions could do to enhance it. No army has ever been exempt from some bad element.

There was one characteristic, however, that was peculiarly Australian. All soldiers have friends, kindred spirits with whom they spend most of their time because they enjoy and are at ease in each other's company. In the Australian forces the tradition was more exclusive and closer, for every soldier, following his habit in civilian life, possessed a 'Mate'. The term does not carry with it the faintest suggestion of homosexuality as it had done in the armies of ancient Greece and a black eye at least would have been the reward of anyone who even hinted at it. Men in the outback had long been accustomed to working in pairs and it was there that the tradition had grown up. Dr Bean, the Official Historian, tells a story to illustrate it which he himself observed. In a trench on the Gallipoli peninsula a company was waiting for the word to attack when a soldier complete with rifle and fixed bayonet appeared. 'Jim there?', he called out. 'Here, Bill,' came an answering voice. 'Do you chaps mind moving up a bit,' said the first speaker, 'Jim and me's mates and we're going over together'. Never to let down a mate was an article of faith second only to never letting down Australia.

Such were the men who filled the ranks of Bridges' and White's new army. Finding the officers for them was a far more difficult business. Every man of any age who had held a commission of some kind somewhere was considered and the final selection might have given the British regular army cause to wonder whether its misgivings had not been justified. The 1st Brigade was commanded by a barrister, Colonel H. N. MacLaurin, and was recruited entirely from the state of Victoria; the 2nd (NSW) went to a solicitor, Colonel James Whiteside M'Cay, and only the 3rd, drawn from the rest of the Commonwealth and known as the 'All Australian Brigade', was led by a professional soldier, Colonel E. G. Sinclair-Maclagan of the British service. Of the 631 officers in the Force, 68 were serving or recently retired members of the Australian permanent forces, 16 were British regulars, 2 were retired from the same service, 402 were drawn from the old Australian militia, 33 were former members of it, 9 had been

British, colonial or foreign Territorials and the remainder were young officers under the new compulsory service scheme. The whole of the senior year at Duntroon was commissioned and embodied, stirring uneasy memories amongst older men of the destruction of the cadets of the Virginia Military Institute at Newmarket half a century before. Their ages varied between the early 20s and the mid-50s, the doyen of them all being a medical officer aged 67 who had been present at the siege of Plevna in 1877. Two officers of the divisional staff were to be heard of again in a future war, Major Thomas Blamey and Lt R. G. Casey.

On 1 November, 1914, the transports containing the first contingent of the Australian Imperial Force and the New Zealand Expeditionary Force sailed from King George's Sound in the south-west corner of the continent where they had been concentrated for some time because the whereabouts of the German cruiser *Emden* were still a mystery. Thirty-eight ships, crammed with men whose training had been carried out as far as possible in camps on racecourses and similar open spaces, put to sea under escort of HMS *Minotaur*, *Psyche* and *Philomel*, HMAS *Sydney* and *Melbourne* and the Japanese cruiser *Ibuki*. Nobody knew their destination. It nearly became South Africa, where the old Boer War leader Christian de Wet had raised a rebellion in the south-west, but this was put down by his former comrade in arms Louis Botha, now a British general, just in time. HMAS *Sydney* left the convoy for a while to sink, burn and destroy the *Emden*, *Ibuki*, to her chagrin, having had her offer of help firmly rejected. In these ships sailed all that was best in Australia, but John Monash was not with them.

He was, after all, only one of a brilliant generation of citizen-colonels and, although Bridges had long ago marked down his talent for thorough and meticulous organization, there was no reason to suppose him to be in any way superior to others of the same rank and seniority. At the beginning he had to be content with the position of Chief Censor in which capacity he had the uncongenial task of interning a number of German savants whom he had invited as guests of the Association for the Advancement of Science. He did not, however, have long to wait for the chance

to show what he could achieve as a trainer and leader of men.
The number of men who had flocked to the recruiting offices (one
cannot say to the colours for these were not used by the AIF)
and who would not be denied their right to bear arms was so
overwhelming that on 3 September another brigade of infantry,
the 4th, was offered to Britain and again was gratefully accepted.
The Chief Censor was taken from his office and given its command.

The 4th Brigade was a heterogeneous cross-section of Australia.
Of its four battalions the 13th was drawn from NSW, the 14th
from Victoria, the 15th came from Queensland and Tasmania in
about equal proportion and the 16th was made up of men from
the sparsely populated states of South and Western Australia.
Unlike the brigadiers of the first formations, Monash did not have
his staff officers provided by the professional army and only his
staff captain, Carl Jess, was a regular officer. His brigade major,
upon whom would fall all the planning of operations, was also a
citizen officer, J. P. McGlinn; the quality of both men can be
judged from the fact that within four years each was commanding
a brigade of his own.

Monash assumed his command at the camp which had been
formed at Broadmeadows, a grassy plain ten miles from Melbourne, where he had the advantage of being left for three months
to begin the task of turning 5,000 sturdy individualists into a
formation of trained and disciplined soldiers. The records of these
early days are scanty and much must be left to the imagination,
but the task is one which did not vary much between the days of
Hannibal and Ironside. Training was carried out in exactly the
same fashion as with Kitchener's Army at home, the instructional
manuals used and the standard set for attainment being those of
the British regular army for which the Australian officers had an
open, and their soldiers a covert, admiration. They could not yet
have known that that army was fighting for its life at Mons and
Le Cateau in a way that would have won their unstinted praise,
nor that it would soon cease to exist after the slogging soldiers'
battle known to history as First Ypres.

At Broadmeadows the 4th Brigade received its clothing, the
sensible tunic cut loosely on the lines of a Norfolk jacket complete

with pleat down the back and integral cloth belt. Breeches of the same cloth, a shade of khaki rather the colour of pea-soup with a soft, felted surface, and puttees of the same material completed the outfit. Some were lucky enough to receive the famous Australian slouch hat but there were not nearly enough to go round and many men had to sail wearing the British flat-topped cap. Boots, web equipment, mess-tins (billy-cans to the Australian), water bottle and all the other items of a soldier's kit were available in far greater plenitude than they were for Kitchener's unfortunate men, shivering on Salisbury Plain in weird civilian great-coats and drilling with broomsticks. Rifles, ammunition and clothing were all produced in Australian factories, though of the first there were already in the country enough and to spare. Two new words were added to the language at Broadmeadows. The first was the Australian synonym for the British 'latrine rumour'. Every day there paraded through the lines a number of scavenging carts bearing in proud letters across the stern the name of the manufacturer, Furphy. From that time onward, a furphy became the well-understood colloquialism for a rumour. The other word was 'Sir'.

There is no need to follow in detail the steps by which the 4th Brigade began to build itself up into a formation with a soul and a mystique of its own. The miners of Western Australia, railwaymen from the South, clerks from Melbourne and Sydney dockers discovered early that Australia was a greater focus for loyalty even than their own state, and a useful rivalry between units from opposite ends of the continent did nothing to hamper progress. During the long and arduous hours of training men strove to outguard the Guards in their drill and bearing and acquired greater skill at arms than they had ever dreamt possible. Muscles, already hard, became harder still and the relationship between officers and men became workable. The suspicion of the whole system which produced this unknown, privileged class still lingered but common sense and good nature on the part of both leaders and led resolved it into a tolerable state of affairs. Much Australian blood would have to be shed before the need of the soldier in battle for the guiding hand of his officer and the need by the officer for qualities which a private soldier could do without would become accepted as natural and not derogatory to the dignity of man. By the time the brigade embarked, just before Christmas, it had already developed into a formation of which its commander might well be proud.

Their officers, nearly all of whom had come from the militia, had trained them as well as any Sandhurst graduates could have done and had taught themselves a great deal in the process. They had even managed to overcome the prejudice which every self-respecting Australian harboured against moving any noticeable distance on his feet. Long route marches with full pack had been daily occurrences and, like all soldiers everywhere, as they marched they sang. 'Tipperary' had reached Australia some time before and its overworked, raucous lyric was heard as frequently around Melbourne as in the lanes of Kent. They had, however, another song entirely their own with which the king's enemies were shortly to become acquainted; the Australian never indulged in the more blatant forms of exaggerated patriotism, but 'Australia Will Be There' not merely suited the mood of the moment but amounted to a simple statement of fact.

Comparison of the soldiers at Broadmeadows with those at Aldershot soon flags; these men had more in common with other, earlier, armies which had spoken with the English tongue than with their contemporaries at home. In many ways they resembled Cromwell's men of the New Model in their single-minded dedication to learning their business, though their picturesque blasphemies would not have made them welcome in the camps of those gloomy men. More than any other, the army they most closely resembled was that of Robert E. Lee and the Confederate South. They had the same sardonic wit, the same extreme political awareness and, above all, a capacity for unbridled criticism of higher authority and all its works far exceeding that enjoyed by the more docile Englishman. Off parade, they regarded themselves as civilians who were grown up and desired no restrictions put upon the manner in which they employed their leisure beyond those which they had grudgingly endured in their previous status. For any place to be designated 'Out of Bounds' was regarded as an affront to the dignity of man and was treated accordingly. Nevertheless, the moment the bugle sounded 'Reveille' the soldier in them displaced the civilian of the night before and even a taskmaster as perfectionist as Colonel Monash could find little to fault in the rate of progress they made.

In December they sailed from Sydney, to be brigaded somewhere with the now companionless New Zealanders. The 1st Division had been for some weeks in Egypt and the New Zealanders were also there, so it was reasonable to infer that Suez would be their place of disembarkation. Sydney gave them a fitting send-off and on Christmas Day Monash was able to write to his wife that 'I have made a rough calculation of the cost of this convoy, and it works out at £8 per minute (exclusive of pay of the 13,000 men we are carrying)'. After describing the heart-raising sight of a great convoy of troopships at sea in perfect weather, he ends, 'The men are all in the best of good humour, and there is very little crime, although the "jug" generally has a few lodgers for disobedience or answering back.' Monash had the kind of brain that can never allow itself to be idle; very considerable work and many inquiries must have been needed to make the calculation of costs, so rich in academic interest but utterly barren of practical importance. Even so, he would have argued, it was a great deal better than doing nothing at all. His letters written during the voyage across the Indian Ocean and through the Red Sea have little to differentiate them from countless other letters written by countless other officers in the same circumstances before and since. The ships were well found, the soldiers surprisingly tractable (except for an escapade at Colombo when a number of them reckoned that the loss of a month's pay was cheap at the price of a run ashore) and there was nothing about the voyage that need detain us.

Turkey had entered the war on 29 October, just before the convoy had sailed, but it was not expected that this would have any effect on the future of the Australians. Egypt, however, had been left virtually undefended by the withdrawal of the small peacetime garrison and, in order to make sure that the vital Suez Canal should not fall into enemy hands, remote though such a contingency seemed, the 42nd (East Lancashire) Division of the Territorial Force had been moved there. A brigade of regular Indian troops—the 9th—had also been taken, together with a brigade of mountain artillery, from the 3rd Indian Division as it passed through the Canal on its way to France. The Lancastrians were material as good as any in England but the state of their training and equipment had a long way to go before they could be considered fit for battle.

The Turkish army was something of an unknown quantity; it had not shown to advantage during the Balkan Wars, but the recent political changes had brought in their train a German Military Mission which could be relied upon, given time, to make a very fine army indeed out of the tough and undemanding peasants of Anatolia. Lord Wavell, writing in 1927, remarked that he 'had occasionally amused himself by making a handicap—on the lines of a golf handicap—of all the nations which took part in the late war, according to their martial qualities. [I] have found that the Turk is usually set to receive five or six strokes from the nation placed at scratch. On mentioning this to a distinguished officer, the latter replied that his handicap was always on racing lines, and that the Turk carried about 8st 12lbs when top weight was 9st 7lbs.' Be that as it may, Wavell had a number of other and more specific comments: 'The Turk was a fine marcher, and could dispense with many of the impedimenta necessary to European armies. On the defensive, his eye for ground, his skill in planning and entrenching a position, and his stubbornness in holding it made him a really formidable adversary to engage. In the offensive he always attacked gallantly though often with little skill. The Turkish artillery-man handled his guns well and shot accurately.'

As the convoy bearing Monash and his men was passing Aden, the first Turkish stroke was being prepared. Around Beersheba an army of about 20,000 men, two divisions of infantry plus nine batteries of field artillery and another of 5·9 howitzers, was being assembled. Nominally it was under the command of Djemal Pasha, Minister of Marine, and one of the triumvirate then ruling the Ottoman Empire, but its brain was a Bavarian colonel named

Kress von Kressenstein. After the event, Djemal gave it out that this was no more than a reconnaissance in force, though there can be little doubt but that it was a serious attempt at the invasion of Egypt. Kress chose to make his approach march by the tracks leading from Beersheba to Ismailia, for, although it meant very difficult going, he would there be free from attention by the Royal Navy. He carried with him a pontoon train and, by great exertions, his force drew near to the southern end of the Canal at the end of January, 1915.

On the 29th of the same month, the convoy entered the Canal. 'A revelation of Empire', Monash called it as his ships sailed past the huge British cruisers which first paid them the traditional compliments of the sea and then cheered them to the echo. They anchored that night off Ismailia, 'a bright moonlight night, and although all ships are darkened it is a beautiful scene, and it is difficult to realize that we are in the midst of war, and that a considerable Turkish and Arab army is within a few miles of us, led by German officers'. Kress had overlooked the new air arm which, rude though it was, had kept the British precisely informed about his movements.

Monash wrote to his wife of 'the most astonishing medley of military activity, and such a wonderful moving panorama of war in full being surely was never before presented to view'. That was not quite how it appeared in Cairo where the current pleasantry was, 'Is the garrison of Egypt defending the Canal or is the Canal defending the garrison of Egypt?' Monash's judgment of the strength of fortifications had not yet reached maturity. However, the revelation continued to display itself as they sailed on. 'The first section of the Canal was held by Gurkhas, several battalions of them spreading along the first few miles, the men coming down to the water's edge and cheering as we passed. Presently on the southern bank the colour changed to white. "Who are you?" The reply came in semaphore, "NZ, NZ, NZ", to which we yelled "Kia Ora". "Where are the Australians?" "Up at Ismailia and Kantara." Then there was a rush to the other side where there were again English troops, but in an unfamiliar uniform. Then there was a great cheer from the western bank, and, rushing over, we were welcomed by mile after mile of Sikhs, infantry, cavalry, Bengal Lancers. At the entrance of the Little Bitter Lake stood a warship ... [she] raised the French flag and the band burst into the *Marseillaise*. The excitement on the warship was indescribable, the ship's company yelled and danced with delight. Round a bend we found ourselves again steaming between company after company of sepoys, then more Gurkhas, some more New Zealanders, an Egyptian Camel Corps ... then a battalion of King's Own Scottish Borderers and lots more Territorials and Indian and Egyptian soldiers.' A vanished world indeed.

The 4th Brigade moved into camp five miles out of Cairo, 'nowhere near the rest of the Australians', on 2 February. There Monash noted that 'the canal campaign seems to have fizzled out for the present'. The next night Kress attacked across the Canal just south of Tussum. For some reason, he struck first with his 25th Division, Arabs and unreliable troops, leaving his good Turkish 10th Division in reserve. The result was never in doubt. The rafts and pontoons which had been dragged so far with such Herculean efforts were launched and loaded with troops by 3 am. Within a few minutes the garrison of the West bank had shot them to pieces, only three pontoons reaching the other side and their crews being taken prisoner to a man. They made a further effort at dawn but with no better success. The Turkish army began its withdrawal at noon on 3 February, the only pursuit being by two companies of Gurkhas who launched a private counterattack without waiting for orders. The affair cost the British about 150 casualties while Wavell reckons that the Turks had lost not less than 1,500 or even 2,000. Certainly 716 prisoners appear in the records.

Although the attack on the Canal had ended in failure, one can see in retrospect that it did the Turkish cause far more good than harm. The very ease with which the victory had been gained led those in authority on the British side, from section commanders upward, to believe that the Turk was an antagonist about whom one need not worry too much. If this was the best he could do, then half-trained Territorials would be quite good enough to see him off. This splendid euphoria was paid for at a very heavy price before the year was out. Nobody yet knew for certain what the ultimate destination of the Australians would be. Kress was still at large somewhere in the desert and would remain a nuisance until the Battle of Romani in August, 1916, but that was no reason for their indefinite detention in Egypt. Wavell, who would have known, wrote that 'it had also been decided to disembark the first Australian and New Zealand contingents in Egypt to complete their training in a more favourable climate than that of an English winter'. That, to be sure, is what happened.

While his staff was working on the training programmes, Monash met for the first time the man who would be his chief. Lt-General Sir William Birdwood had been carefully selected by Kitchener as the senior officer most likely to get on with the idiosyncratic Australians, and he had chosen wisely. Birdwood was no Stonewall Jackson and as a book-soldier he was probably surpassed by quite a number of his peers. However, as a fighting commander of men who expected to see their leaders showing themselves where the bullets were thickest he was the ideal man for the job. His actual position was a little odd; with the arrival of the 4th Brigade it was possible to make up a complete corps, the Australian division providing one component and the New Zealanders with the 4th Brigade making the other. The corps commander and his staff were all British, provided and paid by the British government; this state of affairs continued almost to the end of the war, by which time Corps HQ had expanded to about 70 officers and more than 500 men, of whom most were Australian. Bridges, of course, commanded the 1st Division and Godley assumed command of the 2nd, originally called the New Zealand Division.

Birdwood realized from the start that these were not men to be treated in the same way as the soldiers to which he had long been accustomed. To take up time in insisting on the niceties of dress and the cardinal importance of saluting would have been a disaster in this army. On his first day, says Dr Bean, the corps commander was seen strolling round Gizeh Zoo talking to the soldiers he met as a man talks to his friends. Monash thought him 'a fine, dapper little chap with whom I am sure I shall get on'. It was no play-acting on Birdwood's part, for he had an unforced love for these men and a rare talent for getting the best out of them without stooping to cheap tricks for winning popularity at the expense of respect. His new charges met him more than half way, for they were sound judges of a man and had no difficulty in distinguishing between the genuine and the spurious. Monash certainly approved of him, writing that 'I think the Australian Army Corps is most fortunate that Kitchener chose Birdwood as their corps commander'. His own divisional general, Godley, he admired also, 'tall, elegant, graceful, genial and expansive — he also shows great ability'. Both generals were always immaculate in their turn-out (Birdwood had once been adjutant of the viceroy's bodyguard) and it began to dawn on many people that smartness in dress was not, after all, strong presumptive evidence of unmanliness.

The 1st Division had begun its collective training immediately on arrival in Egypt, starting in the conventional way with section training and working upwards. The New Zealand and Australian division, camped at Heliopolis, was more ambitious despite the fact that it was in many ways incomplete. Godley was right to aspire to bigger things, for the New Zealanders were already well advanced in their training and the 4th Brigade was probably the best formation ever to leave Australia. Most of the soldiers had been a little later in joining than those of the first three brigades, not because they lacked their ardour but because they were, for the most part, men of some substance who had had to sell a farm or a business of some kind before they could enlist. Dr Bean says of them that 'the huge men who at this time began to appear in the streets of Cairo gave the appearance of being built, if anything, on an even larger scale than those of the first contingent.'

Godley and Monash decided that there was no need, figuratively speaking, to teach these men to walk and that they could start running at once. Within less than a fortnight of their arrival they were sent out into the desert on a complete divisional exercise. True, it was far from a complete division, for the only guns they had consisted of a single NZ battery of 18-pounders and of engineers and most other services they had none at all. Nevertheless, this was a very considerable feat which Bridges never attempted at all with the 1st Division.

The Australian soldier had an invaluable gift, denied to his cousin, in that he was not road-bound. He found nothing unusual in moving swiftly by day or night over open country where the young Englishman would have floundered vaguely about. The speed and certainty with which the brigades could deploy in the open was a source of great encouragement to their generals. Bridges worked his division at least as hard, to the extent of having several men die from pneumonia as the result of exposing sweat-soaked bodies to the bitter desert wind.

All the training was based on the experiences of the British army in South Africa, for little or nothing of any use had filtered through from the Western Front for which they were, it was supposed, intended. There was, however, a small but useful practice on which Godley insisted; signal equipment was scanty and crude, so much play was made with the passing of messages by word of mouth. This was to pay a handsome dividend later. Another matter that received much attention was 'mateship'. This was a phenomenon so uniquely Australian and now so much a part of folklore that it still continues to inspire articles in learned journals. The British soldier, as a rule, did not very much mind who was on either side of him as he scrambled out of his trench to go forward, provided that it was not somebody he actively disliked or distrusted. Not so the Australian. The difficulty arose when one of the pair was hit. The British doctrine from time immemorial has been that no man is ever to fall out on the pretext of taking wounded to the rear. The reason is obvious and the crime has always been regarded as a serious one. Necessary and elementary though the prohibition was, it did not square with outback philosophy. To desert a mate in distress was the bushman's sin against the light that knows no forgiveness, and how could a mate be in more distress than lying on the ground in a pool of blood? Gradually and grudgingly the thing was accepted; when it happened, Bill must go on and Jim must take his chance.

It was at this time that Monash began to appear as something rather more than a British general had any business to expect of the equivalent of a Territorial colonel. The planning of a single operation by a brigade of four strong battalions is not a job which many non-professionals could perform at all. To do it as well as the results demonstrated demanded a talent far removed from the commonplace. 'The methodical, painstaking thoroughness with which he worked out every detail of the activities of his brigade, and the extreme lucidity with which he could explain to his officers any plan of coming operations', was how Bean perceived his quality. Monash would probably have replied that methodical, painstaking thoroughness had been a life's habit with him and that it was only by the exercise of such qualities that the Anderson Street Bridge had been built. The exact discipline of the engineer left nothing to chance and by comparison with some of the problems he had overcome in that field the planning of brigade manœuvres was not very difficult. Indeed, by contrast with what he would have to do during the next few years, it was a game for children. Godley took his measure and, at the conference which followed the scheme, his comment was, 'As to our new Australian brigade, all I need say is that they fell into their place and did what they were ordered to do with a punctuality, precision, steadiness, and thoroughness which make further comment unnecessary.'

On 17 February, Godley sent for Monash and said, 'General Birdwood and I have been closely watching the work of your brigade for the past ten days, and we have quite made up our minds that your brigade is the best Australian brigade in Egypt. This consideration has entirely modified the plans for the disposal of the whole army corps, and has greatly contributed to its fighting efficiency.' He went on to say that Monash could now move on to the most advanced forms of night-work and training in trench warfare. It is interesting to speculate on exactly what Godley meant by 'modifying the plans for the disposal of the Army Corps'. So far as anybody in Egypt knew, they were there, as Wavell explained, because it was the most convenient training ground available. There was no doubt in the minds of any of its members in February, 1915, but that the AIF was going to fight its first battles in France or Flanders. That was where the great battles had been going on for months and there was no other major theatre of war.

The most likely explanation is that Birdwood already knew something of what was in the wind and had taken Godley into his confidence. The events which were to lead to the campaign on the Gallipoli peninsula had indeed been in train for the last six weeks or so. They had begun on New Year's Day when Mr Lloyd George had circulated his memorandum to the effect that an unwarrantable spirit of optimism was abroad, that the Russians were not doing at all well and that a stroke was called for in the Balkans in order to rally Greece and Bulgaria on the side of the Allies. This may seem a singular document to emanate from the Chancellor of the Exchequer but strict departmental functions did not seem necessary to Mr Lloyd George until he became Prime Minister. The sentiments expressed agreed exactly with those of his colleague at the Admiralty, who had wanted the Dardanelles attacked as soon as war had been declared.

On the following day Kitchener received a telegram from the Grand Duke Nicholas in which he admitted the Russian army to be hard pressed in the Caucasus and asked whether it would not be possible for the British government to stage some sort of demonstration which would have the effect of drawing the Turkish reserves. Before the day was out, Mr Churchill had put to Lord Kitchener his proposal for an attack on the peninsula; the Secretary for War 'did not dissent' but made it plain that it would be of no use to ask him to spare troops for such an enterprise. Mr Churchill was not put out; the use of troops was not then in contemplation and if a small number should be needed, they could be drawn from the Royal Naval Division of seamen and Royal Marines surplus to the requirements of the Fleet.

On 4 January, Russian and Turk met head on at the Battle of Sarikamish, of which few details have ever penetrated to the West. Enver Pasha, the self-appointed Caesar of the triumvirate, led a Turkish army of about 90,000 men to force his way into Russia from the south during the depths of winter. Something under one-seventh of them ever came back, bringing with them the scourge of typhus. The need of the Grand Duke for help was past, but the news was kept from those upon whom he had called for it.

During the next few days Vice-Admiral Sackville Carden, commanding in the Mediterranean, gave it as his opinion that the Dardanelles could not be rushed but that a systematic bombardment of the forts by the great guns of his ships, delivered from anchorages which the cannon of the forts could not reach, might stand a decent chance of pulverizing them. The enormously increased power of naval ordnance which the last few years had brought about seemed to outdate the 'Ships can't fight forts' lessons of earlier wars. It had been demonstrably true when ship and fort had carried much the same sort of gun, but it could no longer be so when the ship could do all the shooting and the fort could only provide a target. No senior naval officer raised his voice to say otherwise.

It is worth noticing one suggestion made by Carden which nobody ever mentioned again. After enumerating the ships he would need, Carden added that four of the old battleships should be fitted with mine-bumpers. His estimation of the importance of this weapon was correct. The sea-mine had been invented by Mr Nobel, of Peace Prize fame, in the 1850's and very serviceable ones had been used by the Russian navy as part of the defences of Kronstadt during the Crimean War. The Turkish navy had recently been receiving training from a British Naval Mission under Admiral Limpus and were known to be well supplied with mines and quite skilful in their use. At one point the Narrows are less than three-quarters of a mile across and the employment of mines in such a place in large numbers must have been a foregone conclusion. Nevertheless, when the time came to sweep the minefields under fire, the task was given to the civilian fishermen and merchant seamen who manned the trawlers requisitioned for the purpose.

On 12 January the Cabinet minuted the preparation of a naval expedition in February to 'bombard and take the Gallipoli peninsula with Constantinople as its objective'. How fleets take peninsulas was not explained. Carden was told that his plan was approved and, further, that the last word in battleships, HMS *Queen Elizabeth*, should be put at his disposal so that she might carry out calibration tests of her prodigious 15-inch guns on the unfortunate Turkish garrisons of the forts. Experts worked out precisely how it should be done, though they were a little handicapped by the fact that the British ordnance factories, unlike the German ones, did not then know how to fill shells of that size with high explosive and so they were packed with black powder only.

Kitchener blew hot and cold over the use of the 29th Division, the last regular formation in England and made up from units returned from India. He would accept advice only from people he knew to be competent to give it and of this select band Birdwood was a member. So Kitchener sent him off to the Dardanelles at the end of February to see things for himself and to report back to his chief what he thought of the chances of the navy doing the job unaided. On 5 March, Birdwood sent the first of several reports, saying that he was 'doubtful if the navy could force the passage unassisted'. Though he did not leave Egypt until 24 February, the fact that Godley was able to speak to Monash six days earlier about 'plans for the disposal of the whole army corps' makes it reasonable to believe that he and Birdwood had already obtained a shrewd idea of what the future held for them. His departure was kept a well-guarded secret for, on 4 March, Monash was writing home that 'General Birdwood left yesterday for an unknown destination' and offered the choice of several 'furphies' as to where they were likely to be going. All of them were wrong.

For the Australians, meanwhile, life had not been wholly occupied in training. For one thing, they had made the acquaintance, for the first time in the lives of many of them, of the English. In a way, it was an unlucky one. The regular garrison had long departed and in their place had come the 42nd (East Lancashire) Division TF. These men have enough feats of arms to their credit (the most recent being the breaking up of Djemal's attack on the Canal) to need no insincere praise. They could not have been expected to have the bearing of the Brigade of Guards, nor do Bolton and Rochdale breed the largest men in the country. To the huge Australians they were like creatures from another planet; likeable little chaps, generous to a fault within the limits of their resources, utterly without 'dog' but barely comprehensible. Naturally the thought came to many, 'Did great-grandfather really look and talk like that?' The daunting answer was 'Very probably'. Monash, whose ancestors had been very different and to whom dark, satanic mills had been unknown, found them 'a wonder and a puzzle'. On the whole, they got on well together but they had too little in common to encourage much mixing.

There was, however, one unhappy meeting that could not be avoided. Hard work and no fighting had damped down the 'Now all the youth of England is on fire' mood amongst some of the larrikin element and Bridges had cause to worry about the reputation a tiny minority was giving the whole Australian force. Drunkenness, insubordination, desertion and attacks on natives were becoming common and it was noticeable that some of the New Zealand officers were encouraging their men 'to have nothing to do with the Australians, but to show by their neat dress and sobriety that there was a wide difference between the two forces'. Bridges decided that only one punishment fitted the crime and he sent 300 of the hardest cases home in disgrace, leaving it to them to explain as best they could how it had happened. On Good Friday, 1915, shortly after being warned for embarkation, a party of both Australians and New Zealanders decided that they would square a few accounts before sailing. They began by visiting the *Haret el Wasser*, the street of the brothels, where they ransacked one house, in which they reckoned that they had been more compendiously swindled than in most. By stages it developed into a regular riot. The British Military Police, never the most beloved of men, were chased off, an indignity which they sensibly accepted rather than opening fire. It was the Lancashire Territorials, advancing in line with bayonets fixed, who dispersed the crowd, the Australians probably not wanting to pick a fight with the 'chooms'. It is known to Australian history as the First Battle of the Wozzer.

The Cairenes, naturally, did very well out of the rich Australians, who imposed a discipline of their own when they came to understand the mentality of their temporary hosts. From them they learnt several useful phrases some of which are found in guide-books. 'Imshi Yallah', 'Igri', 'Orinjis' and 'Eggs a-cook' passed into the language alongside 'furphy'; these were the genial war-cries which were shortly to ring across the Gallipoli peninsula, entirely suited, in the Australian view, to the pursuit of an oriental foe.

CHAPTER FOUR

## Australia was There

THE Turks were under no illusions about the designs the Allies entertained on the Gallipoli Peninsula. Indeed, short of actually publishing an advertisement in the Constantinople daily press, little had been left undone to acquaint them with the two governments' intentions. In November the navy had bombarded the outer forts of Kum Kale and Sedd-el-Bahr, the Padlock of the sea, for half an hour without achieving very much. Between 19 and 25 February a much heavier cannonade had seemed to produce more impressive results and parties of Marines had been landed at the peninsula's tip to do what damage they could to the deserted guns of the forts. They spent a most pleasant day on the beaches, for there was not a Turk to be seen.

The great effort by the fleet followed nearly a month later and is more than adequately described in many books; for the purposes of this one, it suffices to say that at the moment when the Turks were down to their last few rounds of armour-piercing shell, half their guns out of action and the crews at the end of their tether, the admiral called it off. Some years after the war a senior Turkish officer enquired of the British historian, in Constantinople on a fact-finding expedition, why the attack had not been renewed. He refused to believe the explanation that five ships had been lost by mines and that the admiral had decided that he must not expose more battleships to them until clearing had been carried out. The Turk adhered to the view that it was all part of an elaborate subterfuge to prevent the Russians from having Constantinople.

Before the guns thundered and the clouds of smoke blew over the plains of windy Troy, Kitchener had received Birdwood's reports and had satisfied himself that the navy would never see Constantinople unless the army made it possible for them to do so. He issued orders for the 29th Division to be transported at once to the island of Lemnos, kindly put at the disposal of the Allies by the Anglophile Greek Prime Minister M Venizelos. Since a major undertaking was about to be started, he needed a commander of stature and seniority. Birdwood was rather too junior a lieut-general, and, in any event, it would be a pity to take him away from his Australians and New Zealanders on the eve of their first battle and incur all the general post amongst commanders that would necessarily follow. His candidate was never in doubt.

General Sir Ian Hamilton was among the most senior officers in the army; his record was distinguished and, although he had not yet seen action in this war, he was one of the most up-to-date men in the service. After commanding the Mounted Infantry Division in South Africa with conspicuous success he had gone as an observer to Manchuria, attached to the Japanese army, where he had seen how the machine-gun and barbed wire had come to dominate the battlefield. His subsequent publication, *A Staff Officer's Scrap Book*, had shown that he was not just a simple-minded thruster but a thoughtful man with an excellent brain. Though it had no particular military relevance, Hamilton was also one of the most attractive personalities in the army and men found it a pleasure to work with him. He was to stand in need of every quality he possessed and more, for the task set him, the landing of a large army on a hostile beach and its subsequent maintenance for an indefinite period, was something that had never been done before.

Such amphibious operations as the army had undertaken in the past gave little enough inspiration to the formulating of his plans. Havana had been taken from the sea in 1762 and an unopposed landing at New Orleans in 1814 had been followed by bloody defeat because the army, once landed, had done nothing in particular but had allowed the defenders generous time in which to complete their strong fortifications. There was probably a moral in this somewhere.

Hamilton has come in for harsh criticism and, beyond doubt, his judgment was sometimes at fault. It is not difficult to criticize when one has the benefit of hind-sight and when so much is known that could not have been even suspected by him. He had no voice in the appointment of his subordinate commanders, some of whom were quite unequal to their tasks, he had no plan and no maps. The Gallipoli Peninsula, for all its proximity to one of the oldest capitals in the world, was as rugged and practically as unknown as the moon. A few villages of shepherds and fishermen alone redeemed it from utter desolation and, as nobody ever went there, it is no great wonder that it had never seemed worth anybody's while to have its tangled, scrubby, ridges and valleys properly surveyed. Kitchener was able to furnish the commander of the great expedition which was to burst in the back door of the Central Powers with three useful artifacts: two small guide-books and a textbook on the Turkish army. He tendered advice on how to attack and then hold Constantinople but brushed off the earlier stages as being hardly worthy of discussion. When Kitchener asked Hamilton, in his present capacity as C-in-C Home Forces, whether he thought the 29th Division could be spared, Hamilton replied, 'Yes, and four more Territorial Divisions as well.' 'K used two or three very bad words and added, with his usual affability, that I would find myself walking about in civilian costume instead of going to Constantinople if he found me making any wild statements of the sort to the politicians.'[1]

The next day, 13 March, Hamilton sailed. The first landings, involving about 50,000 men, took place forty-eight days later. The planning of the invasion of Normandy took something over two years. Those inclined to denigrate Hamilton should pause to reflect that, as Dr Johnson said of women preachers, 'It is not done well; but you are surprised to find it done at all.'

Monash, still in Egypt and still hard at training his brigade, was becoming bored. 'My brigade is now a very complete, very well trained, and very formidable fighting force . . . I wish this war were over and that we could resume our lives together on the

[1] *Gallipoli Diary*, Vol. I, p. 5.

lines of some of the happy days we have had.' By the end of the month, however, he began to have some clue as to what was in store for them. Maclagan's 3rd Brigade was known to have sailed off somewhere into the Mediterranean. The French general, Albert D'Amade, whose Territorial divisions had already given a good account of themselves on the fringes of the battle of Le Cateau, was at Alexandria with his troops and the Australians were inspected by Hamilton on 29 March. The two men had met before when Hamilton had visited Australia just before the war. During the march past they rode together and Hamilton 'cocked his head on one side, in the funny little way he has, and said; "Well, Monash, when we sat under a gum-tree together twelve months ago, we didn't think, either of us, we should meet again so soon".'

Monash, at least, appreciated the burden that had been strapped to Hamilton's shoulders. 'What a tremendous responsibility that man must have ... as it looks as if he is going to command the operations of the Allies at this end of the show.'

While Liman von Sanders, the recently-arrived German general who was now commanding all the Turkish forces in the peninsula, was digging, wiring and preparing gun emplacements at all the most sensitive points, Monash had the chance to indulge his taste for archaeology. He was able to spend a weekend amongst the ancient tombs of Luxor, 'by far the most wonderful and impressive sight I have seen anywhere ... Just imagine going down four hundred feet into the bowels of the earth, through galleries hewn out of the solid rock, with spacious and majestic chambers every few feet for six hundred feet, on the incline, with every inch of all the walls carved with the most beautiful hieroglyphics, large and small, all in their original rich colouring, absolutely unharmed, and at the end in a noble chamber, to see a beautiful red granite richly carved sarcophagus, and in it the absolutely perfect mummy of Amenhotep II, the great Pharaoh of Joseph's time, where he has lain asleep, undisturbed for over four thousand years, with all his history and that of his time carved in the stone all around.' This must have carried more of a message to the descendant of one of the dispersed tribes, wandered to a corner of the earth of which Solomon had never dreamt, than the sight and sound of the sons of Lancashire. One can be pretty certain, too, that the engineer in him was busy with calculations of strains and stresses, quantities and labour costs.

On his way back through Cairo, where the newspapers were publishing uninhibited and tolerably accurate accounts of the nature of the impending operations with complete impunity as their country was not at war, he saw an army of another pattern. General D'Amade's division contained every kind of French colonial troops, black Senegalese, Zouaves, Chasseurs d'Afrique and Foreign Legionaries, each more gorgeously dressed than the last. Even these, however, seemed drab beside the Sultan's escort in ultramarine and silver, with a red tarboosh. Contemplation of these did not long detain him, for, as he wrote next day, 'In another week I expect we shall all be pretty seasick and catching colds.'

Three days later, the 4th Brigade marched out, to entrain at Helmieh station. 'Thousands of Territorials and Australians and New Zealand Light Horsemen, many weeping with regret at not being allowed to come, gathered around to give us a royal send-off.' On the following day, they were at sea, slipping quietly out of Alexandria before the sun rose. Monash says that on every day of the three preceding weeks a troopship had left at every other hour and that, although two hundred ships had already gone, it would still require a week more before the last details had left. By this time he had been told officially where they were going and for what purpose. His thoughts as the ships steamed swiftly through the Aegean spring remain: 'As the morning mists lifted we found ourselves abreast of the island of Karpathos on our west, with the peaks of the Island of Rhodes just dimly showing on the horizon to the east. It seems strange to be cruising along in this beautiful sea and mild fragrant air, and yet to know that so near to us is the centre of an epoch-making clash of arms. After all, is it not strange that we should be fighting the Turks and not the Germans? It makes a considerable difference to many from different points of view that this should be so. One probable result of the war will be the freeing of Jerusalem and Palestine from the Turkish yoke.'

No campaign since the Crusades ever began in such an atmosphere of educated romance. Homer's Troy would soon be abeam, the Narrows where Xerxes had built the bridge of boats by which he had passed his army from Asia to Europe lay ahead, Rhodes with its memories of the siege and Master Villiers de L'Isle Adam was in sight, and the ultimate objective was the city of Constantine itself. Hamilton, who had been born in Corfu and to whom no part of the Middle Sea was strange, tried to entice another poet (he was by no means a contemptible one himself) on to his staff. 'Young Brooke replied, as a preux chevalier would naturally reply, that he realized the privileges he was foregoing but he felt bound to do the landing shoulder to shoulder with his comrades.' Hamilton, who had just read *Sinister Street*, transferred the offer to Compton Mackenzie.

Since the fleet had withdrawn on 18 March, much had been done to make the peninsula as nearly impregnable as possible and, in general terms, Hamilton knew it. What he lacked most desperately was up-to-date and accurate intelligence of exactly what these preparations had been. Liman von Sanders had managed to extract another division from Enver, bringing the total force available to six. No force is ever sufficient to enable a defending commander to be strong everywhere, and he had to consider the several courses open to the invaders. One serious possibility was a landing on the Asiatic coast followed by an advance across the plains of Troy to take all his carefully prepared defences from behind. The next most likely seemed to be an assault on the neck of the peninsula at Bulair; true, this would not help the navy and would leave the army advancing on the capital with a strong and fresh force breathing down its neck, but a thrust of such audacity could not be discounted. At the tip of the peninsula lay the old but modernized fort of Sedd-el-Bahr which, with its neighbour Tekke Burnu (sounding far less formidable when translated into Shrimp Point), was particularly vulnerable to the great guns of the ships. An advance from here to the summit of the dominating Achi Baba—Plaster Hill,

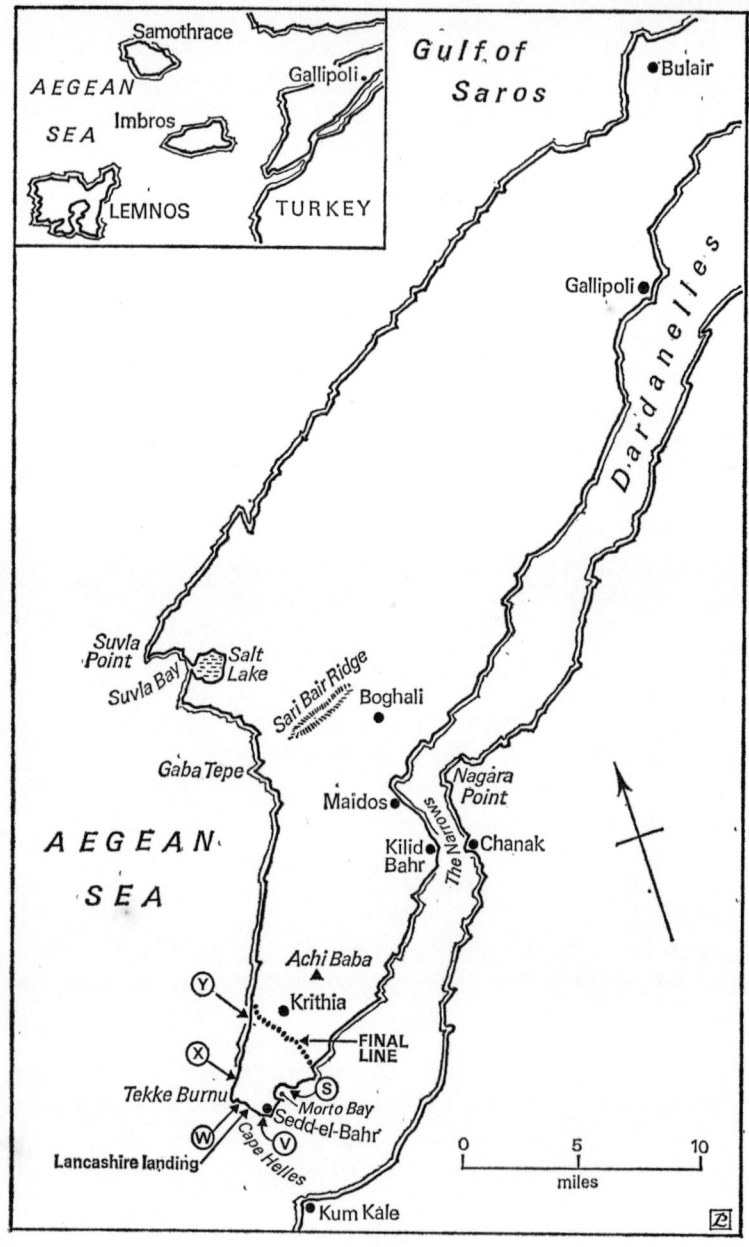

because of its whiteness—could take all the works along the Narrows in enfilade. Lastly, on the west coast, there were possible landing places on the beaches either side of Gaba Tepe—Rough Hill; on Gaba Tepe itself there was a strong position with artillery and machine-guns well wired in, but it could be bypassed and the next objective of the attackers would be Maidos which overlooked the Dardanelles. He decided that he must have a strong force in Asia and two divisions were dispatched there, the 3rd and the 11th. Two more divisions, the 5th and the 7th, were assigned to the defence of all the possible landing places around the coast and his last division, the 19th, was held in general reserve around Maidos. He spent the Allah-sent month in improving communications so that his reserves could be swiftly moved as they were needed, though the commander of the 19th Division could be relied upon not to dawdle. He was a rough, foul-mouthed soldier of peasant stock after the school of Rapp and Augereau, by name Mustafa Kemal. Writing after the war, von Sanders said that 'the English allowed us four good weeks of respite for all this work before their great disembarkation ... [it] just sufficed for the most indispensable measures to be taken'.

His dispositions were as sound as one would expect from an experienced German general, but Hamilton's task was by far the harder. He knew that he had not nearly enough men for a protracted campaign and the administrative problems alone were gigantic. Quite apart from anything connected with fighting, he had to feed, on an alien and inhospitable sea-coast, the equivalent of the population of a town the size of, say, Maidstone, and to provide all the essential services of a local authority in the way of water, sanitation and hospitals. Ordinary requisites of life apart, he must find ammunition of all kinds, evacuate casualties and keep up a steady flow of news bulletins to London. He also had to direct a major campaign in conjunction with the navy. The prospect could hardly have been more daunting and it was of little assistance to be told by most of his generals that they were of opinion that it was impossible. There were shortages of everything, especially of artillery ammunition. The Turks were well supplied with grenades, the most important infantry weapon in trench warfare, but they had been dropped from the British ordnance stores at about the end of the Seven Years War. Until the few batteries he possessed could be got ashore, his would be purely an infantry army. To aid him there was not one single article designed for facilitating amphibious operations and he must make do with the standard equipment of ships and armies.

Hamilton would have liked to adhere to the Napoleonic maxim of 'Scatter to forage, concentrate to fight', but it was simply not possible. His orders from Kitchener contained the words 'The occupation of the Asiatic side is to be strongly deprecated', presumably because any operations there would be exposed to the fire of the forts. An attack on Bulair, tempting though it was, could not be seriously considered because he lacked the transport to carry out an advance to the Narrows with a Turkish army treading on his heels. The single, smashing blow that he would have liked to deliver was out of the question also on the constricted beaches; there remained only the course of making one, or perhaps two, landings in as much strength as he could muster with a good deception plan being employed to try and keep his enemy rushing hither and thither while the landings went on. Such, in essence, was the ultimate decision. He would make two feints, the French landing on the Asiatic shore at Kum Kale where they would occupy the attention and draw the fire of the biggest Turkish guns which might otherwise cover Morto Bay; the second by the Royal Naval Division, which was to cruise in its transports up the Gulf of Saros to induce von Sanders to believe that a landing at Bulair was imminent. Under cover of these diversions, two genuine attacks would be launched, the main one at Cape Helles by the 29th Division aimed at Achi Baba and a subsidiary one by the Australian and New Zealand Army Corps north of Gaba Tepe, with the object of seizing the high spine of the peninsula and intercepting the retreat of the defenders of the southern tip on the plateau of Kilid Bahr.

Covering fire would, of course, be provided by the fleet in accordance with a carefully-worked-out timetable. In addition to the common shell which she carried for her 15-inch guns, the

*Queen Elizabeth* had been provided with a quantity of shrapnel, each shell containing something like 10,000 balls.[1] Taking into account the resources available and the almost total lack of any useful information, it is difficult to think of a better plan. The beaches for the landings were selected and the old tramp steamer *River Clyde* was converted at great speed into the first landing ship. In case the spies who abounded in Alexandria had missed this interesting detail, the Egyptian newspapers painstakingly set out all the details, with pictures. The landings were planned for St George's Day—23 April—but bad weather compelled a postponement of forty-eight hours. Thus it happened that the most hallowed anniversary in Australia has ever since been celebrated on 25 April, Anzac Day.

Since Monash was in no way concerned with the landings at Cape Helles they need only be dealt with in an outline which falls far below their deserts. There were five of them in all, each taking place on a cramped beach identified by a letter. Well away to the north-west was Y Beach, at a point which Hamilton reasonably supposed unlikely to be strongly defended; two battalions were assigned to the task, the King's Own Scottish Borderers and the Plymouth Battalion of the Royal Naval Division. Following along the coast X Beach came next and, passing Tekke Burnu, there came then W and V Beaches, right under the guns of the forts. At the eastern end of the arc of Morto Bay, about a mile and a quarter from Sedd-el-Bahr, was the last beach, S, which was intended largely as a diversion. It was well within the range of the guns at Kum Kale on the Asiatic shore but D'Amade's Frenchmen could be relied upon to deal with them. The troops were to be taken ashore in ship's boats towed by warships until near enough for the unarmoured picket-boats of the fleet to complete the journey. W Beach was to have the addition of the *River Clyde*, which was to be run ashore with her troops (the

---

[1] During an ammunition crisis in 1941 a number of these were found still in store at Malta where they had lain for more than twenty-five years. When they came to be fired it was found that the passage of time had congealed all the balls into one solid chunk of iron. In their day they had been reckoned to sweep a full acre but it would have been hard to think of any use to which they could then have been put.

Royal Dublin Fusiliers, Munster Fusiliers, half the Hampshires and a Territorial Field Company RE from the West Riding of Yorkshire) landing from a bridge.

The attack was timed to go in at dawn, a little after the Australians and New Zealanders had been set in motion towards the beaches around Gaba Tepe, away to the north-east. No operation of war can compare in difficulty with the co-ordination of the actions of a number of dispersed bodies of men each aimed at a different objective. When there is added the factor of having to concert arrangements with another service, it becomes nearly impracticable. Only by having the best and swiftest of communications, ample reserves and the means of moving them at speed to the place where they are needed, can there be any hope of success against serious opposition. One thing only can be regarded as certain; the plan, however excellent, will miscarry. In some places a column will manage to fight its way through, in others it will be held up. All military philosophy demands that in such a case success must be reinforced but failure never; throughout history wars have been lost by rigid adherence to plans.

Not one single essential was available to Hamilton. For signals he was utterly dependent on the navy, who had a battle of their own to fight. An adequate reserve, the 42nd Division, was available in Egypt, but he had been forbidden even to cast covetous eyes on it. He decided that the course offering the least of the inescapable evils was to establish himself and his HQ in the conning-tower of *Queen Elizabeth* from which he could get a fairly good view of the earliest stages of the battle and where he would be in the closest rapport with his admirals. He ordered his two commanders, Hunter-Weston at Helles and Birdwood at Gaba Tepe, to remain in their ships for the first twenty-four hours so that he could keep in radio communication with them. The result was disastrous. Hamilton was deafened by the thunder of the ship's guns and the navy required the wireless for their own use. Hunter-Weston, similarly immured off W Beach, was powerless to influence events, desperate though the need soon became for a commander of all the forces ashore. It is fascinating, though unprofitable, to speculate on what Monash would have done had he been in charge of the expedition. In 1918 he was to write that 'the battle plan having been thus crystallized, no subsequent alterations were permitted, under any circumstances, however tempting'. His assertion that 'in a well-planned battle ... nothing happens, nothing can happen, except the regular progress of the advance according to the plan arranged' was clearly not written with this situation in mind.

In any event, the advance did not meet with anything like regular progress. Both battalions at Y Beach landed without any opposition, climbed the cliffs and rested from their labours. Brigadier-General Hare, commanding, at X Beach, issued an order which deserves to survive:
'Fusiliers,

Our Brigade is to have the honour to be the first to land and to cover the disembarkation of the rest of the Division. Our task will be no easy one. Let us carry it through in a way worthy of the traditions of the distinguished regiments of which the Fusilier Brigade is composed; in such a way that the men of Albuhera and Minden, of Delhi and Lucknow may hail us as their equals in valour and military achievement, and that future historians may say of us as Napier said of the Fusilier Brigade at Albuhera "Nothing could stop this astonishing infantry".'

Times had changed and the machine-gun could, and did, stop any infantry in the world. Nevertheless, the Fusiliers of 1915 showed themselves true sons of their fathers. Under the guns of HMS *Implacable,* and in the company of two other regiments with traditions as old and as fine as their own (the Inniskillings and the Border Regiment) they made good their foothold on the enemy shore and were soon locked in battle with the Turks.

The last report of success came from distant S Beach where the South Wales Borderers landed without difficulty and wasted no time over storming the battery there at bayonet point. From V and W Beaches, however, came stories of bloody failure. The *River Clyde* ran her bows into the sand as the morning mist was beginning to disperse and was greeted with a tempest of fire from the fort and the village. Three companies of the Dublins, towed in barges by the picket-boats, commanded by 16-year-old midshipmen, were cut to pieces before they set foot on shore.[1] With a courage beyond all praise, the naval parties in the old ship erected the bridge, men falling dead as they worked and being promptly replaced by others; the Munsters dashed for the beach and died in swathes. The *Queen Elizabeth* came to the rescue with her secondary batteries but could do no more than make it possible for a few scattered groups to reach land and shelter under a low, sandy cliff. Within a day or two the battalions were amalgamated as the Dubsters.

At W Beach things were a little better. The Lancashire Fusiliers, part of Hare's Fusilier Brigade, had disembarked from their boats when the Turkish fire opened on them; seventy men fell at the first burst but the remainder rushed the wire, taking very heavy casualties in the process, and won their way to the safety of the cliffs. Hare made an adroit attack from a flank under the guns of the navy and, with the arrival of the Worcesters, managed to make some headway towards the interior. During the afternoon he was able to link up with the Fusiliers and Essex at X Beach. The astonishing infantry continued to move forward, cutting wire as they went.

This was the moment when a fresh plan should have been made and it might well have been done had Hamilton been in possession of the signals system of a generation later. S Beach was firmly held, but the force there was so small that it could do no more than defend itself. If Hare could have been reinforced by just one of the Lancashire Brigades doing nothing in Egypt, he might well have broken through to the rear of V Beach. The men at V Beach, however, were still in the fight, for all their dreadful hurt. At dawn on the 26th, they rose up under the leadership of the gallant Col Doughty-Wylie, drove the enemy from his trenches and captured Sedd-el-Bahr itself. At Y Beach, however, the easy start was succeeded by a rout. The troops there do not seem to have made any very serious effort to dig themselves in and when the Turkish attack eventually came they were not prepared for it.

[1] One of *Bacchante*'s midshipmen, Douglas Dixon, achieved the unprecedented and probably unique distinction of being twice mentioned in dispatches before his sixteenth birthday.

They lost most of their officers and the survivors, with little idea of what they were supposed to be doing, sent an impassioned plea for boats and the navy took them off. A single brigade landed here would have completely altered the pattern of the rest of the campaign. However, by nightfall on 26 April the line ran unbroken from Morto Bay to X Beach; next day the division advanced a full two miles all along the line against little resistance. It might have been much worse.

One of the chaplains of 29th Division afterwards met a friend newly arrived from Australia. He quoted to him the address given by a wounded Australian officer to the boys of a school at home: 'Now, boys, I want you to understand that there has never been a finer fighting unit than the 29th Division.' He added his own comment. 'The Australian is often accused of having a high opinion of himself. But he certainly knows where and when to praise, and every one of them whom I subsequently met, and who had seen anything of the 29th Division, was unqualified in his admiration for them. Often they would add, "We see now the value of discipline." '

It is time to go back and see what was happening to the soldiers of the two dominions. Their task, to effect a landing around Gaba Tepe, was secondary to the Helles operation but even so it was one of the greatest amphibious attacks ever launched. Maclagan's 3rd Brigade was selected by General Bridges for the honour of being the first Australian formation to go into battle. They travelled in their transports, every man carrying two hundred rounds of ammunition, two empty sandbags wrapped round his entrenching tool and rations for two days (corned beef, biscuit and a tin of tea and sugar) in cotton bags tied to the belt. Packs were fastened in a fashion that enabled them to be slipped off at once; the owner might wish to rid himself quickly of this heavy burden should he find himself in the sea, and, in any event, they were not intended to be carried beyond the shore. The transports anchored off Imbros and, at about midnight, the men were transferred to destroyers, each towing a line of empty rowing boats, or, in the case of those to make the first landing, to battleships similarly appended. The night was utterly still with the moon

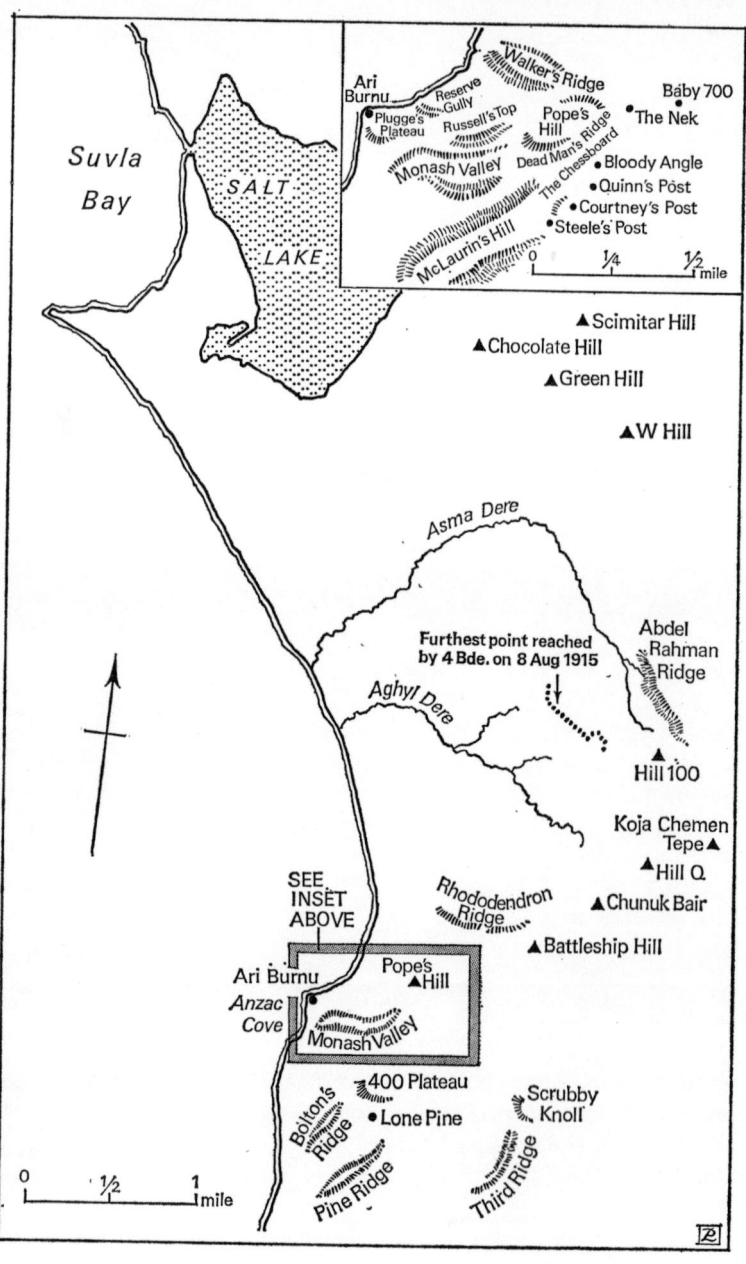

high and bright. Just before it set behind them, the troops were again moved into the waiting boats. At three o'clock the moon sank and twelve tows each of three boats pulled by a naval picket-boat began to move over the last two or three miles to the shore. There was no sound save the wash of the water and the bubbling note of the small steam-engines. This part of an opposed landing is not too bad, even when it is being done for the first time, for in the little vacuum of a boat only the faces of comrades can be seen and excitement alone keeps the spirits high. It is far worse when one actually lands, and the unfriendly, unknown country seems to be alive with cunning and merciless enemies. As they moved slowly through the inky blackness, mitigated only by a few stars, a current, unknown to anybody, was bearing the boats to the north. At about 4.30 the leading ones grounded and the men could make out a plateau of land ahead with a round knoll about two hundred feet high at its foot. It was Ari Burnu Point, a good mile north of where they ought to have been.

For a moment there was dead silence. Then there appeared on the sky-line the figure of a man. A voice called out, a rifle flashed, followed by several others. Men clambered out of the boats and dashed across the strand to a sandy bank which marked the junction between beach and hill. The fire increased in intensity, a machine-gun joined in; and men began to fall. A tiny shrimp of a midshipman, waving a revolver nearly as big as himself, scrambled over broad Australian backs and dashed forward yelling in a squeaky treble, 'Come on, my lads. Come on, my lads.' Having reached the foot of the plateau it seemed to dawn on him that he had no business to be doing such a thing and, sadly, he made his way back to his picket-boat.[1]

Heavier weapons, including 1-inch Nordenfeldts, were adding their contribution now and the battalions were mixed together in the confusion. One thing, however, was firmly in the front of every mind. They were the covering force and it was up to them to get forward as far as possible, even if they had been landed at the wrong place. Packs were dropped and sub-units began to

[1] Doubt has been cast on the authenticity of this story but it was first related by men who were there.

move upwards as best they could; there was no question of keeping in touch with each other. They hauled themselves up the steep sides of the plateau as the light increased, dragging their way up by the roots of the arbutus that grew thickly thereabouts. By degrees they mastered the top of the plateau, shooting and bayoneting those of its defenders who were imprudent enough to linger, and found themselves brought up short by a deep valley. Down the slope and up the other side they went, men dropping to right and left, the line never faltering for one moment. The making of the Anzac legend had begun. As the light improved, the Turkish battery on Gaba Tepe opened fire at their backs with shrapnel. HMS *Bacchante*, an elderly cruiser, which was hovering about to deal with such eventualities, poured in broadside after broadside. Each time the broadside struck, the battery fell silent but each time a destroyer came in to release another tow of boats, it opened up again. It was, perhaps, just as well that the current had taken the first flight away from the designated landing place; Gaba Tepe might very easily have been another V Beach. However, the boats continued to come, the Anzac vanguard continued to advance, and by about 7.30 the remaining two brigades of Bridges' 1st Australian Division were ashore.

From the outset, they were dogged by the cruellest luck. Hamilton's dummy attacks were working quite well, for as the first Australians were swarming ashore at the place which will for ever be known as Anzac Cove, a report reached Liman von Sanders that a fleet of transports was in the Gulf of Saros, apparently making for Bulair. This was, of course, the Royal Naval Division, sent there to induce such a deduction as von Sanders drew, that the Gaba Tepe landing, of which he learned almost simultaneously, was the feint and Bulair the real attack. He was at a fort near there when the news reached him of the fighting at Cape Helles. The warships began to bombard Bulair, and Liman, refusing to believe that the main effort was going to be made elsewhere, entrusted command of the forces aligned against the attackers of the other places to a subordinate, Essad Pasha. To him he gave the 19th Division, still at Maidos, in addition to the 9th which was already engaged.

When the Australians first landed, the only troops opposed to them were some companies of the 27th Regiment and two batteries of artillery which they soon overran. The remainder of the 27th Regiment was hurried to the Gaba Tepe area and arrived in position at about the time the later Australian brigades were disembarking. However, on the day of the landing Mustafa Kemal had arranged an exercise for his 57th Regiment. They paraded at 5.30 am, but before he had finished his inspection a message arrived announcing the Anzac landing. Mustafa did not wait to do more than ascertain whether his men were carrying ball cartridge or blank. On receiving a satisfactory answer, he led them himself across the rough country between his present position and Koja Chemen Tepe – the Hill of the Great Pasture – directly in the path of Bridges' advance. Exactly at what hour he arrived is not certain, but he was in time to encounter stragglers from the line who gave him a highly coloured account of what was happening. Kemal at once saw the seriousness of the situation and sent back for his other regiment, the 77th. He did not wait for their arrival, but attacked at once with two regiments and a mountain battery.

As Kemal was mustering his troops for the counterattack, the covering force was continuing to make headway. The accident of the landing having taken place on the wrong beach, coupled with the fact that this maze of hills and scrub-covered ravines had broken up all co-ordination, compelled it to be carried out haphazardly; battalions and companies were broken up but with the 1st Brigade now on the left and the 2nd on the right of the original force, small parties under any officer who happened to be on the spot pressed forward towards the main objective known as Third Ridge.

Lack of knowledge of the ground had caused Hamilton to set them an unattainable objective, though the distance involved was no more than a mile and a half as the crow flies. Before noon Lt Loutit of the 10th Battalion had led a party of his Queenslanders to Scrubby Knoll on the Ridge itself, the furthest point reached during the campaign, and it is probable that others reached it also. However, so scattered and small were the bands of infantry that their position soon became untenable. Kemal's attack began to develop during the afternoon and the Anzacs were forced back, fighting for every inch of ground they were made to concede. Such was the power of their musketry that the attack failed in its purpose of driving them into the sea but the gaps that existed in the line made it fairly certain that another attempt would probably be successful.

By late afternoon they had been pushed back into a position that was at least more or less cohesive but it was plain to everybody that things had not gone as planned. Far from standing triumphantly on the heights overlooking the Narrows, they had been torn and battered by small arms fire and shrapnel, had lost many of their best men and were clinging as well as they could to half a square mile of waste land bounded by a rough arc of a circle. As stragglers and wounded filtered back to the beach where all the various HQs were jostling each other, alarming messages began to come in. They were men, not demi-gods, and the punishment meted out was more than they could endure. Birdwood, who had no means of checking the accuracy of these reports, took counsel with his generals. The consequence was that at a few minutes after midnight Hamilton was roused from sleep and handed this signal: 'Both my Divisional Generals and Brigadiers have represented to me that they fear their men are thoroughly demoralized by shrapnel fire to which they have been subjected all day after exhausting and gallant work all morning. Numbers have dribbled back from firing line and cannot be collected in this difficult country. Even New Zealand Brigade which has been only recently engaged lost heavily and is to some extent demoralized. If troops are subjected to shell fire again to-morrow morning there is likely to be a fiasco, as I have no fresh troops with which to replace those in firing line. I know my representation is most serious but if we are to re-embark it must be done at once.'

Hamilton in his turn sought the advice of his admirals. Thursby, in operational charge at Anzac Cove, was firm about it. Evacuation would take all of three days and the Turks were already on top of them. Hamilton, who had much experience of war and great confidence in the dominion soldiers, never

1. John Monash with his wife in 1891, the year of their marriage.

2. Colonel Monash with Major J. P. McGlinn at the foot of the Sphinx, 1915.

3. General Sir William Bridges; killed at Gallipoli, 15 May, 1915.

4. Colonel (later General Sir) Cyril Brudenell Bingham White.

5. General Sir William Birdwood studying the map, at ANZAC HQ, Château d'Henencourt, 1917.

hesitated: 'Your news is indeed serious. But there is nothing for it but to dig yourselves right in and stick it out ... Hunter-Weston, despite his heavy losses, will be advancing to-morrow which should divert pressure from you. Make a personal appeal to your men and Godley's to make a supreme effort to hold their ground. PS You have got through the difficult business, now you have only to dig, dig, dig, until you are safe.' No personal appeal was, in fact, made, nor was it needed. This was not the true voice of Anzac; it was the justificatory clamour of the weaker spirits who had forsaken their duty and to which their generals had lent too ready an ear. It was a mistake they would not make again.

At about 6 pm, the first attack having petered out, Monash landed at Anzac Cove with his leading battalion, the 16th, closely followed by half the 15th and a couple of platoons of New Zealanders. He reported himself to Godley, who was already ashore, and was ordered to send the battalion at once to support the 3rd Brigade in the left centre of the line between Courtney's Post and Steele's, at the head of the gully henceforth known as Monash Valley. The valley divided at its eastern end into two defiles which were separated by an unoccupied feature soon to be christened Pope's Hill, after the commander of the 16th. Beyond the northern fork lay the high ground known as Russell's Top, itself connected to the beach by Walker's Ridge. This was supposed to be held by the 2nd Battalion but there was nothing to be seen of them. The Top, whose highest slopes commanded Pope's Hill, rose up black and empty. A staff officer was provided to guide Pope into position but, when half his battalion was moving forward in single file, the mules of an Indian mountain battery which had just landed cut across their path, heading towards the left. Pope moved into position on the hill, plugging one of the gaps in the line, and his men immediately came under heavy rifle and machine-gun fire. The rest of Monash's available men were led to the outpost line at Quinn's Post and Courtney's, while he established his own HQ at the head of the valley. Intermittent sniping came from the direction of Russell's Top and his brigade clerk was killed at his side; at this stage of the battle general officers were no more secure than other men from sudden death.

The furlong of ground between Quinn's and Courtney's was nowhere more than one hundred and fifty yards from the Turkish outposts and firing went on all through the night.

On Pope's Hill the line of forward defences was placed on the slope overlooking the enemy, for during the hours of darkness no great harm could come of it, while the rest of the battalion dug for their lives. By dawn, despite the shortage of tools, a reasonably strong trench system existed. At about midnight, the second half of the 15th Battalion came ashore; such was the need to block up the empty spaces in the line that they were at once sent off with a guide to take over an undefended part of the 400 Plateau in the 2nd Brigade area away to the right. They too spent what was left of the night in digging but for want of tools they could do no more than scrape out weapon-pits.

Still nobody knew what was happening on Russell's Top. The sounds of battle had gone on all through the night and some fire was directed into the back of Pope's position, but plainly there were still Australians there and they were still fighting. In fact Major Braund, with the remnant of the 2nd Battalion, was conducting one of the most gallant and skilful defensive actions of the campaign, weary men clambering to their feet again and again to go in once more with the bayonet. Monash was powerless to do anything at all; he had no troops under his command and spent a sleepless night doing nothing but listen and speculate.

At 6 am on the 26th, just as the sky was flushing pink in the east, came the thunderous reverberations of great guns. The *Queen Elizabeth* was shelling Russell's Top to bring some relief to Braund's hard-pressed men. As usual, the vast shrapnel shells drove the Turks back but within a short time of the fire ceasing they had returned and were again sniping into the rear of Pope's Hill.

During the morning Monash's next battalion, the 13th, came ashore; immediately one company was dispatched to the slopes between the Top and Pope's Hill to cover the last of the unguarded ways to the beach. In a totally exposed position, they were decimated by machine-gun fire and were, with great difficulty, withdrawn.

The day was passed in most places by feverish attempts at reorganization and improving the defences and no further Turkish attack was made in strength. Attacks on Quinn's and Courtney's continued but again the *Queen Elizabeth* displayed that naval gunnery, while not particularly effective against forts, was a potent weapon against troops in the open. Braund continued to hold out on Russell's Top, even mounting another counterattack, and the first artillery was landed. Two batteries of 18-pounders under Colonel Rosenthal were manhandled ashore and, by tremendous efforts, were got into a position at Bolton's Ridge on the extreme right of the line. Monash still had no command.

Much the same thing was happening on the other side of the hill. Kemal's division had been very roughly handled and needed sorting-out no less than did the Anzacs. Liman von Sanders was still unsure of what was really going on and his two divisions at Bulair stayed where they were until late in the afternoon when the 7th was ordered to move to Cape Helles. Clearly Kemal could be trusted to deal with whatever force had been got ashore around Gaba Tepe. The situation in the south was the more menacing and the possibility of a landing at Bulair could still not be discounted. Kemal, in fact, was regrouping his forces with the object of launching an all-out and probably final attack on the following day.

Early in the morning of the 27th, Birdwood ordered the New Zealand Brigade, which had had a very rough time on the left flank after landing immediately behind the Australian Division, to relieve Braund's battered but triumphant band of heroes on Russell's Top. His next action was to summon a conference, to which Monash was bidden, to meet him on Plugge's Plateau at 10.30. Here he divided his front into four sectors and assigned commanders to them. From north to south (or left to right), Walker with his New Zealanders would be responsible for the area from the sea inland along the ridge that bore his name and then swinging south to Russell's Top which was in his area. Next came Monash who, with his 4th Brigade, was to hold the left centre from, but excluding, Russell's Top to Courtney's Post, inclusive. Both these sectors were to be under the general control of Godley, from whose NZ & A Division the troops were drawn.

Continuing southward, the right centre was given to a mixture of the 1st and 3rd Brigades under MacLaurin and the right to M'Cay with the 2nd Brigade. General Bridges was similarly in control of the sectors drawn from his own division. There were no reserves, except for some units of the 3rd Brigade, withdrawn to the beach for rest and reorganization.

Of the four sectors, that entrusted to Monash was by far the most difficult to defend. There was not, could not be, a continuous trench line. The gap between Pope's Hill and Russell's Top was impossible to cover except by fire, for any troops put there would be presenting an unmissable target to the Turks who overlooked the defile from two sides at least. Quinn's Post was even more impossible. It was open to fire from both flanks as well as from the left rear and the garrison could only stay alive by remaining on the reverse slope, while the Turks continued to swell their numbers on the other side of it. The troops, though for convenience they were called the 4th Brigade, were heterogeneous elements of the 3rd, 11th and 12th battalions and of a New Zealand battalion lying alongside Monash's own 13th, 14th and 16th. His 15th Battalion was still away to the south in MacLaurin's parish. A company of the 13th was part of the garrison of Quinn's while the remaining three were detached to join Pope on his hill. There the mystery of what lay on their left was so great that during the afternoon the 16th opened a smart musketry fire on the Otago battalion in the belief that they were Turks. It was probably not the only incident of its kind.

In this disjointed and haphazard defence, Monash and his brother brigadiers awaited the next Turkish onslaught. He established his HQ in the valley at the foot of Steele's Post and went off to concert his fire-plan with MacLaurin and Bridges. With the troops on his left he had no sort of communication except such as could be got by way of the telephone lines which ran from both sectors to Godley's HQ near the beach. The sector boasted not a solitary field gun. There were two NZ howitzers on the beach; the Indian mountain battery that had caused such disruption was under Walker's command on the left and Rosenthal's two batteries were very fully employed with M'Cay. Only the guns of the ships could help him and communication with them was almost non-existent.

All through the wild night of Tuesday the Turkish attacks continued. At Quinn's and Courtney's they were near enough to toss grenades—crude affairs, like iron tennis-balls with a length of fuse, but better than no grenades at all—into the trenches. But the machine-guns and rifles of the Anzacs drove them back. When dawn came and the line still held men began to look over their right shoulders for signs of the 29th Division advancing from the south. Unflattering comparisons were drawn between their own prowess and that of the British army. However, there was no time to discuss the matter or even to enquire for the current 'furphy', for daylight brought yet more Turks yelling their way towards the line with cries of 'Allah'. Down came the shrapnel again as once more the heartening roar of the *Queen Elizabeth*'s 15-inch shells set the hills and valleys trembling. At noon, Kemal put in his last reserves, the 33rd and 72nd Regiments, and yet again haggard men who had forgotten what sleep was put their rifles to their shoulders. Colonel MacLaurin and his brigade major were both killed by a sniper. A few Turks infiltrated between Courtney's and Pope's Hill but did not live to boast of their exploit. Enver had issued an order that they should drive the invaders into the sea or never look upon his face again. They were denied that pleasure, for once more the Anzac musketry strengthened by Monash's last battalion (the 14th) which had arrived during the afternoon, and the naval gunfire brought every attack up short. Nevertheless, it was a situation that could not endure much longer. Men had been stretched to the limit and beyond and some relief must somehow be found. Hamilton had little enough on which to draw, but one source remained. The Royal Naval Division had completed its bloodless task off Bulair and, although some battalions had been committed at Helles, there still remained four at his disposal. The Anzacs were informed that before the day was out they would be relieved by the Royal Marines. This was good news, for they had seen something of the marines while they had been guests of the navy and the reputation of that fine corps stood high with the Australians.

# CHAPTER FIVE

## Gallipoli Summer

WHEN the reliefs landed, the large men of the 3rd Brigade, many of whom were enjoying a swim, could hardly believe their eyes. Surely these weedy boys, made to look weedier still by their huge Wolseley helmets, could not be the robust and tough 'Jollies' they knew? In truth, the Portsmouth and Chatham Battalions RM were not the veterans seen on visits to the seaports of Australia; they were youngsters from English coastal towns, surplus to the requirements of the fleet, whose training had been measured in months or even weeks. Nursed by their officers, they were led wondering into the wretched line of weapon-pits which represented the defences of the vital 400 Plateau, on the right of Monash. He saw them and was not impressed. The following morning brought the other two battalions, the Deal Battalion RM and the Nelson Battalion of the Royal Naval Division, similarly constituted of young seamen not needed afloat. Their officers were sailors rather than soldiers and wore naval badges of rank. Each RND Battalion was named for an admiral of an earlier generation. The Deal Battalion was similarly led by the hand into the trenches south of those held by their brethren of Portsmouth, while Nelson was kept in reserve. The Australians, having got over the shock (the Lancashire lads had all looked Titans compared to these), were kind to them. Many of the 'Diggers', as they were now beginning to be called, took the youngsters under their wings and gave them a lot of good advice.

By Friday, 30 April, the relief had been completed so far as it was possible. Kemal, too, had received an accretion of strength, five fresh battalions, some machine-guns and artillery. He was soon ready for one more try. During Friday afternoon, the Chatham Battalion was edged to the left, part of it being moved to the rear of Courtney's in support. The jigsaw of opposing positions in this closest of country was such that an unsuspected machine-gun, probably about Russell's Top, caught them in enfilade and slaughtered many. Their place was taken by the 14th Battalion.

At dawn on the following morning, May Day, Kemal struck again; this time, in the greatest strength yet, he directed his attack on MacLaurin's Hill, in the part of the sector of the 2nd Brigade held by the 12th Battalion and the Deal Marines. Rosenthal's guns tore into them from Bolton's Ridge, a range of about seven hundred yards, their shrapnel shells being fused to burst almost as they left the muzzle. The effect was like that of some giant duck-gun. However, as Dr Bean recorded, 'The Marines bore the brunt of Mustafa Kemal's third attack. Though better timed and delivered than the last, it completely failed.' The young Englishmen may not have been much to look at but, for all the short length of their service, they were marines. The screaming hordes of Turks swerved to their right in front of Courtney's where a storm of fire from well-sited machine-guns and the rifles of the 14th Battalion and what was left of the Chatham Marines completed their discomfiture. The Anzac position was safe at last and, as the First Lord of the Admiralty later put it, 'the power did not exist in the Turkish Empire to shake from its soil the grip of the Antipodes'.

The sector commander had little to do save watch and encourage, though it is reasonable to suppose that Monash the engineer was for the time being more usefully employed in advising on the construction of field works than was Monash the soldier. There was no plan for him to make, for, in the colloquial phrase, 'all his goods were in the shop window'. Birdwood himself had had but one battalion, the 14th, in corps reserve before Kemal's attack was launched. As soon as that was committed to a place in the line neither he, Godley nor Monash could call upon so much as a corporal's guard for any purpose however desperate. Not surprisingly, the volume of letters fell off during this period, Mrs Monash learning only that 'It is so difficult in the midst of the fighting to get a quiet moment to write at all, that I shall have to discontinue these regular notes until we can have a rest to re-fit and re-equip in some more civilised place than these mountains in which we are existing in the most primitive fashion, living in dug-outs and trenches, and feeding on bully-beef, biscuits, bacon and tea. I am writing within a hundred yards of the firing line and the rattle of musketry and the boom of cannon is incessant.'

Monash was learning the business of command rapidly. In common with the other Australian brigadiers, he had never had the experience of being under fire, or leading even small bodies of troops, which had been the lot of all his British contemporaries. Since the Crimea, there had been wars in China, Abyssinia, Zululand, Burma, Ashanti, the Sudan, Somaliland and South Africa, to name but some, in addition to the traditional training-ground of the North-West Frontier. Plenty of regular officers still only in the middle ranks had had vastly more experience than the new, recently civilian, formation commanders but all of these had taken readily to this novel environment. Monash, naturally, made careful mental notes of all that went on around him and wrote home with an accurate description of the various noises made by bullets as they pass at differing distances. Shrapnel sounded like 'a gust of wind in a wintry gale, swishing through the air and ending in a loud bang and a cloud of smoke', though he is careful to assure his reader that 'unless one gets in the way of the actual fragments of the shell itself, the Turkish shrapnel does very little harm'. It was, however, of the men that he had the most to say. He found them 'as docile and patient and obedient and manageable as children, yet they are full of the finest spirit of self-devotion . . . always cheerful, always cracking jokes, always laughing and joking and singing, and as I move amongst them and ask "Well lads how are you getting on?" the invariable answer is "First rate, sir," or "Ryebuck", or "We're ready for another go" . . . the British officers are the first to admit that for physique, dash, enterprise and sublime courage, the Australians are head and shoulders above any others.'

There was, however, a serious problem that had to be dealt with at once. Quinn's Post was the key to the entire Anzac position and, in theory, it was quite untenable. It consisted simply of a chain of pits on the summit of a narrow ridge overlooked on three sides. If the defenders were forced back only five paces, they would find themselves on a steep cliff where it was not possible even to stand and would have to fall back (almost literally) to the floor of the valley where they would be instantly annihilated. Until the end of the campaign, Quinn's was to remain a miniature of the Ypres salient, with the difference that it could not be given up at any price.

To its topographical impossibilities must be added the Anzac inferiority in arms; this kind of fighting was the apotheosis of trench warfare and in trench warfare the rifle is not the queen of weapons. The short Lee-Enfield was, and remains, the finest military rifle ever produced but in close-quarter work of this kind any rifle is an unhandy tool. Trench battles are settled by bombs and shells, big bombs lobbed into the works by mortars or little bombs thrown by hand. The Anzacs had neither; the Turks had plenty of their crude but effective grenades and, though they had not yet obtained mortars, they had howitzers. Somehow elbow room must be gained around Quinn's and it must be won by infantry alone with such help as the navy could give.

The attack of 2 May gave Monash his first opportunity to display his virtuosity as a brigadier; the task assigned to him was to seize the feature known as Baby 700 and to clear the Turks from the positions they held overlooking Monash Valley. The operation would be carried out by the entire NZ & A Division, the 1st Brigade being brought back into the line to relieve the marines, coming for the purpose under Godley's command, and the NZ Brigade taking the left of the line. The only reserves were the marines and the Nelson Battalion RND, who were disposed around the gullies in rear. The 4th Brigade was responsible for the sector between Quinn's and the summit of Baby 700 where it would link up with the Otago Battalion on the NZ right. The final plan was for the attack to go in at dusk, a course forced upon Birdwood and Godley because the artillery, which should have provided a barrage under whose cover troops could move forward, did not exist. It was generally recognized that the hardest job of all would be that of Monash's men and he made his plan with great care. At 7 pm the ships' guns would open up on the slopes of Baby 700 with the field-guns of Rosenthal and the little screw-guns of the Indian mountain battery supporting. At 7.10 the rifles and machine-guns in the northern part of the line would add their contribution. Five minutes later, all would lift their range by half a mile and play on Battleship Hill and Chunuk Bair; the infantry would then attack.

As the taking of Baby 700 would render the rest of the operation comparatively simple, 4th Brigade got the lion's share of the artillery preparation. Their plan was not an easy one to carry out but, given the nature of the country, it is hard to think of a better. At the end of the eastern fork of Monash Valley, below Quinn's Post, was a point known as the Bloody Angle—a name that, consciously or unconsciously, remembered Gettysburg—up to which two battalions, the 13th and the 16th, would make their way along the valley, the latter leading. On arrival, the 16th would turn right and attack up the side of the valley to seize the crest. At the same moment, the Otago Battalion would be debouching from the western branch of the valley and would assault and capture the seaward slope of Baby 700. The task of the 13th Battalion was to wheel left in single file from the same point at which the 16th had changed direction, make contact with Otago and then the whole line would move forward. A company of the 15th on Pope's Hill would be standing by to fill in any gap that might exist between Otago and the 13th. All this was to be performed in the dark, for the sun set at about 6.30.

Precisely at the appointed time the guns opened up and the hills and valleys shuddered under the cannonade of HMS *Triumph, Dartmouth, Bacchante, Queen, Prince of Wales, London, Majestic* and *Canopus*, drowning in their reverberations the sharper cracks of the field and mountain pieces. Monash's men were waiting, ready and eager, though the 13th had been much harassed by snipers as they formed up. At 7.15, the 16th, in tremendous spirits, moved up the Bloody Angle, made their turn to the right and swarmed up the valley head without a shot being fired at them. As soon as they reached the top, however, they came under rifle fire and began to dig themselves in a few yards from Quinn's; strong voices bellowing out 'Australia Will Be There' could be heard down the valley at Brigade HQ.

The 13th, led by the stalwart Colonel Burnage, 57 years old and a wine-merchant by calling, also did as they had been bidden. There was a bad moment when the rear half of the battalion failed to appear; the NCO detailed to direct the files up the hill had been killed by a sniper. The adjutant ran back to find out what was wrong and saw the last companies heading straight into the Turkish lines. One complete platoon had disappeared, never to be heard of again, before he could get the men moving once more in the right direction.

The 13th and 16th were both more or less in their appointed places on time, though not without casualties, but there was no sign of Otago. Nor was that all, for the left of the 16th Battalion was now found to be only at the end of the Bloody Angle instead of well to its left and the Australian battalions were separated by the head of the valley. About midnight a very battered Otago Battalion arrived, Pope sent out his company to join them to the 13th and a line of sorts was organized. It was not, however, the line planned, for Otago had not reached anywhere near the hilltop which had been their objective. Baby 700 and the ends of both branches of Monash Valley were still in Turkish hands. Both the 13th and the 16th now had completely open flanks and were being enfiladed by Turkish rifles and machine-guns; all they could do was dig. The 13th lost two hundred men during the night but they managed to construct a fairly good trench system upon the Chessboard with a support line on the summit and slopes of Dead Man's Ridge.

Such news as filtered through to Godley was excessively optimistic and led him to believe that the objectives had been attained. He therefore ordered the Canterbury Battalion to advance over The Nek, the feature which joined Russell's Top to Baby 700, where he thought Otago to be. They, too, advanced cheering and singing and were cut down as their comrades had been. What was left of them was then sent down into the valley to draw tools from Monash's Brigade HQ and carry them forward to the Otagos who were in sore need of more than their 'grubbers' (entrenching tools). The left of the line was completely in the air and the Otago men could hear Turkish voices not far away in that direction as they dug. When the light began to thin, fire was opened on their flank and it steadily grew heavier. The Otago Battalion fell back, followed by the company of the 15th. The gallant Burnage and his 13th Battalion were better dug in and they clung grimly to their position.

On the right of the line, things were even worse. Machine-guns from Baby 700 fired long bursts into the 16th Battalion, and Turkish infantry crawled into bombing range. At about 5 am half a dozen shells, almost certainly from one of our own batteries, burst behind them and blew away part of the trench. This was the last straw and a number of men of the 16th leapt over the edge, back into the security of the valley. The two marine battalions were rudely shaken from their rest and placed under the command of Monash, who also received a message from Godley informing him that he would now be responsible for connecting the entire line of trenches from the right of his own brigade to the left of Otago. His valley was filled with wounded, over whom the marines blearily picked their way in the half-light as they made for its head.

Before long there arrived Major Tilney of Pope's battalion bearing an order to the Portsmouth Battalion, over the signature of his CO, requiring it to move under Tilney's guidance to support his left. This did not tally with the orders already given to the marines but Tilney was a persuasive man and they followed him. The Deal Battalion attempted to scale the eastern slope of the valley, in broad daylight, to thicken up what remained in position of the 16th. They presented a splendid target and were driven down by the machine-guns behind them on the left. Attempts to reinforce the 16th by sapping through to them having also failed, they were withdrawn during the afternoon. After various efforts to relieve or support the 13th by the Nelson Battalion had come to nothing, they too were withdrawn after dark. Monash's first battle of manœuvre had ended in dismal and utter failure.

The entire strength of the 4th Brigade on 3 May amounted to

just over two thousand. The 16th Battalion alone had lost eight officers and three hundred and thirty men while the casualties in Otago amounted to 'at least ten officers and two hundred and fifty-two men'. The whole miserable business had cost about one thousand in dead and wounded; for this there was nothing to show, not an inch of Turkish soil nor a solitary prisoner. Quinn's was as vulnerable as ever and the strength of the garrison had been seriously depleted. What on earth had gone wrong?

Monash pondered on the lessons to be learned and in this he was not alone. First, there was one obvious basic error common to the entire peninsula; the Turkish soldier had been ridiculously underrated. In part the reasons were historical, for Turkish troops had not shown to advantage in the Crimea and the legend still lingered in the army of a comical, baggy-breeched character with little stomach for a fight but addicted to the pleasures of hubble-bubble pipes and pederasty. The Balkan Wars had done little to raise this reputation and the ease with which Djemal's attempt on the Suez Canal had been repulsed completed the illusion. In fact, three years under German instructors had transformed the Turkish army out of recognition. Tough, undemanding Anatolian peasants might not prove the most intelligent of soldiers but they were material from which brave and well-trained regiments could be made. On their own ground, well supplied and decently led, they could be as formidable as any troops in the world. On the Anzac front Mustafa Kemal had inspired them with a fanatic courage reminiscent of the earliest days of Islam and, although they were not strong on initiative, they would attack again and again in spite of huge losses. Their snipers, in particular, merited respect, for they worked in groups varying from a couple of men to a platoon and were expert in the art of concealment.

Secondly the objectives had been chosen from a map and were far too ambitious. Night operations by well-fed and well-rested men on Salisbury Plain did not always turn out exactly as intended; by tired and hungry men, trying to find their way through a wilderness where every feature looked exactly like every other one and involving changes of course of an exact right-angle, they could never have succeeded. The failure of the Otago Battalion to arrive at the time and place ordered was the biggest single factor which made this operation collapse but it was entirely understandable. The CO had to choose between moving forward over the exposed Russell's Top or a long detour back to the beach and then forward again up the valley. Quite rightly, he adopted the latter course. An officer was sent to walk over the ground and calculate the time needed to reach the forming-up place, which he did correctly. Unfortunately, at the time he did so the valley was almost empty; when the battalion came to move it was jam-packed with the marines waiting in support and great numbers of wounded, many of whom could not be shifted. In future, somehow, police must be provided to keep clear all ways by which units moving into the line must pass.

Lastly, the bombardment, however Wagnerian a noise it had made, was quite ineffective. For country like this howitzers and mortars in substantial numbers were essential. Until they could be provided, the only way to move forward at Anzac would be below ground.

Monash's next letter home seems to indicate that his introduction to the attack on a strong position followed by a bloody repulse had not put him in the least out of countenance. 'During an attack a few nights ago on a ridge in front of us (which did not succeed owing to an accident)' is his euphemistic description of it before he goes on to extol the gallantry of his men. He also mentions that although Birdwood, Bridges and Trotman (one of the marine brigadiers) had all been hit and about a dozen of his own Brigade HQ people killed and wounded, he had so far come through unscathed. He may well have been whistling in a graveyard, for the situation in his sector, especially at Quinn's, which was almost permanently under attack, was precarious. The Turk could dig as well as he could fight and, with the advantage of dead ground below the Post, he was creeping his works nearer and nearer. At the end of the first week in May less than fifty yards of tortured earth separated the two sides.

Fortunately, no army contained more skilled and experienced miners than that at Anzac. Many of them were taken from their units and formed into tunnelling companies (though the name was not yet in use) and they did much to improve matters. First a series of T-shaped saps were driven forwards and, when these were completed, the diggers connected them by burrowing underground. The last stage was to break through the roof from below and a new front-line trench came into being.

Even then affairs were not all that much better, for the Turkish snipers were in such commanding positions that it was death for a man to show his head over the parapet even for an instant. The ingenuity of the Anglo-Saxon race soon came to the rescue. First, a periscope was obviously needed. The engineers and the naval artificers provided them; the first ones were simply stout sticks with a small mirror fixed at each end, appropriately adjusted. Looking-glasses disappeared from ward-rooms and cabins and were cut to size and shape either on board ship or in workshops on the beach. There were never enough of them for the snipers soon learnt to pick them off, but they were a great help.

However, although a man could now see something of what was going on in front of him, he could still not interfere with it. The next step was a gadget made by an Australian soldier of remarkable enterprise. A wooden frame was contrived into which the periscope and a rifle could be fitted, the whole being held above the trench and the rifle sighted by the mirrors. It worked far better than might have been expected and the demand for periscope rifles to replace those shot to pieces became insatiable.

Bombs were a *sine qua non* and their production became the speciality of Colonel Joly de Lotbinière, Birdwood's CRE. There was no novelty about them, for an efficient grenade had been used in England during the civil war and the first regular issue dated from as long ago as 1677. In 1739 there had come into service a discharger cup fitted to the muzzle of a musket almost exactly the same as that shortly to be used in France. Though they had gone out of service before the American war they had been revived in the trenches before Sebastopol and there would have been a few serving officers with experience of them as they had, for some obscure reason, been handed out to the Gordon Relief Expedition in 1885. After that campaign, in which they were almost certainly quite useless, they once more vanished from the G 1098.

De Lotbinière and his henchmen had as raw materials slabs of gun-cotton, lengths of slow fuse and precious little else. With this unpromising equipment they began to manufacture grenades of two kinds. The smaller was a jam tin packed with a mixture of scrap-iron and gun-cotton ignited in the traditional manner by a fuse. Its length was a matter of guesswork and the fuse had to be lit from a cigarette end. Its description coincides almost exactly with the original civil-war model though it lacked some of the latter's refinements. The bigger one, known as the 'hairbrush', consisted of a slab of wood about the shape of that article, but with the bristles replaced by a slab of gun-cotton. Neither were particularly efficient — though the hairbrush was reckoned by far the superior model — but the Turks hated them. A cricketing nation had advantages when it came to delivering them by hand.

The power of invention was not yet exhausted. An unknown minor genius in the RND at Cape Helles fabricated a device resembling a large trough of wood in the shape of the letter Y. A strong rubber cord was wound back by a handle operating a simple screw like that which works a tennis-net until it reached a catch. The jam-tin bomb was placed in a sling, catapult fashion, a blow from a pick-helve released the cord and shot the bomb in the general direction of Constantinople. The idea caught on and a quantity of these arbalests was provided at Anzac also. They had an interesting quality of unpredictability which gave some spice to a life that was, at times, tedious. To such grotesque shifts was the army of the world's greatest industrial nation reduced.

But the Turks were not to be outdone. Before modern trench-mortars arrived, they raided a museum and came back with an enormous weapon which dated back to the Crimea. It threw an ancient iron shell, eleven inches in diameter, which seldom exploded; when it did, the noise and smoke were fearsome, but nobody seemed to be hurt. Fortunately for both sides it soon ran out of ammunition.

The rear of Quinn's, in the bank of the valley, soon became a jungle of shelters, 'funk-holes' ('pozzies' in Australian) and shanties, reminiscent of some early mining camp. It was not until the end of May that this was taken in hand, when Colonel Malone's

6. Lieutenant-General Monash presents the Victoria Cross to an officer of the 2nd Australian Division, 13 August, 1918.

7. King George V confers a knighthood on General Sir John Monash at Bertangles, July, 1918.

8. 'Billy' Hughes, the Australian Prime Minister, with Keith Murdoch, Bertangles, July 1918.

9. The Australian Imperial Forces entertain the Prince of Wales to dinner in London, 1919.

New Zealand Battalion took over the Post. Malone somehow obtained iron plates with loop-holes, corrugated iron sheets and quantities of rabbit-wire. With these aids Quinn's was turned into a good defensive position where the garrison could actively attend to its defence instead of waiting to be bombed or shelled without ability to retaliate. His men terraced the slopes behind and made tiers of neat dwellings where the shanties had been. So pleased was Malone with the work that he was heard to say that if only he had the time he would grow roses over it.

But this is running ahead of events. In the first days of May men used to pass Quinn's Post as they went about their business in the valley with averted eyes: 'like men going past a haunted house', was one soldier's description of it. Mining and counter-mining went on incessantly and it soon became clear to the Turks that men who had learnt their trade at Coolgardie and Ballarat were too good for them at this sort of warfare.

The real defence of Quinn's, however, lay not with its own garrison but with the two groups of machine-guns at Courtney's and on Pope's Hill whose beaten zones effectually crossed each other in front of the Post.

On 19 May the Turks attacked again with a far greater force of infantry and with more artillery preparation than before. It was a complete failure. The Anzacs were ready for them and chose their targets with skill; every fresh wave was met with a storm of small-arms fire above which could be heard derisive yells of 'Backsheesh' or 'Imshi Yallah'. They had become far more artful, for this time whenever a Turkish officer appeared standing in front of a trench nobody fired at him. It was far better to wait for him to collect up his entire company and then shoot down the lot. Nearly a million rounds of small arms ammunition was fired together with about fourteen hundred rounds each from the 18-pounders and the mountain guns. The paucity of shells from the howitzers can be judged from the fact that their contribution was exactly one hundred and forty-three. Shortage both of this type of weapon and of ammunition for such few as he had were among the heaviest crosses Hamilton had to bear.

On 24 May came the famous armistice, generally understood

7

to have been arranged by Temporary Lt-Colonel the Hon Aubrey Herbert. Monash gives a rather different account of it. 'It really began on 22 May by our hearing from a trench about 50 yards in front of what is known as Courtney's Post, during a lull in the firing, cries of "Docteur, Docteur", and the waving of a Red Crescent flag. I sent out Dr McGregor and Dr Loughran with an orderly carrying a Red Cross flag, and instantly from all over the place sprung up Turks out of their trenches waving white flags, white rags and Red Crescent pennants. The doctors called back that the enemy wanted an armistice for the burying of their dead (at this time there were quite 5,000 of their dead lying in front of our trenches), so I asked for a staff officer to come forward, and a very smart young Turkish officer, smartly dressed, came up and spoke in very good French. I told him I had no power to treat, that this would have to be arranged, if at all, between the Army Corps Commanders and with proper Articles of Armistice; that his commander had better send an accredited *parlementaire* half way to discuss the matter. This was at 4.30, and I gave them 10 minutes to get all their men back into their trenches or we should fire on them. That same night General Birdwood sent out to General Liman von Sanders practically repeating the terms of my offer, and sure enough next day a meeting took place and drew up an agreement for an armistice from 8 am to 5 pm on 24 May.'[1]

Both sides were glad of it; the sweet, sickly smell of rotting flesh permeated everything, especially around Quinn's. The air they breathed, the water they drank and the disgusting food they had to eat all carried it. The weather was getting hot now and visitors complained that it took a fortnight for them to get the stench out of their nostrils. What it must have been like for men condemned to hold the place is not susceptible of description.

Herbert arrived early on the scene and so did Compton Mackenzie; the latter was nearly sick when it was pointed out that the object under his boot which resembled a mangold was, in fact, the black and green rotting remnants of a Turkish head. Herbert, a most cultured man with a rare gift of tongues and

[1] The British army did not adopt the twenty-four-hour clock until 1 October 1918.

knowledge of the Near East (a strong school of thought insists that he was the original of John Buchan's Sandy Arbuthnot), was certainly invaluable in making the truce work and, on the whole, it was scrupulously observed by both parties. Monash and Godley watched events from Pope's Hill. The former, looking through field-glasses, descried a small piece of cheating. A Turk about a hundred yards away was busy mending a loop-hole in front of his trench. Monash signed to a Turkish officer and pointed out the offence; the officer ran to the scene of the crime and gave the offender a 'sound belting with a stick'. He then returned to the complainants, expressed his regret at the incident and politely suggested that they in turn were not playing fair by standing where they could never have stood before and examining the terrain with the aid of glasses. One cannot avoid a feeling of game and set to the Turk.

The armistice had a curious result in changing the Australian view of their enemy. At the beginning, probably influenced by the old regulars who had seen service against Waziris or Mohmands, they regarded him as a poor sort of soldier whose only talent lay in the murder of prisoners and the torture of wounded. The fact that no prisoners seemed to have been taken during the rush that had followed the landing lent colour to this. Seeing him now face to face, they found it difficult to believe the atrocity stories, for the simple soldier seemed a decent enough chap and he was certainly a brave one. When the time was up little groups who had been conversing in dumb-show or in a sort of French broke up with expressions of mutual goodwill. The compliment that deserves most to endure was paid by a 'Digger': 'Saida (Good-bye). Play you again next Saturday.' The more courtly Turkish leave-taking was translated by Herbert. 'Smiling may you go and smiling may you come again!'

Herbert had not always been so popular a visitor; one of his contributions to the war effort had been to call to the Turks from some forward position and to invite them to surrender. This was probably done against Herbert's better judgment for he liked and admired the Turks and cannot have been surprised when his kindly offer was answered by a shower of grenades. More subtle was the approach of Mr Ellis Ashmead-Bartlett, the only accredited war correspondent except for Reuter's man. Mr Ashmead-Bartlett's father had written a book nearly twenty years earlier praising the Turks, unlike most people, for their behaviour in Thessaly against the Greeks and his son therefore spoke with authority about their psychology. His suggestion was that they should be offered not merely asylum but a free pardon (pardon for doing what is not clear), a good meal and 10/- in cash if only they would come over with all their arms and equipment. Hamilton wondered what Mr Ashmead-Bartlett's own price would have been. Probably nothing less than luncheon at Simpsons and a modest but regular pension. Mr Ashmead-Bartlett was not universally liked.

The armistice over and the dead of both armies decently interred, the war began again. Positions on both sides continued to be strengthened and at Quinn's Post the two lines were nearer to each other than ever. A communication trench, relic of earlier fighting, ran from the heart of the Anzac position into the Turkish works known as the Chessboard. Only a bank of earth called a bomb-stop kept the two sides from sharing it. So long as the Turks had a monopoly of bombs they retained mastery of the whole length but the supply to the Anzacs slowly improved. In June there arrived from Japan six mortars which threw a 30-lb bomb on a stick; they were distributed throughout the front in pairs and were the most useful weapon yet issued. Their supply was almost certainly thanks to Hamilton who had come across them in Manchuria and, as he says, he had been demanding them for the past three months. The Anzacs thoroughly approved of them and were understandably furious when they were told that after they had used up the two thousand bombs that came with them no more could be had. They would be available in about ten weeks, but only in Japan. Hamilton demanded to know why they could not be copied in Birmingham. He received no answer. Instead he was furnished with two 6-inch howitzers of startling antiquity from the Royal Malta Artillery, served by marines crews. There were only one hundred and thirty-seven rounds with them, but as these usually failed to explode their loss was not much felt.

# GALLIPOLI SUMMER

Early in May Birdwood, on Hamilton's orders, sent for Bridges and Godley to ask each of them for the loan of his best brigade to be sent to Helles for the Second Battle of Krithia. Monash was not chosen, the honour, if such it was, going to M'Cay's 3rd Brigade. They and the New Zealanders left the line on 5 May, their places being taken by the marines and some of the Light Horse who had been brought from Egypt to fight on their feet. Hamilton had also, at last, received authority to take from the swollen garrison of Egypt the 42nd (East Lancashire) Division and a brigade of Gurkhas. It would have done the Australians' hearts good if they had been able to witness how the 'chooms' could fight. In the later battle of 4 June a brigade consisting entirely of Territorial battalions of the Manchester Regiment wrested two lines of trenches from the well dug-in Turks after a splendid charge. When the troops on their right had given way and their flank was in the air the Manchesters refused to budge until they finally received a direct order from Hunter-Weston to withdraw. 'The boldest and most brilliant exploit of the lot,' Hamilton called it.

Monash sent home a description of his life at this time. 'We have been amusing ourselves by trying to discover the longest period of absolute quiet. We have been fighting now continuously for 22 days, all day and all night, and most of us think that absolutely the longest period during which there was absolutely no sound of gun or rifle fire throughout the whole of that time was 10 seconds. One man says he was able on one occasion to count fourteen but nobody believes him. We are all of us certain that we shall no longer be able to sleep amid perfect quiet, and the only way to induce sleep will be to get someone to rattle an empty tin outside one's bedroom door.' For a man very near to his fiftieth birthday who had for many long years been accustomed to living the civilized life of a professional man of means, the strain must sometimes have been well-nigh unendurable. No word of complaint or self-pity ever escaped him.

However, he did have one short break. Hamilton's diary for 26 May tells of it: 'Entertained a small party of Australian officers as my private guests for 48 hours. Col Monash, commanding

4th Australian Infantry Brigade, was the senior. He is a very competent officer... I was prepared for intelligent criticisms but I thought they would be so wrapped up in the cotton-wool of politeness that no one would be very much impressed. On the contrary, he stated his opinions in the most direct, blunt, telling way. The fact was noted in my report and now his conduct out here has been fully up to sample.' Hamilton should not have been surprised. At a private gathering of gentlemen, under no constraint other than that imposed by good manners, Monash was not the kind of man who would wrap things up. He spoke of the dinner in his next letter, though it was some days before he felt himself free to reveal that it had been on board RMS *Arcadian*, now the HQ ship. Sir Ian was 'as usual most gracious and charming and considerate... his recollection for names and faces is remarkable, and he plied me with questions about our doings'. The saddest thing about this enjoyable interlude is that no record survives of what they talked about. For Monash and his fellow guests the clean linen, excellent food, well served by peacetime stewards, and the opportunity for thoughtful and cultivated conversation while he smoked pipe after pipe of his favourite Havelock tobacco must have been a time never to be forgotten. Perhaps Hamilton confided in his guests his own philosophy of never interfering with the man on the spot; in theory, nothing could be more sensible and Monash would certainly have agreed with it. In practice it had led to Hunter-Weston (Hunter-Bunter of the Kaiser moustache and the cackling laugh) being left free to do nothing at all, not even to take the obvious step of transferring troops to Y Beach when the opportunity was there and probably of seizing Achi Baba on the first day. It was well that the future development of Hamilton's *laissez-faire* attitude could not yet be guessed at.

The party over and the appropriate naval compliments having been paid to the parting guests, Monash went back to his hole in the ground, to the stench and the flies; 'I have never experienced such savage flies. They fight you for your food, and make for the eyes, nostrils, ears and mouth.' It was better not to speculate about where their last port of call might have been. Like everybody else Monash was suffering from dysentery, an ailment that might have been designed to remind suffering humanity that it is indeed a little lower than the angels. He could have been forgiven had he come to the conclusion that war is not the business of the over-fifties and that the plate had rubbed off the noble sentiments of August, 1914, to reveal the base metal below. No such thought ever seems to have crossed his mind, unless the sentiments expressed in his letters conceal a remarkable gift for dissimulation.

The greatest danger, disease apart, was still from the snipers. Their most notable victim was Gen Bridges. On the morning of 15 May, in company with his ADC Lt R. G. Casey (the future Governor-General) he punctiliously asked permission from Godley to visit the Light Horse of Colonel Chauvel who were in the NZ and A Division area. The two men walked up Monash Valley where Bridges, contrary to his usual custom, complied with the advice given to him to cross certain points at a run. Behind Steele's Post somewhere he seems to have stood erect for a moment and a Turkish bullet caught him in the groin, severing the femoral artery. His last order to his Anzacs was 'Don't carry me down — I don't want any of your stretcher-bearers hit.' So died the first of Australia's great commanders. His body was taken home and he lies overlooking the military college that he founded.

His death posed many problems for in addition to being GOC 1st Australian Division, Bridges was also commander-in-chief of the AIF. The Government of Australia decided to fill the vacancy by sending out Colonel Legge, then Chief-of-Staff at home, to assume both the appointments held by Bridges. A curious coda to his new assignment was that Bridges' wide powers over the AIF were to be exercised by Birdwood 'in the absence of the general officer commanding it'.

This caused a storm. Promotion was in the air, for Australia had long ago decided that in peacetime the size of her army did not justify the existence of a rank above that of colonel. The same situation prevailed in America. The result was that all the Australian brigadiers found themselves junior in rank to their counterparts in both the British and the Canadian forces and they did not regard this as fitting. The War Office in London took the same view and had been for some time past making polite suggestions that the time had come for all the officers concerned to be given a step up in rank. To make things even more difficult, the number of reinforcements arriving in Egypt had now reached such a quantity that the creation of a 2nd Australian division must soon take place.

Legge was two years older than Monash and a permanent officer, but he was a stranger to Gallipoli and the AIF had now got into the habit of making its own promotions from amongst the men who had passed the ultimate test of showing their mettle in real war. Legge arrived in Egypt in the middle of June, already wearing the badges of a major-general.

Monash did not learn of his own promotion until he received a cable from his wife dated 10 July and announcing, in the staccato style of cables, 'Congratulations on promotion brigadier-general well love.' With their unfailing resource, 'my staff set to work and, by some mysterious means, managed to materialize for me a pair of new shoulder-badges all ready to put on when the formal announcement is made'. He had no enthusiasm for being passed over by Legge; admittedly Legge held a permanent commission, but he was junior to both Monash and M'Cay in point of date, to say nothing of experience. M'Cay took the same tone. At Bridges' death the command of the 1st Division had passed to Walker who had until then been commanding the NZ Brigade and whose reputation as a fighting soldier stood high. Walker, however, suffered from the disadvantage that he was a British regular officer; he himself made no difficulty, for he was a loyal man and felt it to be natural and proper that the Australian government should want an Australian officer to command an Australian division. M'Cay was pacified by being given the new division but misfortune overtook him. He had been wounded in the leg some time previously and it seems that, although he had returned to duty, the hurt was not completely healed. On the day before he was due to leave Anzac he slipped and the leg snapped. He was sent back to Australia, Legge was transferred to the 2nd

Division and command of the 1st was entrusted to Walker. Monash was left to sulk alone. He himself makes no mention of the incident but Bean says that 'some even spoke of resigning, until Birdwood urged that resignation was not to be thought of in war'. It looks as if Monash was the only person to whom he could be referring, but if that be so it can only have been done in a moment of dysentery-inspired pique. Years afterwards he wrote to John Gibson, his partner, apologizing for his long neglect of the firm's business and asserting flatly that an officer could not on any account resile from his duty until the war was won. He soon got over it.

It seems slightly absurd to describe the months of June and July as restful, but by contrast with what had gone before and what was soon to come the word is not wholly inaccurate. Fighting went on without ceasing at the two most sensitive places, Quinn's Post at one end of the line and Lone Pine at the other; on 28 June the Anzacs again sallied out of their position to stage a demonstration in order to draw off such Turks as they could while Hunter-Weston again attacked from Helles. Once more they sustained heavy casualties with nothing to show in return.

After this date a malaise set in throughout the whole area. There was hardly a man in the two attenuated divisions who might not have joined the daily sick-parade with a good conscience but, until then, it had been a point of honour not to do this unless the illness was nearly disabling. Dysentery; horrible, warm, greasy corned beef day after day, mitigated only by teeth-breaking biscuit; milkless tea and coarse bacon, had reduced the giants of the landing to great gaunt skeletons. Their fighting power seemed unimpaired but only so long as it involved holding existing positions; it was very doubtful whether the originals, though they were now in a minority, would still have the stamina to carry through another attack.

Monash, who was half a doctor himself, called together all his medical officers and reported their findings to Birdwood. They were unanimously of opinion that the men's health was below normal, was getting worse and advised that the only way it could be ameliorated was by rest. Quite apart from fighting, fatigues of one kind or another, most of them involving digging or hauling, were taking up nearly all a man's time and the law of diminishing returns was beginning to operate. Monash was more optimistic for he added a note to the effect that he did not regard the situation as very serious and that all the soldiers needed for a swift recovery was the prospect of battle. It is quite true that when the battle came this is exactly what happened but Monash has been criticized for believing himself to know more of what his men were feeling and thinking than he really did. There may be some substance in this; soldiers, especially Australian soldiers, are not usually garrulous about their private thoughts when senior officers are about.

There was, at any rate, one great improvement: Colonel Malone had taken the sniper problem in hand as firmly as he had tackled other difficulties. His own picked shots, under an officer who had been a mighty hunter before the war, had now mastered the business and the less intelligent Turkish marksmen were becoming the targets. This made life in Monash Valley infinitely more endurable.

Its temporary tenant celebrated his fiftieth birthday at his home, 'a hole in the side of the hill, about 6 feet by 7 feet and 4 feet deep. The sides are built up with sand-bags and the roof consists of 3 waterproof sheets lashed together. Biscuit boxes serve as tables, chairs, cupboards and other furniture. I have my valise to sleep on, and get a daily bath out of a canvas bucket with a sponge, and at rarer intervals a dip in the sea.' None could call the brigadier a sybarite but he was a little better off than most under his command; the story lingers on of the 'Digger' looking contemplatively at a mess-tin full of water and eventually observing that 'if I was a procreative canary, I could have a bath in that'. Monash celebrated his half-century fittingly for somehow the news had got about. Lady Godley, who was running a nursing home in Alexandria (where, according to rumour, the patients were ordered to 'lie at attention' whenever she passed by) cooked him a birthday cake which her husband had sent over, and 'all my C.O.s lined up at my dug-out at 6 am to congratulate me and shake my hand, the Army Service Corps sent me a present of tobacco and matches (a most welcome gift: wooden matches at 1/- a small box), Norman Young gave me a bottle of champagne, 14th Battalion sent collective greetings and the headquarters cook scoured around and prepared for me a specially sumptuous four-course dinner. All day long officers from near and far came to wish me happy returns — so that, with the feeling that I have earned the good wishes of so many people, I have really had a very happy birthday under the circumstances.'

It does no harm to remember this little incident in later years. Monash has been accused of inordinate ambition, vanity and self-delusion. When a large body of strong-minded individualists, who could with perfect decorum have let his birthday pass unremarked, go to so much trouble to give pleasure to their commander, more particularly at a time when he had not emerged from battle as a famous victor, there can not have been very much wanting in him as a man.

His second chance as a field commander was soon to come. Only the briefest sketch of the Suvla Bay operation is possible here and the story has often been told before. It was plain to Hamilton that matters could not continue as they were. The Helles force was worn out and was now facing very strong Turkish lines, constructed under German surveillance, with the result that the original plan must be considered not postponed but abandoned. From the Anzac position, about the size of Regent's Park, he could do nothing more. Any move forward over this dreadful country — Hamilton said it was worse than the Khyber Pass — would demand guns and troops which could not be crammed into the available space.

There was a third point at which a strike could be made, the idea for which was first put forward by Birdwood. North from Ari Burnu to Suvla Point there was flat beach, lightly defended, and from the foothills beyond lay a relatively easy way through low hills to the back of the range called Sari Bair — the Yellow Slopes. A quick dash in this direction should be able to join up with the main thrust made by Birdwood's Anzacs, reinforced by fresh British troops from home, breaking out from the North to Chunuk Bair while a feint was carried out in strength at Lone

Pine. The Helles force, now about 35,000 strong, would make its contribution by attacking yet again towards Krithia thus keeping von Sanders' divisions in the south from interfering. Birdwood would have, in all, about 37,000 men under him with another 25,000 going ashore at Suvla under a commander yet to be chosen.

Hamilton was quite clear in his own mind as to the kind of man he needed. 'Only men of good stiff constitution will be able to do any good', he wrote, and suggested the names of Byng or Rawlinson. He was told firmly that neither was available. The force to be landed would amount to a full corps, a lieutenant-general's command, and officers of that rank did not abound in 1915. The list of candidates was further shortened by the fact that the officer chosen must be senior to Lieut-General Mahon; in spite of his rank, Mahon still remained in command of the 10th Division for reasons related to the affairs of Ireland, where that formation had been raised, and the division was to form part of the new corps. This reduced the field to Lieut-Generals Ewart and Stopford; Kitchener, in whose gift the appointment lay, had a scrupulous regard for seniority strange in a man whose own progress from subaltern to field-marshal had not exactly followed the usual path. Ewart had been a good man in his day but he now carried too much weight and his girth disqualified him from being involved in trench-warfare. Only Stopford remained.

Hard things have been said about Lieut-General the Hon Sir Frederick Stopford. The greater condemnation should surely be of the man who ordered him to assume a burden which he was totally incapable of supporting. Stopford was 61 years old; he had left the army six years previously, partly for reasons of health, and had probably been the least considered officer of his rank. Apart from some service in the Sudan towards the end of the previous century he was a complete stranger to the battlefield and had never held the smallest command save in peacetime garrison towns.[1] The zenith of his career had been as Military Secretary to Sir Redvers Buller in South Africa. Buller has been well described

---

[1] His last appointment before Suvla had been Lieutenant of the Tower of London.

as 'a superb major, a mediocre colonel and an abysmal general'. It was during his last period that he had been Stopford's mentor. The latter must have realized his own incapacity, for his personal qualities were excellent, but he would have considered himself to be failing in his duty had he made difficulty about accepting the command; one cannot easily imagine Stopford arguing with Kitchener. Stopford was considered a man well-read in military history and indeed he had a reputation as a teacher of that harmless subject. It was unfortunate that, like some other military historians, he knew a great deal about war but nothing of it. Hamilton was horrified. He wrote a personal letter to Sir John French, saying, 'Who is to be commander of the new corps I cannot say, but we have one or two terrifying suggestions from home.' Stopford would have recognized the words as being almost exactly those used by the Duke of Wellington on the same subject. Kitchener, however, had spoken; Ian Hamilton had asked for a Rupert or a Wolfe; he had got a Buller.

To compensate for Stopford's shortcomings, Kitchener had given him for his Chief-of-Staff a thoroughly up-to-date soldier. Brigadier-General Reed was a gunner and a good one; he had won a VC in South Africa and had seen service in France with the BEF. Unfortunately, the capacity of his mind was limited to one thing at a time. The battles of Neuve Chapelle and Festubert had driven home the lesson that infantry could make no headway against a strongly fortified line unless the attack was preceded by the heaviest possible bombardment to smash the defences and to tear gaps in the enemy's wire. The task was best performed by the biggest guns available. When that had been satisfactorily accomplished, the field-guns would lay down a barrage in front of the advance so that hostile machine-gunners and riflemen should not be able to fire at the oncoming infantry. So it had been in France and so it must be elsewhere. The suggestion that a quick move against a lightly held position, under cover of such fire as the ships could give, might succeed in taking it before enemy could arrive strong enough to need guns and a fire plan to dislodge them was the kind of nonsense a regular soldier might have expected from amateurs. If it was Birdwood's idea, he should have known better, but Indian cavalrymen could not be expected to understand these things. Reed was quite determined that no infantry should be committed until the guns had been landed in sufficient quantity, emplacements completed, ammunition dumped in suitable places and ranging carried out. The other elderly generals, all of them recalled from retirement by the outbreak of war, agreed that Reed must know best. The combination of young troops (all either Territorial or New Army), who as yet knew very little, and old commanders who had forgotten whatever they may once have known, was not promising. There was nothing wrong with the troops nor with their regimental officers as time would show. Flung ashore after weeks at sea, many of them dizzy from recent inoculation against enteric, they had little idea of where they were or why. It was as different from the Anzac landing as is darkness from light.

Birdwood and some of his most trusted officers had been busy reconnoitring the land over which the Anzacs (a term which during the Sari Bair battle must include the British and Indian troops lent to Birdwood) would have to fight. It was even more rugged than that which they had already experienced and it was impossible to produce accurate maps from sketches made under the noses of the Turks in broad daylight. Major Overton, a 38-year-old New Zealand sheep farmer, was the acknowledged expert; he crawled and scrambled day after day in and out of the horrid gullies and ravines that cover the approaches to Chunuk Bair and it was on the strength of his reports and sketches that the plan was made. No officer can ever have been given a more difficult or less rewarding task for, in comparison with the ground over which they were soon to go, the earlier battles had been fought on a bowling green.

Hamilton, with Birdwood's approval, allotted to the Anzac force the 13th Division of the New Army, the 29th Indian Brigade and a brigade of the 10th Division. These, together with his own NZ and A Division, were to come under the operational command of Godley, whose orders were to seize the summit of the range known to the British as Chunuk Bair. Originally it was to have been Hill 971 itself but Overton and his people had discovered just in time that a series of precipices separated this point from the remainder of the ridge. From the top of Chunuk Bair there is an unobstructed view across the Narrows to the plains of Troy. With this in his hands and with Stopford's Corps driving energetically round from his left front, Birdwood might reasonably feel that a great victory had been won. Nobody expected it to be a bloodless one, for the Turkish position was well sited and strong and there was little room for manœuvre, but this was to be the decisive battle that would finish with Hamilton hammering on the gates of Constantinople.

Birdwood's intention was that the heaviest fighting should be carried out by the troops best fitted for the purpose, the experienced Anzacs. Their battleground would be over country far worse than that to be traversed either by the raw British troops at Suvla or by the exhausted men at Helles and it is debatable whether this was the wisest course. It might have been better to transfer the Anzacs from their impregnable stronghold to Suvla and replace them by Stopford's corps, but the practical difficulties would have been immense and, if the Turks attacked during the changeover there is no knowing what might have happened. The new formations would not have been able to make much headway and the conditions of fighting at Lone Pine, on the right of the Anzac position, would have been beyond them. Even so, with the usual advantage a critic possesses of knowing what subsequently happened, it now seems that a mere holding battle on the old position would have given a better chance of success by letting the men, or the successors of the men, who had carried out the original landing loose over the sea-plain and then into the lightly held hills beyond.

That, however, was not how it happened. The main thrust was to be made to the north of the old Anzac position with the object of carrying the Sari Bair range and the men who would do it were two New Zealand and three Australian brigades with the bulk of 13th Division and 29th Indian Brigade in reserve. In corps reserve Birdwood retained three battalions of 13th Division and a brigade of the 10th. For artillery there were the Anzac batteries and the howitzers of 13th Division, all placed in the old

Anzac enclave. The vital part of the operation would be the seizure of the dominating feature of Chunuk Bair. The direct route to it lay through the strongly held Baby 700 position and Birdwood rightly deemed this to be a suicidal way by which to approach the objective. On the advice of Overton, he selected another way, across the spur running down to the sea which, from the colour of the oleanders which covered it, was called Rhododendron Ridge. The task of clearing the foothills leading to the ridge was given to the New Zealand Mounted Rifles Brigade with the 40th Brigade of the New Army on their right. When they had accomplished their purpose, the New Zealand Infantry Brigade would pass through them and take Chunuk Bair itself. On their left, another column would attack and take the next feature to the north, Koja Chemen Tepe otherwise known as Hill 971. This was to be the duty of the 4th Australian Brigade and the 29th Indian Brigade, three battalions of Gurkhas and one of Sikhs, the whole being under the command of Brigadier-General Cox with Monash as his subordinate. Their route, far more difficult even than that to Chunuk Bair, lay up the Aghyl Dere valley which at its furthest point inland divides into five branches which in turn subdivide into 'at least 30 steep scrub-covered gullies and ravines', as the Australian Official History puts it. Overton and some of his guides had been there, though not for the full length of the last-mentioned ravines, but, as no reliable maps existed, it could not be considered as explored, let alone properly reconnoitred. Cox's plan, of necessity based in part on guesswork, was for his entire column to go along the beach until they reached the mouth of the Aghyl Dere, move up the valley for three-quarters of a mile and then two Australian battalions should defile to the left forming an outpost line to protect the remainder. The main force would keep moving as far as the fork where it would turn north-east under the foot of Hill Q, between 971 and Chunuk Bair. From that point, two of the Gurkha battalions would be sent off to swarm up its side and take Hill Q. The depleted force would still keep moving up the ravine, cross two ridges and wait for orders for the final assault. When these arrived, they would advance for three-quarters of a mile along the last ridge to master Hill 971 itself, this last stage being executed under heavy Turkish fire and over ground of which nothing was known save for the fact that it was as wild as any place in the peninsula. The final task would be to dig a defensive line which would link the summit of 971 with the Gurkhas on Hill Q and the New Zealanders on Chunuk Bair. When this had all been accomplished, reserves would move up to take over and some of the troops on Chunuk Bair would move down to join with another force emerging from the old Anzac position and, between the two of them, they would pinch out Baby 700. At about the same time as the attacks on Chunuk Bair and 971 were launched, a powerful diversion would be taking place at Lone Pine. The business of Stopford's troops would be to attack and seize the hills known as Chocolate and W, two miles to the north-west of 971. It is not necessary to continue with their intentions for the next phase, for no next phase ever came.

## CHAPTER SIX

## Sari Bair and Evacuation

THE last day of the first year of the war saw the opening of the new campaign. Twenty-five thousand men with all their impedimenta were smuggled ashore at Anzac and moved into a troglodytic existence in the caves that had been dug for them. Aerial reconnaissance reported no sign of unusual activity on the Turkish side. On 6 August, under cover of a bombardment at both Anzac and Helles, Stopford's men began to go ashore at Suvla. The only force present to oppose them was one of three battalions under command of Major Willmer, a very competent officer of the Bavarian cavalry. With less than 1,500 men he had to prohibit the disembarkation of 20,000 and he performed his hopeless task as well as it could have been done. All the same, he could not seriously interfere with the landing and by 2 am on the following day Hamilton learnt that his men were ashore, having suffered few casualties. General Stopford did not accompany them. He remained on board HMS *Jonquil* resting, for he did not feel very well and had hurt his leg.

A brigade from Mitylene arrived and their commander, intent on carrying out his orders to march without delay and seize a certain hill, was met by Major-General Hammersley, in command of the 11th Division, who instantly countermanded them. As soon as the brigade began to move out towards its new objective, Hammersley cancelled the orders completely. Such was the tone of things in general. Having got themselves ashore, the old gentlemen considered their duty done and, until the guns arrived, they found nothing for their troops to do but brew up and go for a swim. The day was very hot, shade temperatures exceeding

90 degrees. Not at all the sort of day on which to go rampaging through scrubby hills and thorn-choked ravines. Later in the day, however, there was a spasm of energy when the young soldiers took Chocolate and Green Hills which they carried in the best style. As, however, no officer above the rank of lieut-colonel was present, all the brigadiers remaining well behind, and no communications existed, they stayed there and lost all contact with the enemy also. General Stopford may have comforted himself with the thought that his behaviour would have won praise from his old chief, Buller, who had behaved in exactly the same manner at Colenso.

At Anzac, things were not done quite in that fashion. Monash, with the aid of his staff captain, Eastwood, had painstakingly worked out a march table by which he reckoned that he would reach his objective on the Abdel-Rahman Ridge by 1.40 am. His troops appeared to be in high fettle for all the sick had miraculously recovered and regimental police had had to be posted in order to prevent those who had no business to be present from joining their battalions. Nevertheless, these were not the same men who had landed in April; apart from the fact that only about six hundred of the originals were still present, the dysentery, lack of sleep and vile food had had the effect of debilitating all of them.

The New Zealanders moved out at 8.30 pm on 6 August and by a 'magnificent feat of arms, the brilliance of which was never surpassed, if indeed equalled, during the campaign', the Mounted Riflemen (dismounted, of course, for the occasion) were in their designated position amongst the foothills soon after 1 am. Cox and Monash led out their column about an hour later and, as the latter wrote afterwards, 'It was like walking out on a stormy winter's night from a warm, cosy, home into a hail, thunder and lightning storm. We had not gone half a mile [along the beach] when the black tangle of hills between the beach road and the main mountain range became alive with flashes of musketry and the bursting of shrapnel and star shell, and the yells of the enemy and the cheers of our men as they swept in [he refers to the New Zealanders] to drive in the enemy from molesting the flanks of our march. By 11.30 we had reached the farthermost point of the beach road, and came abreast of the northern end of the mountain range. My column had the role of a vast turning movement, to get completely around the enemy's right as it faced the sea. From this point we turned sharp into the foothills of the main range, with a tangle of gullies and low ridges covered with prickly gorse. It was a black, gloomy night and one could not see 10 yards ahead.'

Already, according to the march table, they were badly behind time; once again congestion in the rear areas was the cause. The left covering force had become mixed up with the 40th Brigade as each groped its way through inky darkness trying to find an unfamiliar place. The time so lost was never regained. Exhilarated though they were by the idea of getting away from the claustrophobic conditions under which they had so long lived, the Australians were already beginning to tire. There was a welcome halt for half an hour while officers sorted out their men and the movement began again at about 11 pm. The pace was that of a funeral with frequent halts when those at the head encountered some sort of obstacle, while the great naval shells rumbled overhead and the yellow flames of bursting lyddite momentarily lit up the still distant hills. From time to time the searchlight of a destroyer would sweep round turning everything into an instant silhouette of black and white. Packs and rifles became imperceptibly heavier. At 1 am, as the triumphant New Zealanders were making their last attack, the left column was still shuffling past Godley's HQ, the Indian Brigade parallel with the tail of the Australian and a little inland from it. Godley took the opportunity of sending Monash a message desiring him to make better speed; his comments on its receipt are, mercifully, unrecorded.

Though neither of them knew it, the difficulty was that one of Overton's Greek guides at the head of the column had lost his way. Overton himself with ten scouts, an interpreter and the local expert formed the van of the column and Overton had noticed that the way they were going was not the one he had reconnoitred. They halted to discuss the situation; the Greek insisted that, although they were going half-right instead of straight ahead, he was taking a short cut which he knew well. Overton, mindful of the possibility of treachery, needed some persuading but in the end he accepted that the man was honest and probably knew best. Accordingly, with the Greek leading and Overton close behind with his pistol loose in its holster in case he had been mistaken, the column filed into a valley which soon narrowed to such an extent that they could move only in single file with pioneers cutting through the thorn-choked bed. Some resistance was met and a couple of platoons were sent forward to deal with it. At this point, the column still being some way short of the Aghyl Dere ravine, Monash came forward to take charge. He found Overton again in conclave with his Greek and, after hearing him out, gave orders that the column must adhere as far as possible to the original plan and move down the northern side of the defile into the bed of the Aghyl Dere, a matter of about six hundred yards.

This done, the brigade found itself on a flat stubble field between two spurs of the ridge which faced them; it was now 2 am and a crescent moon was rising in a cloudless sky. It gave sufficient light to make them visible, for some scattered rifle fire came down on them from the hill on the right. Overton frankly admitted that he had never been there before and was lost. Monash, uncertain what he ought to do for the best, sent two battalions to form an outpost line on the ridge to the north. No sooner had they gone than Colonel Cannan of the 15th Battalion arrived with the 16th, the Indian Brigade and the mountain battery trailing behind him. Monash directed him eastwards along the flat beside the Aghyl Dere, with orders to turn left up one of its branches and then straight towards Abdel Rahman Bair. This was the point at which the two Gurkha battalions were to break off for their attack on Hill Q. The 15th soon came under heavy fire and by 3 o'clock, with dawn approaching, Cannan sent for Overton and asked him to point out the direction of the two-hundred-metre contour on Abdel Rahman which was to be his forming up place. The Greek assured them that it was no more than a quarter of an hour's walk away. The weary Diggers moved on again though the opposition had stiffened and there was a Turkish rifleman behind every boulder and bush. As the light cleared so did Cannan realize that he was nowhere near his objective. Colonel Pope of the 16th who was on Cannan's inland flank, had the same truth brought home to him. Abdel Rahman was a long mile away and the brigade, instead of being closed up to fight, was deployed in line and exhausted. They had suffered about three hundred casualties and men were falling asleep where they lay. It was all of a mile and a half to Hill 971 and Monash accepted that no attack was now to be thought of. He issued orders to his battalions to dig in where they found themselves.

Dr Bean has something to say of the brigadier at this point in his career and one cannot gainsay him: 'Monash was a leader of whom it was already said that he would command a division better than a brigade and a corps better than a division. His powerful intellect was obvious to all who knew him. His knowledge ranged over an extraordinarily wide field of subjects, and his width of outlook was combined with a grasp of detail which in social intercourse immediately raised him head and shoulders above most of his colleagues. The care with which he prepared an operation and the lucidity with which he could explain it, were the marks of an organising brain capable of undertakings of the first rank whether in the army or in civil life. But he was not a fighting commander of the type of Walker, M'Cay or Chauvel, and the enterprise in which he was now engaged was one calling for still more — the touch of a Stonewall Jackson, and the recklessness of a J. E. B. Stuart.'

A similar but less inhibited description comes from Major Allanson, then commanding one of the Gurkha battalions. He came to Monash's HQ for orders and judged the brigadier apparently to have lost his nerve, unable to give coherent orders but repeating over and over again 'I thought I knew how to command men'. Allanson was brusquely dismissed, being told that Monash had no use for his battalion. He is not a witness whose evidence can be lightly discounted, but if he were correct it is hard to understand how Monash was permitted to continue his upward career. Armies have very efficient grapevines, especially when a senior officer is thought to be lacking in necessary personal qualities, and the thing was not done in a corner. The fact that he was selected afterwards for command of a division answers the criticism, but some after-taste must remain. Perhaps Monash had this incident in mind when he made the remark to his staff that he cared nothing for their loyalty when they thought him to be right; when he needed it was when they thought him wrong. However, not all the loyalty in the world could have covered up for a brigadier who had gone to pieces in a crisis. Clerks, signallers, orderlies, batmen and all the other minor but necessary members of a brigade staff must have been aware of how he conducted himself. Monash himself certainly harboured no hang-dog feeling, for he was soon to write that 'there was a check, a momentary confusion, and a few tense minutes when anything might have happened. I had to go forward personally to the head of the column to push things along, and put vigour into the advance. By dint of yelling and swearing I got the head of the column going on and soon as company after company deployed and dashed forward, I had the whole brigade going in fine style, and they swept forward in a magnificent dash of two miles, on a front of fully a mile, carrying everything before them, and just as day broke we established ourselves on a line of ridges overlooking the valley of Asma Dere.' It is a little difficult to identify the incident to which he refers. Probably Monash, a middle-aged man whose best attribute was his excellent brain, liked to fancy himself more as a man of action. The state of mind is not unknown. The letter contains two palpable errors of fact; in the first place, 4th Brigade was still a long way from the Asma Dere and was separated from it by another sizeable valley; in the second, Monash blames the loss of direction on the assertion that 'I had a guide from the New Zealand Rifles, and two Greek farmers who were supposed to know the country, but Major Overton, the guide, was killed almost at the beginning'. In fact Overton was not killed until a concealed rifleman brought him down on a ridge above the last fork of Aghyl Dere just about dawn when he was leading one of the battalions of the Indian

Brigade into its presumed position. The mistakes are all the odder as the letter was not written until 16 August.

The same dawn found 4th Brigade facing roughly north, instead of east, and a full thousand yards from the nearest point in the Asma Dere valley. Everybody, Monash and Pope included, was firmly convinced that they were far more advanced than they were and so it was reported to Cox. He, not surprisingly, ordered them to advance and complete the capture of Hill 971 and it was not until Monash went forward again to confer with Pope that the ugly truth forced itself upon them. Monash, in Bean's words, 'who was inclined to caution, represented the situation strongly to Cox, and after considerable demur was permitted for the present to fortify the line he had won'.

This, to all intents and purposes, ended the part played in the battle for Sari Bair by the left covering force. Once again Monash had failed. By contrast with the splendid performances of the New Zealanders who had won a foothold on Chunuk Bair, the Australians at Lone Pine whose exploits can be judged by the fact that seven Victoria Crosses were won in a matter of hours, and the Gurkhas, some of whom under Allanson had won to the heights and for a time looked down on the Narrows, it was not an exploit of transcendent merit. Monash says that, after digging hard all through the next two days, 'I was ordered (much against my advice) to make another sortie to ascertain the enemy's strength on the opposite ridge' in which he incurred another thousand casualties without achieving anything. He personally captured a couple of Turks and acquired a copper bath tub and a camp bed 'as my share of the loot'.

At Suvla a languid chaos reigned supreme. Sir Ian, isolated at Imbros and with three major battles to concert, had received only one message from there announcing that the landing had been successful. This had reached him at 8 am on 7 August and silence then fell. At 4.20 pm Hamilton could stand it no longer and dispatched a signal exhorting his subordinate to get a move on. Some ten hours later Stopford vouchsafed a reply, to the effect that his position was on a line running north and south about a mile from the sea. It can hardly have been first-hand information, for Stopford was still aboard *Jonquil* resting his leg. At 5.10 he signalled that Chocolate Hill had been taken, that another brigade had advanced about a mile east of the Salt Lake and that Hammersley and his men deserved great credit for their accomplishment. Hamilton, though he politely agreed with the sentiment expressed, was aghast. The corps had been on Turkish soil for thirty-six hours, the time allotted for the capture of the Suvla hills, and it was not half way there. He determined that he must go himself to Suvla and infuse some energy into the commanders there. The destroyer put at his disposal by De Robeck did not appear; instead there came a courteous message from the navy that her fires had been drawn and her boiler was being cleaned; any inconvenience was greatly regretted but no other ship was available. Six hours later, Hamilton arrived in De Robeck's own yacht. It is a pity that so long had elapsed and that his temper had had time to cool. At the beach he met Colonel Aspinall of his own staff who was eloquent about the total inertia he had encountered and the opportunities that were slipping away.

Hamilton did what he could to put fire into non-inflammable bellies, which had the result of precipitating some confused and objectless fighting, but the corps commander was not there to listen. The situation was plainly one of extreme urgency and Hamilton travelled in a borrowed launch to interview Stopford. The corps commander was well content with the situation. His men were tired, they were short of water and the guns had not yet been landed in sufficient numbers so the attack might as well wait until tomorrow. Hamilton gave him the nearest thing possible to a direct order to occupy the heights at once. Stopford demurred. Sir Ian then demanded to see the subordinate generals. Sir Frederick assured him that nothing could please him more. Would Sir Ian excuse him from joining them? His leg still needed rest.

Hamilton again went ashore, to Hammersley's HQ. The conversation with Stopford was practically repeated and the same feeble objections raised. It ended with the commander-in-chief outraging the decencies by giving a divisional general direct orders to attack at once. It was just too late, for Willmer had been substantially reinforced and the attack, put in at dawn on 9 August, was a complete failure.

There is no need to dwell on the painful sequence of events at Suvla. The greatest chance of the war was thrown away by the most abject collection of general officers ever congregated in one spot. While the New Zealanders and the Gloucesters were fighting like heroes for Chunuk Bair, while Allanson's Gurkhas with a company of the 9th Royal Warwicks were clinging to the top of their hill and a fearful battle, part above and part under ground, was raging at Lone Pine, the man who should have been urging on his fresh troops to clinch a great victory was engrossed in applying embrocation to his extremities. Asquith had his measure when he learnt the truth, writing to Kitchener on 20 August that 'I have read enough to satisfy me that the generals and staff engaged in the Suvla part of the business ought to be court-martialled and dismissed from the army'. It was an understatement. By comparison with the sins of Sir Frederick Stopford and his band of brothers, the sins of Admiral Byng had been venial. Stopford appears only once more; after he eventually came ashore, his leg being better, he was observed on the beach giving his personal supervision to the construction of a bomb-proof shelter for his personal occupation, observing to the sapper subaltern in charge of the work that it should be well built as he expected to be there for a long time. His reign lasted exactly three days more, for on 14 August came the signal from Kitchener giving Hamilton leave to dismiss Stopford and Hammersley. Hamilton responded with alacrity. Soon afterwards he was told that Byng (who had only recently been pronounced irreplaceable), Maude and Fanshawe, some of the best generals in the BEF, were on their way to join him. Fortune, however, had forsaken the suitor who had rejected her and they could only act as receivers of a bankrupt business.

We must go back to Monash, whom we left with his brigade digging like badgers in the boiling sun. For a moment of time, in a myrtle-covered ravine without a name, the paths of two great soldiers crossed, one who was in a few years to become Australia's first general of international reputation, the other who, a generation later, would prove himself the greatest fighting commander the army had known since Wellington. At the head of the company of the Royal Warwicks on its way to join Allanson on Hill Q walked its commander, a Territorial soldier holding a temporary commission, Captain William Joseph Slim.

Cox's own 29th Brigade had come to a halt also on the right of the 4th Brigade and Godley had moved up behind it a brigade of the New Army, the 39th, which arrived at about dusk on the 7th. No more troops were sent to back up Monash, whose brigade was suffering a steady rate of casualties from Turkish snipers and field artillery firing shrapnel. Digging, for which only the men's entrenching tools were available, became a hazardous business and some units had to be withdrawn a little to the reverse slope of the valley which Monash believed to be the Asma Dere. Late in the afternoon Cox sent for him to report his situation and, by reason of Monash's insistence that his men were in the last stages of exhaustion, he obtained the loan of a battalion (6th King's Own) from Corps reserve to thicken up the line. The price for this was that three of Monash's original battalions should make one more attack across what both generals imagined to be the Asma Dere up a spur of Abdel Rahman. As we know from his letter, Monash protested about it but he could not disobey, especially when a signal arrived from Godley saying 'The GOC wishes you to close the troops . . . well up the slopes towards the enemy during the preliminary bombardment of the position so as to be ready to reach the crest as soon as the gun-fire stops to-morrow morning. The assault should be carried out with loud cheering. I feel confident that, after today's rest, and starting comparatively fresh, your brigade will make a determined effort to capture the key of the position.' How Godley can have thought the brigade to be 'comparatively fresh' is a mystery and Monash's comments must have been pithy. Their condition did little enough to encourage spontaneous cheering but as they never came anywhere near the crest it did not greatly matter. At 2 am on 8 August they moved out and blundered about in the dark whilst the naval guns again pounded the hills. At 4.15 the bombardment ceased and the three

Australian battalions attacked blindly in the general direction of Abdel Rahman, their commanders having little idea of where they were or of how far they had to go. A devastating fire met them and, after some initial progress, they fell back to a line not far in advance of that from which they had started. Such was the confusion, honest men asserting flatly that they had reached the Asma Dere and beyond, that it was not until 1919, when the Australian Historical Mission under the ubiquitous Bean visited the scene, that the truth was discovered. They had never, in spite of putting up a splendid fight, reached even the Asma Dere.

Monash, completely out of touch with his battalions since the telephone wires had been cut by shellfire, received no news of them until seven o'clock, when an intrepid sapper managed to get the line to Pope's battalion mended. The disheartening message came through that the task was beyond their powers. Machine-guns and artillery were killing the men in large numbers and there seemed no object in staying where they were. Monash passed the message to Cox who ordered him to withdraw his men to the old position.

Bean links 8 August, 1915, with the battle of Fromelles a year later as the two 'Black Days' of the AIF. He also adds, from personal experience, that 'so rugged was [the country in front of 4th Brigade] that from the supposed starting-point [which the column had barely reached at the end of its calamitous advance] the climbing of Abdel Rahman Bair, even in daylight and in peaceful manœuvres, would have taken troops, though at the acme of fitness and health, longer than the time allowed for the whole operation. Leaving out of account the fact that the brigade was intended to proceed up an exposed spur with the enemy possibly on several sides, the natural difficulties which were still in front of the column at day-break were considerably greater than the sum of those encountered by any column on the night of August 6.' The Archangel Michael himself could not have led a brigade to victory in such conditions. The bill amounted to twenty-two officers and 743 other ranks, though most were only lightly wounded.

Another attempt was made on the following day to storm the

same heights, this time by the British 38th Brigade of Brigadier-General Baldwin. The 4th Brigade was spared from any part in it. Suffice it to say that it was a 'carbon copy' battle. Units became lost and found themselves either facing sheer cliffs or entangled in thorn choked gullies. Baldwin was killed and the attack petered out with nothing to show but dead and wounded men for its pains. The Sari Bair range, like Anzac, was now too strongly held ever to change hands.

Mustafa Kemal had been adequately reinforced, thanks to the timidity displayed at Suvla, and the story ended with all the assaulting troops, even the New Zealanders and their comrades of the New Army being driven from the positions they had gained so bravely and at such cost. The only advantage that remained was described by Godley as 'about 500 acres of bad grazing'.

There was a last, despairing attack at Hill 60, the feature which some of Monash's commanders had taken to be a lower spur of Abdel Rahman, to coincide with the Scimitar Hill battle at Suvla, which began on 21 August and which lasted for two days. All the 4th Brigade could provide was a detachment totalling 500 men. Again the same things happened and it would be tedious to write of it in detail. Monash was only engaged to a small extent; his greatest concern now was the shrinking size of his command, due to a recurrence of every kind of sickness to which his worn-out men had little resistance. 'Where, I wonder, are the 15 per cent per month reinforcements which Australia promised us?'

During the minor operations of late August he had time to ponder on events and the opportunity, at last, to put his thoughts on paper. They are worth reading, for they mark a subtle change in his earlier, rather naïve, faith in the capacity of those responsible for the higher direction of the war. 'I am afraid it must be admitted that Ian Hamilton's plan in its entirety has so far failed to achieve the main objectives and this has tended to overshadow the many minor successes and the brilliant achievements of the Australian troops and the New Zealanders. It is the old story — insufficient troops, inadequate munitions, attempting more than was possible with the means available... The Turkish losses have been enormous, but our losses have been very heavy too — so heavy that we can now do no more than hang on to what we have gained and wait for reinforcements. As an index of our losses, I marched out of Reserve Gully on 6 August with 3,350. My parade state to-day is 1,037. I have left in the Brigade 2 lieutenant-colonels, 5 majors, 3 captains and 22 lieutenants (out of a total of 136 officers) — of course many of these are lightly wounded, or sick, and will re-join later.

'Much of the fault with the British troops lay in the leadership; the officers do not mix with the men as we do, but keep aloof, and some senior officers appeared chiefly concerned in looking after themselves and making themselves comfortable... Result — although we have gained enormous new tracts of country, our strategic or tactical objectives are still unreached although within easy reach with a few brigades of fresh, good troops and plenty of gun ammunition. I am still on a very strict daily ammunition allowance, which is rather a bother when one gets good targets or wants proper preparation for an infantry offensive... I am more than satisfied that after the destruction of the regular army in France no other troops at the Empire's disposal could have got and held a footing on Gallipoli except the Australians and New Zealanders.

'I still keep in the very best of health, and the active life has made me fit and hard and strong, and I never seem to tire; also my spirits keep up, although, as I lose good officers, the work of keeping up efficiency gets harder and harder. I cannot tell you how much all your full and interesting letters cheer me up.'

'Enormous new tracts of country' was something of an overstatement, but at least the two positions of Anzac and Suvla were now connected up and the 4th Brigade was the formation linking the two. On Monash's left, the 54th (East Anglian Territorial) Division, milked of its best men and technical units for France before leaving home, looked out towards the unattainable heights of Sari Bair and on his right lay the New Zealanders.

Health was now a far greater problem than Mustafa Kemal, and a lowering of the spirits had set in after the succession of failures through which they had passed. In mid-September, the brigade was withdrawn from the line and sent to recuperate on the island of Lemnos. Here for the first time Monash experienced real muddle and confusion. Hamilton had been forced to start his campaign with no 'A' or 'Q' staff at all and the only trained officers of those departments were, of course, in France. The quality, apart from the inexperience, of those holding down jobs in the rear areas was unequal. Nothing was ready for the troops, the island was plagued with amoebic dysentery, and the men had to fend for themselves. Monash went down with both lumbago and dysentery and was, for a time, very miserable. He soon recovered and, with the aid of a horse borrowed from the remount depot, set out to explore the island. What he saw delighted him. 'Did somebody say there was a war on somewhere? To bask in the sun here, looking out over rolling meadows and the hills topped with windmills, the sails turning around lazily in the gentle breeze, with flocks of ridiculous little black and white sheep about the size of poodles, and caravans of picturesque Greek peasants in national dress on lines of little donkeys — one would never dream that close by are armies of men fighting and killing and maiming each other.' He observed other, and less picturesque, things also. 'In this island one can see the cult of inefficiency and muddle and red-tape practised to a nicety. There are ever so many gentlemen earning their war medals on board luxurious transports, decked all over with gorget patches and arm-bands and lace, acting as deputy-assistant-acting-inspector-general-of-something-or-other . . . As to the British hospitals, here, well, the sooner they hang somebody for gross mismanagement the better.'

At Lemnos he learnt for the first time the truth about the early days at Suvla; his comments are, understandably, bitter.

Away from the war, Monash felt a touch of homesickness. A long letter to Mrs Monash demands information about his beloved garden and reads like a seedsman's catalogue. Not a bed, not a tree is neglected, from the Mary Manifold roses and bougainvillea over the tennis pavilion to instructions for the pruning of fig and almond trees. At least he would see them again one day; that other rose-fancier, Colonel Malone, had died in a very gallant charge up the slopes of Chunuk Bair.

He passed most of his month on Lemnos expostulating with the authorities there about the shameful incompetence of the postal service, the hospitals, the food and the disappearance of comforts sent from home, some of which mysteriously fell into the hands of Greek contractors who sold them back to their owners. These aggravating tasks were relieved by ten-mile walks and an occasional camp-fire concert, his reception at which showed that the opinion of him expressed by Allanson was not shared by the Diggers.

At the beginning of October he was given a holiday in Egypt where he soon realized that muddle, inefficiency and general skrim-shanking were in their infancy on Lemnos. It was in Cairo that he received news of his CB, 'for distinguished service in the field', but it did not excite him. Neither did the news that Bulgaria had entered the war on the side of the Central Powers, one of the things the Dardanelles expedition had been designed to prevent.

Nevertheless, while Monash was choosing silks for his wife in the Muski, in Downing Street words like 'evacuation' and 'Salonika' were beginning to be heard. The undermining of Hamilton had been completed and, on 14 October, Mr Lloyd George lit the charge. Fisher had deserted back in May, and, within a matter of a few weeks, Churchill was to be shut out. Hamilton's last task was to prepare an estimate of the loss to be expected if an evacuation were to take place and he was then dismissed. History has been unjust to Sir Ian Hamilton, interesting itself only in his failure to achieve success but ignoring the reasons for it; in fact, his accomplishments had been very great, but with the commanders given to him he might as well have been ordered to make a table with a set of rubber tools. The final insult came when, at a meeting of the Dardanelles Commission, he was accused by his old enemy Field Marshal Lord Nicholson of undue interference with his subordinate generals.

Monash was back with the brigade on 10 November; he found it built up again to its war establishment and well dug in. The main business was preparation for a winter on Gallipoli and there was much to be done to make ready for the gales and rain, ice and snow, to which that inhospitable place is subject. He found time to send home some acorns, with the surprising comment that the scrub so often mentioned was a species of holly and presumably wishing for a memento of a horticultural kind. A couple of days later came an ominous signal. He was to meet the corps commander next morning ('service dress, belts') but was to leave his escort at least a quarter of a mile from the meeting place. He arrived to find Birdwood, with all the commanders of divisions and brigades, gazing intently out to sea at a picket-boat threading its way towards them through the lines of anchored ships. No word was spoken until a very tall officer with a heavy moustache and dressed in the khaki of a field marshal stepped ashore. Lord Kitchener had come to see things for himself. The Secretary of State shook hands with all the party and, as Monash was the first of the Australians he met, he spoke to him. 'I have brought you all a personal message from the King. He wants me to tell you how much he admires the splendid things you have done here.' Kitchener spent a couple of hours at Anzac, walking round every place of importance, and left as unobtrusively as he had come. He gave no indication of what his thoughts might be.[1]

At the beginning of December, the smiling Aegean showed its teeth. It started with thunder, followed by torrential rain and concluded with a snowstorm that left the entire landscape covered in six inches of snow, something that few Australians had ever seen. The thought of a winter at Anzac, once the novelty had worn off, suddenly became even less atttractive. The rest of the campaign was fought almost entirely by patrols and machine-guns. General Sir Charles Monro—bitterly summarized by Mr Churchill as a man swift to make up his mind, 'he came, he saw, he capitulated'—had taken over Hamilton's command, but it does not appear that he and Monash ever met.

---

[1] During the perambulation a small incident took place that deserves better than oblivion. The YMCA had established a canteen at Anzac and as he passed it Kitchener, probably for the first time in his life, spoke directly to a private soldier emerging from the tent. The soldier was an Australian. 'What can you buy there?' asked the war lord. 'Nuts,' replied the soldier politely. 'Yes, but what else can you get there?' 'Nothing.'

Monash could have spared his pains over making ready to withstand the winter. On 12 December 'like a thunderbolt from a clear blue sky has come the stupendous and paralysing news that, after all, the Allied War Council has decided that the best and wisest course to take is to evacuate the Peninsula, and secret orders to carry out that operation have just reached here ... I need not say I feel very unhappy ... I am almost frightened to contemplate the howl of rage and disappointment there will be when the men find out what is afoot, and I am wondering what Australia will think at the desertion of her 6,000 dead and her 20,000 other casualties.'

The operation of withdrawing hundreds of thousands of men by sea from enemy territory was one for which the British army had, so far, little precedent to guide it. At the affair of St Cas, in 1758, about half the rearguard had been lost in a furious battle on the beach; at Corunna, in 1809, Moore had dealt his pursuers a smashing blow and his army had slipped away before the French had had time to recover themselves. Neither gave much encouragement. Hamilton had reckoned on losing anything up to 45% of the troops engaged. The only crumb of comfort was that the Turks were also believed to be in a bad way and there was a school of thought convinced that any evacuating would be done by them.

The staff work involved was entrusted mainly to Cyril Brudenell White, who had only recently been appointed Birdwood's Chief-of-Staff. His plans were a masterpiece of synchronized detail and comprehended the entire Anzac and Suvla areas. Helles was to be held by the four divisions which still garrisoned it.

The absolute essential was secrecy, though it was too much to hope that the troops could long remain in ignorance of what was going on. Furphies of staggering ingenuity were abroad; they were all going to Salonika, to Greece, to Italy, to France and to other even less likely places. The Turks were allowed to attack trenches unresisted, so that they would learn that a position that did not open fire was not necessarily empty. Again Australian inventiveness came in useful with the self-firing rifle, a kerosene tin full of water dripping into another which, when sufficiently full, tumbled over and jerked a string tied to the trigger which fired the weapon. Few men seemed stricken at the prospect of leaving Gallipoli, but the prevailing mood was one of humiliation at giving up a job when it was only half done.

When the time came, it was plain that White's deception plan had worked perfectly. The Turks had no idea of what was happening and the divisions thinned out unmolested. It was the thought of deserting their dead that troubled people most; one man spoke for them all, observing quietly to Birdwood as he passed him, with a gesture towards one of the little cemeteries, 'I hope *they* won't hear us marching down the deres.' Demand for places with the last to embark greatly exceeded needs. 'I was here at the beginning and I have a right to stay to the end' was an expression frequently heard.

The 4th Brigade began to embark on 13 December; Monash had expressed the intention of being the last man to leave, but he was appointed second-in-command of the division to go to Lemnos to supervise the arrangements made for its reception there. Before leaving, however, he bent his mind to the problems of evacuating his men. The whole operation was to take place over a period of two nights and the most elaborate arrangements were put in hand to make sure that another complicated movement in the dark should not go astray in any particular. Men were divided into parties, each of which had to leave by a specific path at a precise time in order to meet up with the correct number of motor lighters which would ferry them to the waiting transports. Absolute silence was necessary; even one blunderer could give the game away. Amongst the other precautions taken was the destruction of every drop of drink in the Anzac and Suvla positions. As they could afford to be prodigal of the stores of food which would have to be abandoned, paths were marked out by lines of flour or salt and, so far as was possible, men were rehearsed in what they would have to do on the night. In the 4th Brigade, Monash took his usual pains to ensure perfection by having every man issued with a card telling him plainly what his duties were and setting out an exact timetable.

The whole business ran on oiled wheels, and all that remained was for the chaplains to pray for fine weather. Not for the last time Providence was kind to the British army when engaged in getting itself off a hostile shore; the nights of 18 and 19 December were dead calm and not a man got his feet wet. They left behind great quantities of food, clothing and tentage but managed to get away all but eleven of the guns, and even these were suited more to the museum than to the battlefield.

In spite of his new functions, Monash contrived to delay his own departure until the last night. At nine o'clock the final patrol came in, an hour later the strength of the brigade was down to 170 men and at 1.45 on the morning of the 20th the remaining three parties, the machine-gunners being last of all, trooped down to the beach at ten-minute intervals. Barbed wire knife-rests were placed across the gullies, the fuses to the mines under Russell's Top and other places lit and the 'beetles', as the motor-lighters were called, chugged quietly away. The mines went up with a tremendous flash and roar and the whole length of Sari Bair exploded in rifle and machine-gun fire.

From Anzac they had taken off forty-five thousand men and several millions of pounds worth of guns, stores, mules, provisions and transport. Monash, on a bunk in the pantryman's cabin of the small transport *Arran*, was wide awake and undisturbed by the hand-shaking and back-slapping going on around him. He got out his pocket-book and, as dawn broke over the island of Lemnos, he jotted down his last impressions. 'It was a most brilliant conception, brilliantly organized, brilliantly executed, and will, I am sure, rank as the greatest joke — and the greatest feat of arms — in the whole range of military history.'

CHAPTER SEVEN

## The Western Front and Salisbury Plain

ON the last day of 1915, a black year for the Allies, Monash steamed into Alexandria as GOC Troops aboard RMS *Cardiganshire*, an Atlantic liner which he had armed *cap-à-pie* with his field artillery and machine-guns as a precaution against attack by submarines. Nothing, however, happened to disturb the cruise. In beautiful weather he found time to catch up with his neglected correspondence and gleefully set down the current pleasantry about the comfortable staff officers aboard the transports having been awarded three clasps to their campaign medals for 'Imbros, Mudros and Chaos'.

Now came the time of the great reorganization. Already in Egypt there was a large number of Australian troops and one glance soon made it clear that not all of them were of the quality of the original AIF. Lithgow had proved incapable of keeping up the supply of rifles and many of the new men arrived without ever having handled one. Their equipment also was uneven, for supplies of webbing had run out and a large proportion of the new drafts had to make do with the heavy, old-fashioned, leather belts and pouches. Plainly there was a lot to be done before the newcomers would be fit to take their places in the ranks. It was not surprising that voices had been raised in the Australian Parliament asserting that their men had been uselessly sacrificed in Gallipoli while the British forces had got off more lightly. Publication of the figures of the casualties soon put paid to this but for a moment men wondered whether Australia would still be willing to send her sons to fight in a war that bore so heavily upon her small population. The enemy and some of the neutral press naturally made the most of this. Australia's stern answer came in the announcement that a new division would be raised at once to make good some of the gaps in the British ranks.

From the remnants of the existing formations and from the mass of details in Egypt two more divisions were constituted in that country. A Fifth Brigade had arrived in Gallipoli a little before the evacuation, bringing the total available to fifteen Australian and three New Zealand brigades. In February, the order appeared for the formation of four new Australian brigades which were to be created by each existing battalion being divided into two. It was not a popular expedient, for obvious reasons, but it was effective. The War Office copied it in 1939 when the doubled Territorial Army was subdivided in the same way. Most of the commanding officers played fair by resisting the temptation to rid themselves of their undesirables, but few went as far as the scrupulous Gellibrand; he divided his complement into two wings of about equal merit and then tossed a coin to decide which was to go and which to stay. The 4th Brigade bisected to form a nucleus for the 12th but Monash contrived to retain all his own HQ staff, his machine-gunners, signals and battalion commanders. The NZ & A Division ceased to exist. From its ashes rose the 4th Australian Division of 4th, 12th and 13th Brigades and the New Zealand Division.

The sister dominion took its leave by staging a campfire concert at which the principal entertainment was a 'haka' specially composed for Monash and danced by the Maori contingent. The spectacle of their doctor and chaplain, both gentlemen of education and refinement, stripped to their underpants, hideously tattooed and 'going through cannibalistic dances with their men' amused him hugely.

Among senior officers there was much interest in the question of the likely recipients of these fine new commands. Everybody knew that the new divisions owed their existence largely to Senator Pearce and 'Billy' Hughes, now Prime Minister, since Sir Andrew Fisher had gone as High Commissioner to London, and they were expected to exercise considerable influence over the choices to be made. Monash, of course, was on terms of close friendship with the former and it rather seems that his wife had been doing a little gentle lobbying on her own account. Her husband airily wrote that he was not at all sure that he wanted the extra responsibility as he had quite enough to worry about already. 'I have firmly resolved not to intrigue or canvass for promotion in any way, and if Australia chooses to let her forces be exploited to find jobs for unemployed senior British officers, that is not my affair.' This is almost certainly a dig at Cox, who does not seem to have been Monash's favourite general.

The truth of the matter was that the last word lay with Birdwood; he has been accused of being an advertising kind of man, bent only on his own advancement but it has never been suggested that he was anti-Australian. On the contrary, Birdwood is on record as having said that he would prefer to give high commands in the AIF to Australian officers fit to fill them even if more competent British officers were available. By far the most competent of the Australians was Brudenell White, a man in every way fitted for the highest position, but he could not be spared from his post as Chief-of-Staff. This was hard on White for had he not made such an outstanding success of the most difficult task of them all he might easily have succeeded to command of the Australian corps in April, 1918. Such are the fortunes of war.

As to Monash, Birdwood recognized his great planning and organizational qualities but he plainly felt, as did others, that his métier was not that of a hard-fighting leader, swift to respond to a changing situation and able to get the last ounce out of his men. Monash was not of that opinion: 'My thoroughly successful command of my own brigade performance of every task set my brigade is quite good enough for me [sic], and I know what Cox and Godley and Birdwood and Murray think of me and my brigade.' Perhaps it was as well that he did not know it all. The letter begins breezily enough with 'Now, good people, don't worry about me or my advancement. For me it counts for very little. If they want me to command a division, they know where to find me. So far nobody has passed over me. M'Cay, Chauvel and Legge are all my seniors. I might have had the 4th Division. Pearce cabled Birdwood asking that White or I might get it; but Birdwood preferred to entrust it to Cox, a Kitchener man, and an old Indian colleague.' Pearce had done nothing of the kind. Birdwood had written to him that no Australian officer was yet fit to be promoted to a divisional command and he had put forward the names of Cox and Sir Herbert Lawrence, sweetening it a little by suggesting that if M'Cay were sufficiently recovered he should have the 3rd Division, still forming in Australia. Pearce sadly accepted the recommendation but added a rider to impress upon Birdwood the strength of national feeling on this sensitive subject, and saying that one of the two named generals must wait for the arrival of the 3rd Division in Egypt. As both men knew, Lawrence could not be kept idle in Egypt for so long and Pearce suggested that, if he could not stay, White or Monash should be considered; but this recommendation was for command of the embryo formation in Australia, not for the extant 4th Division in Egypt.

In the event, the appointment of GOC 3rd Division was left, for the time being, unfilled. Cox was given the 4th Division and M'Cay returned in March to take over the 5th. Lawrence left Egypt; in course of time he became Chief-of-Staff to Sir Douglas Haig in France. Monash was obviously disappointed; he would not have minded in the least if White had been given his division, for it was on this occasion that he referred to him as 'far and away the ablest soldier Australia has turned out', adding, for the edification of Mrs Monash, 'You will remember meeting him at the Roosevelt reception at the Ritz. He is also a charming good fellow.' He had too the advantage of a regular Staff College training, whereas Monash, for the moment, was obliged to make good the gaps in his military education either by drawing upon the other discipline in which he had been trained or simply by the light of nature. Nevertheless, to be passed over by Legge and then to have Cox preferred to him was, undeniably, a blow to his pride, no matter how much he might try to disguise it.

There remained plenty of work for him to do, some of it of an uncongenial kind. The defence of Egypt still worried the authorities even though there was no substantial Turkish force within threatening distance. The 4th Brigade was given the task, concurrent with its training, of guarding the crossing place at Serapaeum, almost exactly the spot where Djemal had come to grief in the previous year. The first anniversary of the landing was fittingly celebrated with a blend of the sombre and the frivolous. In the morning the entire brigade was paraded; each man who had served on Gallipoli wore a blue ribbon on the right breast and each who had taken part in the landing wore a red one also. They looked pitifully few amongst so many. The massed bands played the *Dead March in Saul* — music older by far than Australia — and at its conclusion the massed bugles sounded the Last Post. When the parade was over, the rest of the day was given up to carnival; there was a cricket match, swimming races in the Canal and a 'screamingly funny skit' on the landing. An unexpected guest was the young Prince of Wales, packed off out of harm's way in France by Kitchener, despite his indignant reminder that, if anything happened to him, he still had four brothers. Kitchener's deflating answer was that he would not mind too much if the Prince were killed but he could not face the prospect of his being taken prisoner.

The task of re-shaping the AIF was formidable indeed. First and foremost, there was the problem of the quality of the 'new chums' who made up about three-quarters of its present complement. Most of the recruits were of good quality, for all their rawness, but a substantial larrikin element had now arrived and was threatening to contaminate many of the others. The most dangerous element of all was a handful of professional criminals who had enlisted only because the word had got about at home that there was easy money to be made in the army; quite apart from the generous rates of pay, there were substantial pickings to be had from the running of gambling schools and the fleecing of local inhabitants. The number involved was never great but such a leaven has a way of inflating the appearance of bad behaviour. It was exceedingly difficult to control them because the dearth of officers, especially in the junior ranks, was now acute.

It had become official policy to appoint to commissions only men who had proved their worth in the ranks, Duntroon graduates apart, and the practice was not always successful. In the first place, men with officer-like qualities did not abound, though the ranks were combed and combed again in order to find them. There were still no schools of instruction for aspirants and the promotion from corporal to second lieutenant was marked by little more formality than had attended the grant of a lance stripe. The custom was for the new officer to give a farewell dinner, at which no holds were barred, and on the morrow relations became formal. The Diggers had learnt by hard experience that officers were, after all, something more than a parasitic growth demanding an obsequious homage that transcended all sense. More than one veteran had been heard to say that 'by God, our officers were wonderful'. Nevertheless, the attributes of a good officer have always been slightly different from those that make a good NCO and not all the new bearers of the King's commission were ideally suited to their additional responsibilities.

Amongst the seniors, too, all was not well. Some of the battalion commanders, men well advanced into middle age, ought to have been sent home with the thanks of their country for past services and put to work as trainers rather than as leaders. Bean had noticed that one of the causes of the failure before Sari Bair had been a lack of cordiality between some battalions. Colonel Pope, for all his gifts, seems to have been a difficult man to work with; after the battle of Fromelles he was sent home 'for disciplinary reasons', though he was back again in time for Messines. He was probably not the only one. Amongst the captains and majors there were first-class young men, fit in every way for promotion, but the government insisted that it would not be fair to remove from their commands older men who had not done anything positively wrong.

The battalions themselves suffered a continual bleeding; first, the artillery had to be expanded from thirty-six to sixty batteries to bring its establishment to parity with that of the New Army divisions in France. Next, a Pioneer battalion had to be raised for each division. 'Pioneer' is a rather loaded word, suggestive of an elderly gentleman with a walrus moustache and flat feet reluctantly wielding a shovel. White could see the folly of this and the men selected were required to be the best rather than the worst the battalions could find. The result was that the Australian Pioneers became numbered amongst the best units in France, closer to the American Engineer Regiments than to the usual run of Pioneers, but capable of fighting with the best infantry when the need arose. Many deeds of valour were performed in the later stages of the war by men armed only with a sharpened shovel which, in the right hands, can be an extremely formidable weapon. If this were not enough, yet more men had to be given up to form such useful adjuncts as field butcheries, bakeries and a dozen other ancillary services.

All this was done under the eye of Sir Archibald Murray, Maxwell's successor, whose HQ was hard by the areas occupied by I Anzac Corps and II Anzac Corps as the formations were now called. I Anzac comprised the 1st and 2nd Divisions, under Godley, and II Anzac was made up of the 4th and 5th, nominally under Birdwood. Murray had served in France from the beginning as Chief-of-Staff to Sir John French. He was a professional soldier of great experience but the unaccountable rages of his incompetent chief had proved too much for him and he had suffered a nervous breakdown. He was, naturally, wedded to the traditional ways of the British army and what he saw of the Australians during the period of reformation did not greatly impress him. Slovenliness in dress, permissible in Gallipoli, was general, march discipline was poor but the worst of all was the matter of saluting. Whenever he passed an Australian camp, whether mounted with suitable attendants carrying his flag on a lance, or driving in his motor-car, the result was always the same, either complete indifference or an interested stare. Saluting, of course, did not come naturally to Australians and it was hard to make the point that it was something more than a cringing obeisance from low to high. Lectures were given to unconvinced audiences with the theme that it was the soldier's traditional greeting owing its origin to the raising of the visor by the helmed knight in order to make himself known. Nobody believed it. Surprisingly, no play seems to have been made with the reciprocal nature of the salute; a private soldier failing to salute an officer of course gets into trouble, but it is nothing like the trouble that comes, in a good regiment, to the officer who fails to return it properly. There is a famous story of three Diggers at Anzac who, quite deliberately, gave a crashing salute to a colonel when they could see that he was looking in the opposite direction and was unaware of their presence. As they passed by, one of them observed loudly, 'I suppose that's what they call breeding.' Saluting must seem, to the unmilitary mind, a silly thing about which to become excited and a feudal relic. It is not. Thirty years later, Sir William Slim was to write that 'we tried to make our discipline intelligent, but we were an old-fashioned army and we insisted on its outward signs. In the Fourteenth Army we expected soldiers to salute officers — and officers to salute in return — both in mutual confidence and respect.' Note the 'we'. No 'them' and 'us' about it. But with the Australians it was a losing battle. It had the effect on Murray of hardening his view that this was not an army but an undisciplined mob, unfit for the serious business of war on the Western Front, and so he reported to the War Office.

In consequence, when the AIF went to France, a bad reputation preceded it. It was the critical situation at Verdun that settled their future. On 26 March Murray received a signal from Robertson, now CIGS in succession to the ineffectual Wolfe-Murray (Sheep-Murray, Churchill called him). Things were not going well with the French and they must be given every possible support, even at the price of denuding Egypt. Murray had at one time intended to send the Australians to France first of all his troops but his opinion of them had become so poor that they had sunk to fourth place, after the 29th, 31st and 11th Divisions, in that order. Robertson, however, was not satisfied. Three Australian divisions now, he asserted, will be worth more than double that number in April. Murray responded to the obvious emergency and dispatched all six divisions as quickly as he could.

I Anzac Corps disembarked at Marseilles on 19 March, their artillery being brought up to strength by drawing whole batteries from the formations left behind in Egypt. As to their discipline, the base commandant assured Birdwood that no troops had ever given him less trouble. On the express orders of Sir Douglas

Haig, who knew Murray well and had no doubt heard his opinion of the Australians, they were moved by train across France and into a fairly quiet sector behind Armentières. Once again the fates seem to have conspired to give them a grotesque view of the English. When the time came for them to take over frontline trenches they, or some of them, relieved the 35th Division. The 35th were known as 'The Bantams' because the men were of a stature even below the modest 5 ft 2 ins demanded as the minimum height for infantry recruits. One result was that a great deal of digging was called for since what was to a Bantam a deep trench was about belt-level to most Australians. If the juxtaposition of an enormous Queenslander and a diminutive Bantam did not engender the famous cartoon characters of the time, Mutt and Jeff, it should have done.

We must leave them to their labours and return to Egypt. M'Cay came back on 22 March and assumed command of the 5th Division. He had never been a popular officer; many felt that he exacted a brand of discipline that was needlessly rigorous. He did not make himself more loved by his first action. Because the Egyptian railways had no rolling-stock available it became necessary for his division to march across the desert from Tel-el-Kebir to the Canal where they were to take over the posts left vacant by the departure of I Anzac. Cox's 4th Division was to do the same, the distance being about forty miles mostly over heavy sand. The British army trained Cox insisted on care being given to the state of men's feet, the checking of boots and the loading of every possible thing on the camels which accompanied them. M'Cay, or his staff officers, decided that such precautions were grandmotherly. His division marched with full packs, water-proof sheets and one hundred and twenty rounds of ammunition apiece. Inevitably, though many men fell out in each case, M'Cay's troops arrived in no sort of order and suffered the humiliation of seeing the Prince of Wales watching as they shambled in. The 'Desert March' loomed large in memory for years to come and M'Cay never lived it down.

At about the same time Cox fell sick and Monash found himself in command of a division of all arms. The appointment could hardly have come at a more challenging moment and it was, perhaps, poetic justice that the lot fell upon him in the place where his ancestors had been bidden to make bricks without straw. His own task was not dissimilar but infinitely more difficult. The first two divisions had taken with them practically every trained artilleryman in the AIF and, while the training of foot-soldiers is not too complicated a business, the making of gunners from raw material is a task that would have taxed the genius of Moses to the utmost. The credit for the hard, slogging work that produced a divisional artillery of passable quality within a matter of weeks is due entirely to a handful of Australian militia officers who happened to be the only men present to whom the gunner's art was not a closed book. Fortunately the general himself had been an officer of the Royal Regiment, even though he was a little behind the times with his knowledge, and he was able to keep an eye on his men's progress and to give some practical assistance.

Mrs Monash, at home in Australia, also had a part to play; she and the ladies of the Purple Cross League were put to work providing horse-bandages which were otherwise unobtainable. With shade temperatures touching 109, plagues of flies by the million and with sandstorms raging around them, the 4th and 5th Divisions managed to guard the Canal, train as best they could for France and somehow to stay alive. Epidemics of mumps and measles, which few Australians had endured in childhood, added to their difficulties and there was almost audible relief when the orders arrived for them to embark.

The Canal defences were taken over by Chauvel and his mounted division and at the end of May II Anzac entrained at Serapaeum for Alexandria. The corps was commanded by Godley, for he and Birdwood had changed places when I Anzac had sailed for France. The voyage to Marseilles was uneventful except for two wireless messages. The first gave news of the Battle of Jutland; the second told of the mining of HMS *Hampshire* and the death of Kitchener. This was grim news and, from the British point of view, it marked the end of an epoch. Whatever his constitutional position may have been, Kitchener had been the head of the army.

Certainly he had made his tally of mistakes. Nevertheless, only K had had the insight to see that the German armies would go through the French 'like partridges', that the war would endure for years and that the Empire would be compelled before it was over to put into the field armies reckoned in millions. Now he was gone and there was nobody who could take his place.

They arrived at Marseilles on 7 June and Monash, now reverted to the command of his brigade once more, found a train waiting to take him and other senior officers to Paris and onwards, so that they might see what was in store for them. He and his brigade major were decanted at the Gare de Lyons early in the morning after a night journey which had denied them the opportunity of seeing the beauties of unravaged France and, having no duties for the rest of the day, they set themselves the task of exploring Paris. He gave a full report of what they found. 'Although there is a sombre air over the whole city, and very large numbers of people are in black, and the streets are full of soldiers, yet there is a good deal of life in the streets still. Of course the Louvre and many other galleries and museums are closed. But we managed to put in a good deal of sight-seeing including Place de la Concorde, Arc d'Étoile, Luxembourg gallery, Les Invalides (Napoleon's tomb), Eiffel Tower (closed), Musée Grevin, Palais Royal, and Arc de Carousel. On Thursday evening we visited *Folies Bergère* and saw a revue, but as all sale of drinks is stopped after 9.30 pm the streets were deserted by 11 pm and night life was stopped absolutely.'

Next day they travelled on to Calais where, after hanging about for hours, they were put in a troop-train to Hazebrouck. Birdwood's car was waiting for them at the station and whisked them to the little town of Merris which was to be the HQ of the 4th Division. Monash was allotted a brigade area of about sixty square miles, given a car and introduced to the unfamiliar art of billeting. Bean tells us that the word 'billet' conjured up visions of beds with clean linen, beautifully cooked meals and all home comforts. In fact, most of the men were to live in farmhouses of the traditional kind, built in a square around the most important feature, a steaming dunghill. The lucky ones might get the bedroom of some male member of the family who was either with his regiment or, too frequently, *mort sur le champ d'honneur*, but for most it was a matter of dossing down in a leaky barn in company with numerous rats. Monash explains how it was done. 'You pull up at a large farm house, demand inspection of the accommodation available (rooms, barns, stables and kitchens), make friends with the children, or the dog, or in one case the pet pig; curry favour with the old dame who cannot understand my Parisian French, as she speaks only a Flemish-French patois; and finally, after much gesticulation and remonstrance you chalk up on the various doors —

> "3 officers and 6 batmen"
> "Mess for 4 officers"
> "$1\frac{1}{2}$ platoons" (in the barns)
> "2 horses" (riders).'

The brigade area was sufficiently far behind the line for most of the inhabitants still to be in their homes but the monstrous rumble of the guns left no doubt about the proximity of war. The troops arrived a day or two later, enchanted with what they had seen of France *en route* and soon settled down on terms of cordiality with their hosts. It had been carefully explained that every Frenchman of military age was away, fighting for his country, and that the unprotected women, children, cattle and possessions were a sacred trust. The trust was very seldom abused.

Monash, becoming more security-minded, tried to convey his whereabouts. 'Where I am going there are two airmen but they are blind, that is, not an eye between them. Does that attempt at a joke make you shed tears?' The deplorable acrostic is even worse than that of Ian Hay's fictional Roy Birnie. 'I am not allowed to tell you where we are going but it would be harmful to blub about it.' Still, Armentières gets through somehow.

The 1st and 2nd Divisions had been in the line since the middle of April but the Australian reputation did not, at this moment, stand very high in the army. At the top, Birdwood did not enjoy the confidence and admiration that he had received from Kitchener once he became a relatively lowly officer under Sir

Douglas Haig. Murray had not trusted his judgment and considered some of his black swans to be geese; Haig, not yet familiar with the idiosyncratic ways of the Diggers and shocked by the high proportion of them in military custody at most times, held the corps commander to be a slack disciplinarian. The divisional commanders fared no better. 'Some of their divisional generals are so ignorant and (like many Colonials) so conceited, that they cannot be trusted to work out unaided the plans of attack.' The only man spared was White, 'a very sound capable fellow'. The soldiers he considered to be magnificent material but very raw. In part his judgment was based on reports emanating from Murray but he had seen enough with his own eyes to be able to form an opinion.

Sir Herbert Plumer, to whose Second Army the Anzac Corps belonged, was more experienced in colonial ways; he had spent much time in Rhodesia during the Boer War and much of his command had been made up of men of a similar kind. He had got on well with the Rhodesians and they learned to love 'the little man', as they called him. He had also had some previous experience of Australians; at the end of that war the Australian contingent was at Pretoria, time-expired and waiting to go home. Before the train arrived, Plumer received an order to march out immediately to the relief of a column that had got into trouble. The Australians protested and 'signs of incipient mutiny seemed not unlikely'; Plumer had them paraded, told them that he had orders to go to a certain place, that they would move off at 7 am, that he would be there and so would they. 'Cheers broke out and there was no further trouble.' There was no condescension towards colonials in Plumer's mind. Nevertheless, after he had seen them, he too took the view that a lot more training was needed before these men would be fit to face the German army in the field. Haig told him, needlessly, that they must first undergo a spell in a quiet sector and it was accepted by all concerned that they were not yet fit to join the other formations then mustering for the battle of the Somme.

I Anzac, though brimming over with determination to demonstrate that they were in every respect as good as any troops in

France, got off to a bad beginning. Trench mortars were now an accepted essential in the armoury and a start had been made with the provision of heavy patterns, the 9·45 – the famous 'Flying Pig' – and the 4-inch, weapons much the same as those used by the Germans. There was, however, a new and excellent light weapon, the muzzle-loading Stokes mortar, just coming into service and Haig intended to wring the maximum surprise effect from it when his offensive opened. To give the crews experience, some were sent to the quieter places to try out the new gun and the Newton fuse which ensured explosion of the bomb no matter what part of it struck the ground. Strict orders were given that on no account must these be allowed to fall into enemy hands. On the night of 5 May, one of the battalions of the 2nd Division was raided near Bois Grenier by a party from the 21st Reserve Infantry Regiment and the precious mortars were captured having, apparently, been abandoned. News of this reached Plumer by way of the German daily news bulletin and, for once, he was furious. 'The loss of the two Stokes mortars is, as stated by the Corps Commander, inexcusable ... The two officers who were in charge of the mortars will be brought before a Court Martial', read a part of his report to the commander-in-chief. There was a searching enquiry and the battalion commander was sent home in disgrace.

On 18 June, another Waterloo anniversary, the 4th Brigade quitted its billets and took its place in the line, being, for administrative convenience, attached to the 2nd Division. There was less than a fortnight to go before the great attack by Rawlinson's Fourth Army and Haig had asked that everything possible be done by the others to ensure that German troops were kept alert and that they were not allowed to thin out their more peaceful sectors to free more troops to oppose Rawlinson. This could only be effected by artillery bombardments and constant raiding, a course of action common to both sides. While the Second and Third Armies raided their opposite numbers to ensure their immobility, the Germans raided the Canadian corps in the Ypres salient to make equally sure that they did not join Rawlinson. The first of the Australian raids was entrusted to Monash's brigade and he prepared it in his usual fashion. He had a raiding party of eighty-three men carefully selected and command was given to a subaltern named Wanliss. Artillery support was not stinted, though the gunners were still very inexperienced, and, on the terrible first day of July, 1916, when sixty thousand of the finest men of the United Kingdom were cut down in the space of a single forenoon, they were still practising. Next night, the raid went in. We have Monash's account of it. 'France, 3 July 1916 (6 a.m.).

'I have just come in after an all night fight—my first raid. We disposed of over 50 of the enemy. These enterprises are a combination of the highest scientific preparation with the greatest personal gallantry. Our boys are splendid.' This was really a considerable overstatement. All six officers and eighty-three men had indeed crossed No Man's Land without incident and Australian mortars had wiped out an enemy wiring party of ten men; however, when they reached the German wire, supposedly cut by mortar fire, it was found to be undamaged and the machine-gunners and artillerymen were expecting them. Some valiant men hacked their way through the four belts of wire— German wire was far thicker than ordinary barbed wire—or scrambled over the bodies of dead and wounded to reach the German trench; Wanliss, wounded in the face, reached the parapet with about twenty-five men. There was only time enough left for them to club a few defenders and pitch some grenades into the mouths of dug-outs before the timetable required their own guns to shorten range and come down again on the German parapet. They were very fortunate in escaping with only eleven casualties, probably thanks to painstaking individual training, but the figure of fifty said to have been inflicted must be suspect. The raid was a miniature of what was taking place on another part of the front and pointed the same lessons.

This was also the last appearance of Brigadier-General John Monash in actual combat. The 3rd Division was arriving on Salisbury Plain, direct from Australia, and still it lacked a commander. As the division did not form part of the BEF and there seemed no likelihood of it going to France as a complete formation in the near future, Sir Douglas Haig could have no say in the matter;

this was just as well, for his opinion of Australian generals has already been seen and he was to write shortly afterwards (in reliance on a report from Sir Hubert Gough) that 'Legge was not much good'. M'Cay was the only one to arrive with a good 'chit' from Murray but he also was to lose favour after the Battle of Fromelles. No commander of a division in France in 1916 would be likely to be an Australian officer if Haig could help it. The C-in-C Home Forces, Sir John French, fortunately counted for very little. The real arbiter was Birdwood who, though only a corps commander in France, was also commander of the entire AIF, even though the force was now spread from Armentières to Sinai. Senator Pearce cabled him on 12 July to enquire whether he felt his two offices to be compatible; Birdwood replied that, having delegated his powers in the Middle East to Chauvel, he experienced no difficulty. He still retained the confidence of the government for, unlike Godley, he had been at pains to make the force as near to an Australian army as was possible and his views were accepted. The choice was thus very restricted. Once again, he felt White to be indispensable; M'Cay and Legge already had their divisions and no brigadier had manifested qualities so outstanding that he merited promotion. Only Monash remained. He had done nothing that singled him out from amongst so many others and his name remained quite unknown outside the AIF. Nonetheless, he was the senior officer to be considered, he had friends in high places at home and he had done nothing to disqualify himself for preferment. So, with some misgivings, Birdwood proposed him for the new command and the government endorsed his choice. On 10 July, after a visit to Birdwood at his HQ in Château la Motte, John Monash left France and travelled by way of London to assume his new command at Larkhill.

# CHAPTER EIGHT

# The Third Division goes to War

The command of a division of all arms is something entirely different from anything that is likely to have gone before in the experience of a new general. It is an army in miniature, complete with its own horse, guns, engineers, medical and administrative services, machine-guns, trench-mortars, signals, police and a score of other minor ancillaries. The man who has commanded an infantry company for a time should find no great difficulty in taking over a battalion; the commander of a battalion, so long as he knows his job, should not find himself at sea in command of a brigade. He is, after all, only dealing with larger numbers of his own arm of the service and although he will often have to work in concert with others and must understand what they can and cannot do, they will seldom be under his direct orders. For this reason, although brigades are but rarely commanded by officers who have not graduated through the lowlier infantry units (though during the Great War quite a number of under-employed cavalry officers swallowed their pride and accepted the command), the divisional general does not, of necessity, come from any particular branch. It is the first real step to the highest command. Lord Slim called it one of the four best commands in the service, juxtaposed to a platoon, a battalion and an army: 'A Division because it is the smallest formation that is a complete orchestra of war and the largest in which every man can know you.'

Monash was well aware of the state of affairs in Australia. The Commonwealth now had more than one hundred thousand men under arms. To keep this force in existence and without taking into account unusually heavy battle casualties, a monthly replacement of fifteen thousand men was needed and the voluntary system was already badly strained. In August the government decided to submit the question of conscription to a national referendum, an established piece of Australian constitutional machinery. If the country decided against compulsory service and the two corps in France were to be slaughtered as the British army was being slaughtered then the newest division might have to be broken up in order to find drafts, before it achieved a personality of its own. The best way to guard against such a contingency, though obviously this was not the only motive, was to produce as quickly as possible a division so well trained that an unanswerable case could be made out for its retention as a fighting formation. When the matter was put to the vote in October, 1916, the soldiers were solid for conscription but the civil population would not have it. Strong pressure was brought by the War Office to reduce the 3rd to a draft-finding role but by then the case for its continued existence was too strong to be resisted.

By the time the last units had arrived, more than twenty thousand men wore the oval patches, appropriately coloured to identify units, of the 3rd Australian Division. In addition, it comprehended 7,000 horses, 64 guns, 192 machine-guns, 82 motor lorries, 1,100 wagons and 18 motor-cars. At last the conductor had his orchestra.

From the outset he trained the 3rd Division as no other Australian division had ever been trained before. Though Monash's experience of the Western Front was trivial by comparison with that of most other officers of his rank, it had been enough. He realized that the 'ignorant-armies-clashing-by-night' phase of his earlier education was now a thing of the past and that the problem confronting the Allies was that of devising means of penetrating the apparently impregnable German lines. It had been done once, at Neuve Chapelle, but the opportunity had been thrown away by inept disposition of reserves. Conditions, however, had changed so much in little over a year that no lessons were now to be learnt from that costly near-miss. Salisbury Plain was turned into the nearest possible approximation to Picardy, with trench-lines being dug, patrols sent out into No Man's

Land, reliefs practised *ad nauseam* and even mines exploded to give some verisimilitude to the exercises.

During this time, things were still not going well with the divisions in France. Following the policy of pinning down those enemy forces not engaged in the Somme battle, GHQ continued to press for diversions. The Battle of Fromelles does not occupy much space in most of the war histories—the shorter ones, for the most part, do not mention it at all—but it looms large in Australian memories. The village, held by the Germans, stands a little over five miles south of Armentières and within a couple of kilometres of Aubers Ridge. It is on the fringe of the battlefield of Loos and some bloody fighting had taken place there in the autumn of 1915. Such was the speed of events, and so frequently did the participants disappear, that all remaining in the memory was a vague recollection that many English regiments had left their dead thick upon the ground in the narrow space which still separated the trenches. On 17 July, the 5th Division, then part of Lieut-General Haking's VIIth Corps, attacked after considerable artillery preparation and with the 61st Division on their right. The battle, whose description occupies one hundred and twenty pages of the Australian Official History, can only be briefly summarized here. It followed the usual, dismal pattern. The division suffered over 5,500 casualties with practically nothing to show for it. Four hundred Australians were taken prisoner and paraded triumphantly through the streets of Lille. The other side of the account showed practically nothing. White and Birdwood had protested unavailingly against the whole operation and could therefore bear no responsibility for the failure. Every possible explanation was offered: the artillery was not yet good enough; the plans were muddled; the 61st Division had let the Anzacs down. There was some truth in all of them. The CRA thought himself lucky that, with such raw gunners, they had not actually strafed their own infantry. The staff work was equally unskilful and the 61st was by no means a crack formation. The real truth was that the attack should never have been launched at all. All it achieved was to demonstrate yet again the dash and gallantry of the Australian soldier and add to his already poor opinion of the British. Inevitably, all the blame fell on M'Cay. It was quite unfair, for M'Cay, with his eyes open, was deliberately taking great risks in order to succour the hard-pressed British, fighting desperately on the Somme. He had, as we know, never been a popular commander and Fromelles put an end to such chance as he might ever have had of commanding the Australian corps. He was not deprived of his command, for his division was *hors de combat* for some time to come and Haig had other things on his mind than quarrels with governments not his own.

Before the din of the Fromelles battle had died down, there came Pozières. Birdwood's I Anzac Corps had been discreetly moved south to the neighbourhood of Amiens during the preparatory stages of Fromelles and the last remaining division, the 4th, was under his command there also. Pozières is one of the great names of Australian history, second in point of time after Anzac itself. The Official History very properly devotes more space to the battle than is filled by this entire book and its general outline is well known. As with Fromelles, it can only be briefly mentioned for John Monash was not there. It was Pozières, however, that first made the outside world aware of the valour and prowess of the Australian soldier in a way that remoter campaigns could never have done. Before Pozières, the 'raw, undisciplined colonial' jibe that always infuriated Monash probably represented the general opinion of those who could not avoid forming their opinions at second-hand. After Pozières, a new respect for this unique brand of soldier appeared overnight. It cost twenty-three thousand casualties to make the point, distributed roughly equally between the 1st, 2nd and 4th Divisions.

Monash has little to say about it in his letters but he cannot have been unconscious of the fact that his division was now the last formation to be in anything like fighting shape, though such was the resilience of an heroic generation that Haig was able to say that 'luckily, their [the Australians'] losses had been fairly small'. White had assured Sir Douglas that the lessons had been learnt. Monash had learnt them also. 'I had formed the theory that the true role of infantry was not to expend itself upon heroic physical effort, nor to wither away under merciless machine-gun fire, nor to impale itself on hostile bayonets, nor to tear itself to pieces in hostile entanglements (I am thinking of Pozières... and other bloody fields) but, on the contrary, to advance under the maximum possible protection of the maximum possible array of mechanical resources, in the form of guns, machine-guns, tanks, mortars and aeroplanes; to advance with as little impediment as possible; to be relieved as far as possible of their obligation to fight their way forward; to march, resolutely, regardless of the din and tumult of battle, to the appointed goal; and there to hold and defend the territory gained; and to gather in the forms of prisoners, guns and stores, the fruits of victory.' Though this was not written until after the war, it represents, without doubt, the way his mind was working. To most people in the summer of 1916 it would have read like something from the Book of Revelation. Monash was determined that, so far as it came within his power, his 3rd Division was not going to be ruined as all the others had been. There was no brilliant new philosophy about it; it was the mind of the engineer correlating the tools and materials now or soon to be available in profusion, each to be put to its proper use in accordance with a precise plan in order to complete the job with the utmost safety and economy. It was also an elaboration of the motto of the apochryphal Jordan Highlanders 'No advance without security'.

During the gestatory period on Salisbury Plain, two incidents occurred that deserve mention. The first was Monash's introduction to life as it had long been lived in the great country houses of England. His Assistant Provost Marshal was Major Sir Henry Dering of the Royal East Kent Yeomanry, the head of one of the oldest families in the kingdom. In November he invited his general for a week-end at his home, Surrenden, which had been in possession of the Derings since the grant by the Abbot of Canterbury and Prior Leofwine to Swinden fitzDering half a century before the Norman conquest. Monash, with his strong sense of history, was delighted with what he found. Family portraits going back to Queen Elizabeth, tattered standards of forgotten regiments and a park extending to five hundred acres. 'I wandered through fairy bowers where Titania might have lived, and the rich autumn tints made a scene of indescribable beauty.' Monash ever afterwards held Kent to be the most beautiful part of England.

The other great event was a review of his division by the King. Twenty-seven thousand men, in close column of platoons, took nearly two hours to march past their sovereign with whom the Australian general conversed alone for that period and more. In beautiful sunshine, the Royal Standard was broken out and Monash gave the order to 'Present Arms'. Sixteen massed bands crashed out the Anthem and, when the honours were over, the King walked over to Monash 'extending his hand as he came near, with a cheery winning smile. "How do you do, General," he said in a deep, clear, vibrating voice, "I am so very glad to be able to come down to see you all. It is the first time I have been able to see Australian troops in England. Shall we go up to the right of the line?" As they rode on, the King observed, "You used to command the 4th Brigade, didn't you? They've done awfully well. I hear you were on Gallipoli all the time. That was splendid." ' As they walked their horses down the lines, Monash told the King where each battalion and battery had been raised; he found the King, who had visited Australia more than once, surprisingly well informed. At the close of the parade he said, 'Well, General, I heartily congratulate you. It's a very fine division. I don't know that I've ever seen a finer one. The men look just splendid, and so soldierly and steady.' The King, who never forgot that he had been a naval officer, missed nothing. He asked 'hundreds of questions and criticised dozens of small details'. The King told Monash that since the war began he had reviewed one million, five hundred thousand men, adding, 'Isn't it perfectly wonderful? No man could have done it but Lord K. People kept saying he was going to work in the wrong way, but he knew better. He was right after all.' Later on, 'The Germans started out to smash the British Empire—smash it to pieces—and look, just look'—with a sweep of his arm up and down the marching columns—'see what they've really done. They've made an empire of us.' One of his last remarks before leaving was, 'It makes a lump come in my throat, to think of all these splendid fellows coming all those thousands of miles; and what they have come for.'

Mrs Monash was becoming understandably worried about the well-being of the husband she had not seen for nearly two years and suggested that she should come to England. The general assured her that he had never been fitter. 'My face is a bit thinner, less bulgy, for I now get plenty of exercise and make a point of eating very little and drinking less.' He did seriously consider inviting her to come but wisely decided against it. Instead, he posted more souvenirs, a piece of Virginia creeper from his house and a fragment of Zeppelin procured for him by the scientist Dr Rosenhain.

At the end of November, 1916, all was ready. The 3rd Division had been pronounced by the GOC Southern Command to be 'the best trained division that has left since the Old Army disappeared'. They sailed from Southampton to Le Havre, Monash going on ahead to his new HQ, the château of Steenwerck, five miles to the north-west of Armentières.

After allowing them a few days to settle down, the C-in-C paid the troops a visit; only the reserve brigade and some oddments were available for inspection but they made a good impression. This was, for Monash, a most important meeting, for Haig had had no cause to revise his opinion of the Australian generals in France and was under some political pressure to create an homogeneous Australian army after the fashion of the Canadian corps. When that happened, he must find an Australian commander. Could this be the man he sought? 'Douglas Haig looked grey and old. On parting he put his arm around my shoulder (as I rode beside him) and with much feeling and warmth he said, "You have a very fine division. I wish you all sorts of good luck, old man."' This was thoroughly uncharacteristic behaviour; Haig did not know Monash who had, as yet, no great reputation. Though he was a genuine major-general, he was not a member of the coterie from which generals were drawn, men who had known each other since they had been subalterns and who knew everything there was to be known about each other. Haig knew so little about Monash that, two years later, he was to speak of him as being an 'auctioneer by calling'. Plainly, there was something about Monash that struck a spark in the supreme commander for him to unbend and treat an unproved divisional commander as he might have treated Plumer or Rawlinson. Very possibly he had had a good report on him from the King, with whom Sir Douglas maintained a regular, private correspondence. It was a good augury; Haig would never have behaved thus to Birdwood, whose swift promotion to lieutenant-general over the head of Rawlinson had aroused his heavy displeasure.

Monash was now moving out of the parochial environment in which he had hitherto moved. The war was fairly quiet around the turn of the year and Birdwood gave a party at the Château de la Motte to which he was bidden. Amongst the many guests were General Sir Edmund Allenby, recently appointed to command the Third Army,[1] Major-General Chichester (Plumer's MGA) and old friends like Godley, Russell and White. The life and soul of the party was the Baronne de la Grange, 'a remarkably active, witty and clever woman of 50 and the owner of the château'. The baroness spoke fairly good English but apparently there were gaps in it. From her chair between Allenby and Godley she brought Monash into the conversation, referring to the august army commander: 'Oh, do some stop *mon général* here. I asked him to tell me the name for a something and he teached me such a bad word.' Monash, long deprived of the society of ladies, suddenly found himself with a surfeit of it. He struggled manfully to keep up polite conversation in French with the Princesse Bouly, 'daughter of Mme la Baronne, a pretty little brunette, married'. When she dropped her bag Monash retrieved it and she rewarded him with 'Thank you so much. It was awfully clumsy of me, wasn't it, to drop it.' This he considered, not unreasonably, unsporting of her. Every detail of the meal, together with the signed menu, was faithfully reported to Mrs Monash. The party avoided all mention of the war; Pozières had been followed by

[1] Monash writes of his command as being the First Army, a mistake not easily comprehensible.

Mouquet Farm in September, Mouquet Farm by a brief rest in the southern part of the Ypres salient and then, in October by the battle for Flers. There were some things that did not bear talking about.

Throughout the winter of 1916–17 the 3rd Division was separated from the others and was the only Australian division now in II Anzac. The veterans, all part of I Anzac, were still on the Somme doing their best to keep warm around Guedecourt and the sister corps was now made up of the New Zealand Division and a British division as well as the 3rd. Cold was the worst enemy of them all, one sergeant reporting that a waterbottle filled with boiling tea at noon had become a block of ice by 5 pm. All the same, freezing conditions were greatly to be preferred to the ubiquitous mud and sickness fell to smaller proportions.

During the winter there was a shake-up in the higher ranks; M'Cay was sent to Salisbury Plain to command the great complex of base units and Legge was returned to Australia. Cox, the most successful divisional general of them all, was given a staff appointment that could not be considered the Irishman's rise commonly awarded to those whose performance had not been up to standard. In their places came good, experienced Australian officers who were now in every way fit for these exacting commands. Brigadier-General Smyth was given the 2nd Division, Holmes the 4th, and Talbot Hobbs, Australia's best gunner officer, went to the 5th. Monash was, as a result, the senior general after Walker.

His division, however, was an object of sardonic disdain to the older soldiers. Its men had been spared even the discomforts of Egypt and had been subjected to nothing more terrible than a Royal review while their countrymen had been slogging their hearts out at Pozières. Nicknames like 'The Neutrals' and 'The Larkhill Lancers' were hurtful and put the men who had come late firmly on their mettle. For the rest of the winter, however, they were involved in no great battles, though they acquired much expertise in raiding and countering raids.

It might, therefore, be a convenient moment to take stock of their leader at a point midway through the war. His ostensible satisfaction with all that he had done might lead one to think that he took to warfare with enthusiasm but this was far from the case. 'From the far-off days of 1914, when the call first came, until the last shot was fired, every day was filled with loathing, horror and distress. I deplored all the time the loss of precious life and the waste of human effort. Nothing could have been more repugnant to me than the realization of the dreadful inefficiency and the misspent energy of war. Yet it had to be, and the thought always uppermost was the earnest prayer that Australia might for ever be spared such a horror on her own soil.' There speaks the true voice of the zealot. The man who could work out the cost of a convoy was struck more forcibly than most men with the extent of the wounds that Western Christendom was inflicting upon itself. One of his foibles was psychology, then a new word recently emanated from Vienna. In reply to a question put by Felix Meyer, he was to write, 'It is because we do not consider psychology enough that we are taking so long to win the war. Personally I have always found it pays well to consider the psychology not only of the enemy but also of my own troops, to study the factors that affect his actions and reactions . . . and also to study the methods of keeping up the moral and fighting spirit of our own soldiers. Indeed, it is psychology all along the line. As for myself, it did not take me long to learn that the only ways to carry out the responsibilities of command were, firstly, to erect optimism into a creed for myself and for all my brigades, arms, and departments, and, secondly, to try and deal with every task and every situation on the basis of simple business propositions . . . The main thing is always to have a plan; if it is not the best plan, it is at least better than no plan at all.'

Not all his essays into the world of Sigismund Freud were successful; an order to the 3rd Division to wear the brims of their bush hats flat, instead of looped up at the side, was intended to act as a stimulus to morale by showing that they were different and, by inference, superior to the older formations. It was bitterly resented by men whose one ambition was to demonstrate that there was no difference at all. On another occasion, he endeavoured to promote blood-lust just before an attack by publishing an order about the supposed maltreatment of some Australian prisoners. As always happens, it was met with quiet contempt. However, it was probably better than no psychology at all. Today the Australian army possesses a full-blown Psychology Corps.

His passion for minute detail was unslaked; Bean tells that, when summoned to a conference, he would take with him a list of anything up to one hundred questions and not until the last answer had been ticked off would he allow it to break up. Nothing was omitted, from exactitude about artillery preparation to the movements of the YMCA coffee stall. It must have been very tiresome for Godley, but as a result there were no mistakes made due to wrong assumptions and men got their hot coffee when they needed it.

His standard of precision must have been maddening to those not habituated to it. Every day began with the perusal of the list of matters to be dealt with, neatly set out in columns. As each task was finished, he struck it through, in pencil, not merely with a diagonal line but also with a short vertical one. As job followed job, the short vertical lines were joined up so as to force attention on any that remained undone. At the end of the day, a diagonal line was struck through the whole page, anything remaining unfinished transferred to the sheet for the next day and the page filed for use as the basis of his diary. The story persists that whenever the barber finished cutting his hair a note was made of the date and time when it would next need attention and it was documented accordingly. The Duke of Wellington had told Stanhope long ago that 'my rule was always to do the business of the day in the day' but even that meticulous commander could have learnt something from John Monash.

A passion for punctuality verging on the manic was also a prominent feature in his character. He had commented on it in his little book for company commanders: '[It] does not mean readiness before the occasion. This generally involves waste of time, harassing the men or unduly curtailing your previous duty.' He could never be accused of ignoring his own teachings, but the slightest unpunctuality on the part of others was invariably visited by what sometimes seems excessive displeasure.

Early in 1917, great events were being deliberated. On the Allied side, it was the time of the planning for the disastrous Nivelle offensive, to be supported by the attack on Vimy Ridge. On the German, the operation fittingly named for Wagner's malignant dwarf, Alberich, was being clandestinely executed. Harder hit on the Somme than some realized and with heavy preoccupations elsewhere, the German High Command sensibly elected to give up a large tract of France which was useless to them save for reasons of 'face' and to withdraw to the belt of works known as the Hindenburg Line. At the same time, they adopted a new philosophy of defence. Rigid front lines and support lines became a thing of the past and were replaced by deep defended zones. It would not be too difficult for an attacker to break into these and, indeed, it would not in the least matter if he did. Once enmeshed, he would become a target for counterattack both by fire and by men and he ought to be fought to a standstill and swallowed up long before he reached the green fields beyond. News of the fresh doctrine reached GHQ by way of some captured documents later in the year; by then they were out of date, but they formed the basis of the Memorandum on Defensive Measures of 12 December, 1917, which was to plague the British army for the next quarter of a century.

The Allies, who had done nearly all the attacking, except for Verdun, since the end of the first German onrush, had their answers; the first was an artillery enormously increased both in numbers and in power, the second was the tank. Each, however, provided the antidote to the other. If the great shells churned up the land, the primitive Mark II tanks could not cross it; if the guns did not bring down a volume of fire sufficient to neutralize the enemy artillery, German field-gunners would have no great difficulty in killing the slowly lumbering monsters. Their combination would require much thought.

The first of the next great series of battles began in April, but before they were joined Monash obtained ten days' leave and went to Menton. He travelled, of course, by way of Paris and passed a couple of days there, having prudently obtained Dering's expert advice about restaurants. (He found the Café de la Paix, near the Place de l'Opera, much the best.) The train journey to Menton took twenty-four hours with neither wagon-lit nor dining car, but it was worth it. The town he compared, in his letter home, to Lucerne, though it had 'a distinctly Italian air'. He took a tram to Monte Carlo ('I was disappointed—one gets a sense of overcrowding') and noted the scenery, 'a tropical garden all the way—mimosa, cactus, pansies galore, the steep hillsides covered with oranges and lemons'. He was only allowed a quick peep into the casino—strictly out of bounds to all soldiers and sailors—but it was no great loss. It was 'small, dark and dingy' but a performance of the *Barber of Seville* at the theatre cheered him up. It was from Menton that he wrote a particularly revealing letter to Mrs Monash: 'You say I might take up military work as a profession after the war? I hate the business of war, the waste, the destruction and the inefficiency. Many a time I could have wished that wounds or sickness would have enabled me to retire honourably from the field of action—like so many other senior officers. My only consolation has been the sense of faithfully doing my duty... But my duty once done, and honourably discharged, I shall, with a sigh of relief, turn my back once and for all on the possibility of ever again having to go through such an awful time. Of course, if Australia wants my services in some administrative capacity in connection with her future army, permitting me the freedom of an independent citizen, well that is another matter, but not unless it becomes necessary for our bread and butter, and all other means had failed, would I dream of becoming a paid servant of the state in any capacity whatever. I have fought all my life for personal independence, and shall not give up what I have won, except as a last resort.' The devotion to privacy and freedom was as strong as ever though, as will be seen, it did not long survive the war. He managed to get away from casinos and theatres for a few days to walk and do a little climbing, including an excursion to the summit of Le Berceau. Three days later he was back with his division, to find that its front had been extended to include Ploegsteert and Hill 63.

With the coming of April the dogs of war were let slip again. General Robert Nivelle was supremely confident that, by attacking on the Aisne with five thousand guns and fifty thousand men, he would win the war with one devastating blow. Haig, though quite unbelieving, was obliged to conform and to use all his resources to smooth Nivelle's path. Thus came the series of terrible battles that began with the irruption of the Canadians to Vimy Ridge on Easter Monday, followed by the disastrous attack on Monchy-le-Preux on the 14th, when battalions leap-frogged over each other into great salients and disappeared as Ludendorff had intended. In the first forty-eight hours two battalions, the fine Newfoundlanders and the 1st Essex of the famous 29th Division, vanished from the sight of men without leaving a clue as to what had happened. For I Anzac, under Sir Hubert Gough's Fifth Army, the selected killing-ground was at Bullecourt on the old Somme battlefield south of Bapaume. It was to be quite different from Pozières for the attack of the Anzacs and the neighbouring 62nd Division (commanded by Ian Hamilton's old Chief-of-Staff, Braithwaite, still doing his penance for Gallipoli at the head of a Territorial formation) would be covered by an overwhelming artillery barrage and then led safely to their objective by the Tank Corps. In the event, despite an initial success when they broke into the Hindenburg Line, it was another costly failure; the artillery work was imperfect, the tanks — all 11 of them — failed to appear because of mechanical breakdowns, and the attack went in during a snowstorm quite unaided. The battle went on for a fortnight. At the end of it, the Australians had lost ten thousand men and all faith in tanks. In their stead they had acquired a deeper contempt for British staff work and a personal loathing for General Gough. The former was eventually mitigated, even if not entirely dispelled; the latter remained for ever. As for General Nivelle, his attack went in on 16 April, and everybody knows the result. The new system of defence proved its soundness on the grand scale and what remained of the French army afterwards was, for a time, almost out of the war. From April onwards, Britain had to assume the duties of senior partner.

Monash's division, in the quietest part of the front, took no part in these affairs but, after mid-May, they no longer had cause to feel alone. The 4th Division, sadly knocked about at Bullecourt, began to arrive around Steenwerck and settled down as the reserve division of II Anzac. Not unnaturally, they felt that they had been sent there for a well deserved rest. The delusion was of short duration for, before much more than a week had elapsed they were inspected by the commander-in-chief. This might have been no more than a compliment, but when it was followed by a further inspection by Sir Herbert Plumer there was no doubt that something was stirring. On the afternoon of 26 May, the senior officers were let into the secret that they were going to play an important part in the next operation, an attack in Flanders towards the Messines—Wytschaete ridge.

For Monash this broke a spell of comparative inactivity; he had visited the Canadians and stood with Prince Arthur of Connaught, who was on the Canadian corps staff, on the summit of Vimy Ridge. He had found an old man who owned greenhouses which had, in happier times, kept Paris supplied with fresh flowers and had sent home some double fuchsias in the hope that some vestige of them would survive; but he had taken part in no operation of war for the better part of a year. From now until the armistice, however, he was going to be as fully employed as any man on the Western Front.

He was fortunate to find himself under Second Army, for the commander and his chief staff officer were men who had much in common with Monash. Sir Herbert Plumer looked exactly like Colonel Blimp but he was one of the most accomplished generals of his day. 'Tim' Harington, his Chief-of-Staff, had already made a mark on the mind of the Australian with his dictum that 'The staff are the servants of the troops'. Bumptious young gentlemen resplendent in red tabs did not last long in Second Army and Harington gladly helped in the education of the new divisional general. Above all, Second Army was a happy army; 'Trust, Training and Thoroughness' were its watchwords. Seldom can a great organization have been so free from jealousy and seldom have staff officers been so cordially received by the men who had to do the fighting. The cordiality was because they knew that the visitors were there to do their level best to give all the help asked and not to sneak or spy. Plumer and Harington, like Monash, left nothing to chance, for that was not Second Army's way. When the orders came for the Messines battle, all those concerned knew that there would be nothing left unplanned so far as human ingenuity was capable of planning it. For the Australians this was no small thing; apart from the fact that they had suffered again and again from the shortcomings of others, they wanted, above all other things, a victory. For all their hard fights, the dead they had left behind and the high opinions they had gained, the brutal fact remained that they had not yet won a major battle. Perhaps, under Plumer, the day had come.

Plumer had begun his work a year earlier, before the first tank had been seen on the battlefield, and throughout that time a private war of a most fearsome kind had been waged underneath the wet Flanders plain. Men from the mining counties of England, many of them Cornishmen particularly experienced in the peculiar conditions encountered when working in clay, had burrowed out twenty great mines now ready and packed with nearly a million pounds of high explosive. By the taking of great pains their existence had been kept secret from the Germans in their strong fortress overhead and many bloody little battles had been fought by brave men in the galleries in the process. Near the hill of the Scherpenberg there had been built a scale model of the ridge 'about the size of two croquet lawns' and officers down to platoon commanders were all taken there to have the details of the operation explained to them. The gunners had cunningly made the enemy disclose the locations of all his batteries, ample supplies of every piece of material likely to be needed had been amassed and everybody knew exactly what was demanded of him. If the battle of Messines were to fail as those before it had failed, it would not be due to imperfect planning or staff work.

The task of the 3rd Division was to take the southern spur of the ridge and then to form the defence of the army's right flank. It was a job for which Monash was admirably suited. 'For weeks past,' he wrote on 19 May, 'we have been making roads, building railways and tramways, forming ammunition dumps, making

# THE THIRD DIVISION GOES TO WAR

gun emplacements and camouflaging them, preparing brigade and battalion battle headquarters and laying a complex system of underground cables, fixing the positions of machine-guns, working out barrage timetables for machine-guns, field-guns, heavy guns and howitzers. For this operation I shall have added to my own artillery five army brigades of field artillery. The heavy and siege artillery will not be under my command. Then there is a mass of field engineering work to be done, in large dug-outs, approach avenues, assembly and jumping-off trenches; most voluminous orders to be got out, controlling the action of my 20,000 men and animals—feeding organization, transport organization, ammunition supply, cutting the enemy's wire (an operation now in full blast) the preliminary destructive bombardment of his field works, the completion and blowing up of mines and finally the preparation of the 12,000 infantry for the actual work of "going over the top". The army commander spent all yesterday afternoon with me, going patiently and minutely through the whole of my plans, and said he felt sure I had done all that was possible to ensure success.'

On 7 June, 1917, they had their victory. Nineteen of the great mines went up with a roar and a shiver that were felt in London. Harington witnessed it from the top of the hill at Cassel but his chief was not at his side. 'He was kneeling by his bedside, praying for those gallant officers and men who were, at that moment, attacking.' The villages of Messines and Wytschaete ceased to exist, the 3rd and 4th Bavarian Divisions were shattered and the ridge passed into British hands at a price regarded by 1917 standards as absurdly low. The surprise had been complete, the 'mechanical devices' had enabled the infantry to march unhindered on to their objective. The battle had lasted just four hours; the final objectives were reached under cover of a barrage from 2,330 guns and every attempt at a counterattack was smashed. The 3rd Australian was only one of seventeen divisions engaged but it had come out of its first battle victorious. Now they could look I Anzac straight in the eye and the more daring might even patronize them gently. On their left the New Zealanders had done no less well and had left their mark on Saxons, Prussians and

Wurttemburgers alike. Monash published a congratulatory order but it was clear that Messines was no more than a beginning. Harington, looking back from the ridge, observed that he wondered how the British soldier could have existed. He answered himself, saying that no one but the British soldier could have done so.

Monash was not entirely satisfied, for there had been a few discords in his orchestra. On one occasion he had ordered his gunners to shorten the barrage on the strength of an inaccurate report that the 37th Battalion had had to fall back and the result was that some shells fell amongst the leading companies. In addition, there had been inaccurate shooting by some batteries and over-enthusiasm by some infantry units. These faults must be corrected in time for the next battle. Also, conforming to their training, commanders showed a reluctance to leave their HQ even for short periods. Here too was room for improvement, but for the moment there was tidying up to be done to improve the line. Last of all, a quick calculation disclosed that the division had got through about £1,000,000 worth of ammunition in three days.

In the latter half of 1917, the British armies, by contrast with those of the other Allies, were at the peak of their power. The French, debilitated to the point of mutiny by long trials and massive blood-letting, were, for the moment, almost a spent force. The oriflamme had fallen from the hand of Robert Nivelle and it would be a long time before it could be borne forward again. Russia was near to the edge of the abyss, Italy was in serious straits and the USA was not a military power that yet needed to be reckoned with. The offensive in Flanders had to go on, but the six weeks of glorious summer that followed Messines were innocent of major battle. Even so, it was by no means a period of idleness. Before the attack could be resumed guns and ammunition had to be moved forward and this in full view of the enemy, over land as flat as Cambridgeshire. The British artillery was, at last, equal or superior to the German at all levels, from the 18 pounders of the field batteries to the great 12-inch howitzers that required two steam traction engines to move them. Next time the infantry moved eastward, it would be after bombardment such as had never before been experienced and preparations for that could not be scamped. It would have been splendid if Messines could have been followed up at once by another blow of the same kind but it was never a serious possibility. Messines had been unique.

Sir Douglas Haig had more faith in Hubert Gough than the Australians would have been able to muster. Plumer, at 60, he regarded as the cunning slow bowler with an infinite repertoire of googlies, chinamen and the like; Gough, fourteen years younger but still the age Wellington had been at Waterloo, was the pace man and Haig, anxious for quick results, decided to change the bowling. Happily for the feelings of the AIF they were required to find only some artillery units for the Fifth Army and, these apart, they were able to take a rest during the battles of Pilckem Ridge and Langemarck. With every man keeping one eye cocked skyward to watch the weather, Fifth Army began its attack on 31 July in fine style and attained all its objectives. Second Army had a minor but relevant role as a flank-guard to the south of the Menin Road, between Hooge and Hill 60.

The 3rd Division had been extremely busy since 11 June tidying up the line west of Warneton and carrying out extensive field works to make it impregnable. Monash had been asked to suggest something that he could do to assist Plumer's deception plan, an attempt to persuade the German command in Flanders that he was meditating a stroke at Lille. To give some verisimilitude to this, the Canadians were to execute an attack around Lens; Monash suggested an assault on the Windmill Spur, opposite Warneton. Plumer approved. As his division could not expect to have the devastating weight of metal from the guns that was to batter a path for Gough's men, he decided to investigate further the uses of smoke. One of his own subalterns, a young man named Varley, had invented and produced a smoke-bomb that could be fired from the Stokes mortar. Monash was so taken by its possibilities that he passed Varley upwards and his device was formally approved by GHQ. Varley was awarded £300 for his ingenuity and ordered to supervise its début personally. To thicken up the fog of war, the Pioneers were equipped with every

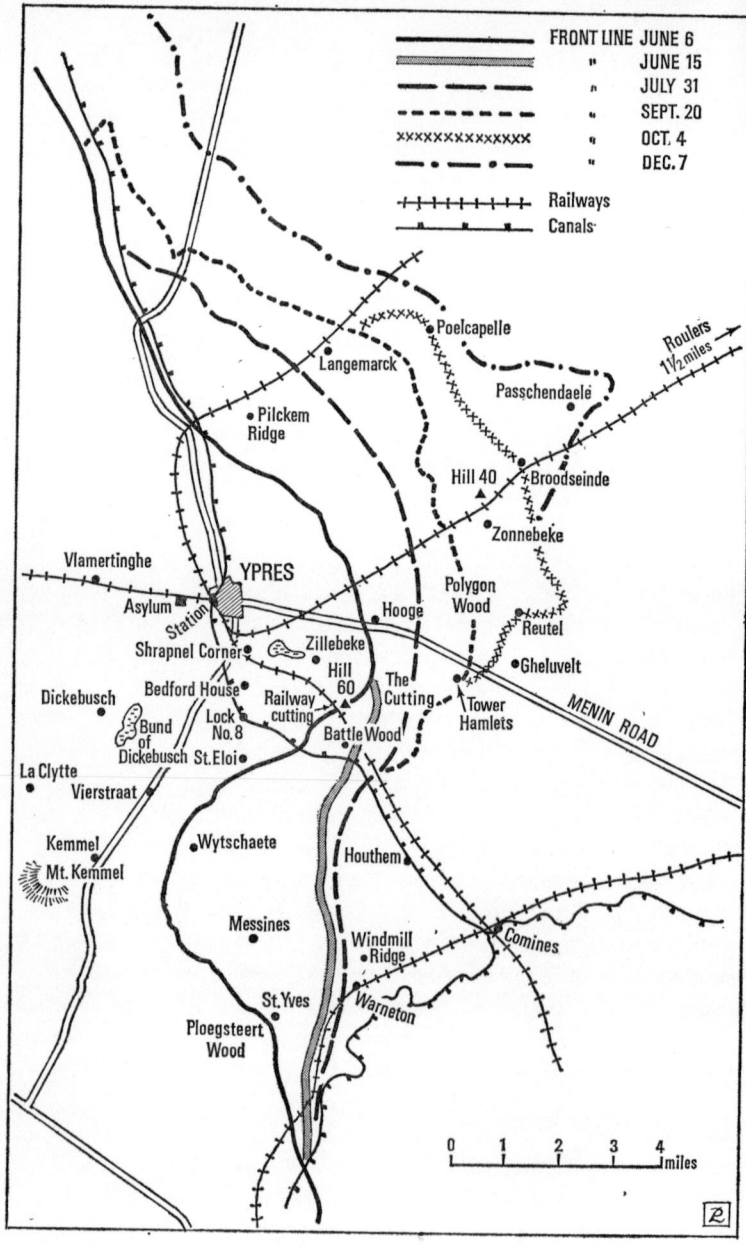

smoke-candle on which the division could lay its hands. The attack, carried out in concert with the New Zealanders, though entirely successful was small beer by comparison with what was happening nearby.

August, as every man who has planned a holiday in advance knows, is a rogue month. It can produce every variety of weather from blazing sunshine to freezing rain, complete airlessness to strong gales. No forecast for August is ever right and sensible men avoid it when they can. In the afternoon of 31 July, it began to rain: by evening, the skies had opened and the water-table of the reclaimed marshland that was the salient had begun to rise at frightening speed. The clay became first slush, then a bog and finally lakes appeared of all shapes and sizes. As the rain thundered down, so did the shells, great spouts of mud which subsided to craters full of filth lying nearly lip to lip. Fifth Army, with General Anthoine's First French Army showing the flag on its left, was brought to a standstill. On 26 August, Sir Douglas again made a change, putting on Plumer to see whether he could not do better. Within a few days the sunshine returned, the bogs began to dry out and dust was more troublesome than mud. It had been the most cruel stroke of the fortunes of war; but for August, Gough and Anthoine might well have struck a blow from which results comparable with those of nearby Oudenarde would have followed. As it was, they had advanced the line by some two-thirds of a mile, incurred more than one hundred thousand casualties and so lowered the spirits even of the dogged British that they no longer, in some instances, tried as hard as they might have done. (In September there was a mutiny at Étaples Base Camp which needed two battalions from the front to quell it.)

Plumer was a more comfortable general under whom to serve. His staff was better, his methodical work more painstaking, and he accepted the axiom that 'Cannon kill Men'. In his battles that was exactly what they were going to do; flesh and blood was not to be pitted against steel until it was absolutely necessary. To Ypres, the 'Mecca of all good soldiers', there came the Anzacs. Brudenell White, who might have been forgiven if his earlier exertions had worn him out, was once more its brains. He and Harington thought alike, approved of each other, and were more deserving than any other two men of the credit for the victories that were to follow. For the battles of the Menin Road, Polygon Wood and Broodseinde were victories by any view and in any language. The evil reputation that will always cling to the memory of Third Ypres attaches to the August battles and to the final ones. The peculiar national talent that ranks Dunkirk as a victory but Ypres as a defeat passes all understanding.

These were the battles in which artillery resumed the part of Queen of the battlefield. Some 1,300 guns opened it, firing more than 3,000,000 shells in a preliminary bombardment spread over a week. The symphony was scored for each instrument with the greatest care; broadly speaking, the lighter pieces were employed in the 'protective' barrage when the time for the attack came while the heavier weapons put down 'roaming' curtains of explosive which, exactly timed, moved over the field like a garden spray, mangling the German counterattack divisions before they could strike their blow. As a small instance of the care taken, the very message pads, down to company level, were ready printed with sketch maps and standard situation reports which called for no more than a tick from a harassed officer.

After the Menin Road battle, in which the 1st and 2nd Divisions had played a considerable part, came Polygon Wood; this was the turn of the 4th and 5th Divisions. Between 20 and 27 September every division but the 'Larkhill Lancers' had been engaged in very bloody fighting and had done everything demanded of them. In the process they had had the opportunity of observing for themselves that there was no shortage of troops from the old country who lacked the grotesque qualities of so many of their earlier acquaintances.

The third step in the Second Army's trilogy was Broodseinde, the subject of Mr Lloyd George's disgusting pleasantry. ('Who remembers Broodseinde now? Try it on your friends'.)

Bean, at any rate, remembered it when he wrote, fifteen years later, that 'in the air was the unmistakable feeling, not to be experienced again by the AIF until 8 August, 1918, that the

British leaders now had the game in hand and, if conditions remained favourable, might in a few more moves secure a victory which would have its influence on the issue of the war'. Three Australian divisions were earmarked for it, the 1st, 2nd and 3rd, the first time the latter had fought alongside its countrymen. They had had a rest of nearly four weeks after Windmill Ridge and were the freshest of them all. Monash was in high spirits, for he had spent a lot of time at Corps HQ and had heard pleasant things from Birdwood and White. 'Birdwood told me the Commander-in-Chief had a very high opinion of my division and of me personally, and had gone out of his way to express himself in terms of praise of my work. B added that it was rare for the Chief to do this. White entirely confirmed these statements.' Monash had had a bird's eye view of the Langemarck battle, for his own HQ was just outside Bailleul and from the top of the nearby Scherpenberg the whole of the salient lay open to view. 'The spectacle in the early dawn of the opening of our artillery barrage on a front of 15 miles from Ypres to the sea was magnificent and terrifying, putting into the shade the most terrible lightning and thunderstorm ever witnessed. The whole country simply trembled.'

There comes a glimpse of the general through other eyes at this time, for Australian political pressure to force the replacement of British staff officers by their own people had just deprived him of his chief administrative officer. Colonel Farmar, a regular officer and a staff college graduate, wrote to his chief on leaving:

'My dear General, I only realised how deeply my affections were rooted with you and the division when the breakaway had to be made. The inspiration of loyal devotion which you are able to give is a personal asset which makes all ways smooth. The poorest instrument will respond unexpectedly well with a master touch, and I have felt always so fortunate to be working in your enveloping influence. The thoughts that will always be mine of the 14 months I have spent with the Australian troops are very happy. At first I accounted my association with them a privilege, the 3rd Division has made it an honour. While its spirit burns as it does now, I know that success will come.' This to the man who was considered by some a harsh master and whose own boast was that he never gave a man a second chance.

Late in September, Haig invited Monash to dine after inspecting the Division in the back areas near Le Touquet. It was not just a social occasion for the other guests were Lieut-General Kiggell—who had the misfortune to bear the name Sir Lancelot—and Major-General Butler, chief and deputy chief of the general staff respectively. 'After each course was served, the mess stewards went out of the room and doors were locked from inside, until the Chief gave a sign for the next course. So you may imagine that some very important and confidential matters were discussed . . . there is no question that we are wearing down the German military power, and it is now only a question of time and weather. Nothing could have been more charming than the affability and camaraderie of these three great soldiers, upon whom rests the whole burden of the British Western Front.' Haig had plainly formed the highest opinion of his guest's potentialities, for such entertainment of a mere divisional general was almost unheard of. It may well have been that the commander-in-chief, under some pressure to have an Australian officer in command of what was virtually an Australian army, was weighing him up as the most probable candidate. Be that as it may, John Monash of Melbourne was being made privy to all the plans for the winter of 1917–18.

In addition to high strategy they probably discussed the manpower situation, for we know Haig to have been disturbed by the number of men absent from the Australian ranks by reason of crime and sickness. A part of this was caused by the refusal of the Australian government to confirm death sentences on men convicted of desertion or cowardice. Monash held firmly to the view that in such cases, few though they were, the law should take its course. The prospect of a ten-year sentence in a warm, cosy gaol in Australia would have been, to a man living waist-deep in mud and under constant shellfire, less a deterrent than a vision of Paradise. The problem was never solved. In one of her endless questionnaires Mrs Monash enquired what the authorities told the relatives of men so executed; she received the rather testy reply that her husband did not know. 'Probably the truth.'

At the beginning of October Monash set up his HQ for the battle in a ratty tunnel inside the ramparts of Ypres, still under sporadic bombardment by German long-range guns though little enough was left of the proud and beautiful town. He made another quick calculation. 'There can be little doubt that it cost the enemy in ammunition fired many times more to destroy the town than ever it cost to build it.' He did his best with the impossible task of describing Ypres at the fall of 1917. 'It is one enormous medley of military activity of every conceivable description, and the traffic on the main roads is simply incredible. Imagine the traffic in Elizabeth Street for an hour after the last race on Cup Day, multiplied tenfold and extending in a continuous line from Flemington to Sandringham, and streams of men, vehicles, motor lorries, mules, horses, and motors of every description, moving ponderously forward at a snail's pace, in either direction, hour after hour, all day and all night, day after day, week after week, in a never-halting, never-ending stream.' He continues with a careful list, running to more than four hundred words, of exactly what the traffic was.

4 October, 1917, is one of the unforgettable dates in Australian military history, for it enshrines the memory of the greatest victory of Australian arms that had yet been achieved.

Harington wrote to Monash on the eve of the battle that it would be the biggest of the war, and so far as it concerned Australia, he was right. Plumer had always intended to make use of the fresh II Anzac Corps but he had been doubtful whether its sister formation, after the hard slog at Polygon Wood, could possibly be fit to be put into the fight again so soon. However, such was their resilience that Birdwood and White readily agreed that there was no reason why, for the first time, four Australian and New Zealand divisions—the 4th was still in the south and the 5th in reserve—should not go into battle shoulder to shoulder. It was by no means an all-Australasian battle for eight British divisions were also to be committed but it was a stirring moment in the military history of the Antipodes and it so happened that the division on the left of II Anzac was that old friend of Gallipoli days, the 29th.

Originally the attack was designed to start on 6 October but a look at the lowering skies made it plain that a race with the weather was one of the most important factors. After anxious consideration as to whether or not he was asking the impossible of his gunners, Plumer decided to advance the date by forty-eight hours. The gunners, as has always been their habit, responded manfully. The change put a heavy burden on II Anzac also; their roads had not yet been completed nor did their units know the terrain in the same way that the senior corps knew it. The divisions, working at speed, made a very good job of it. Harington wrote again to Monash later, saying that the way his division had made its plans at short notice was beyond all praise — but it led of necessity to some things being done less well than they might have been, particularly in the tedious, dangerous, business of laying their cables. In the last days of September and the first of October the divisions of Godley's command marched out through the Menin Gate and quietly took up their places in the web of muddy craters that constituted the front line.

This time also they were neighboured by divisions more representative of the British army than the unusual ones they had encountered before. On the left of the New Zealanders, the most northerly formation, lay the sturdy 48th Division of Territorials from the Midlands, very wise in the ways of war. Beyond them again came the fighting Irish of the 11th, the 4th, veterans of Mons, Le Cateau and almost every battle since and, at the extremity, the 29th. Moving south from the New Zealanders, there came the 3rd Australian Division, divided from the 2nd and 1st by the road from Ypres to Roulers by way of Zonnebeke and Broodseinde. On the right of Walker's 1st Division stood the British 7th, as fine a division as ever trod upon neat's-leather and who had fought their way from the original landing in Belgium to the Somme and Bullecourt; at that engagement they had the distinction of being the first British division whom the Australians acknowledged to be men who could, and did, fight as well as they.

# THE THIRD DIVISION GOES TO WAR 175

Three more good divisions, the 21st, 5th and 37th, carried the line to the south.

It was at this point that the battle began, though not in the way Plumer had planned it. At dawn on 1 October, Polygon Wood was heavily shelled and waves of German infantry advanced towards the part of the line held by the 7th and 21st Divisions. The terrific fire that greeted them soon brought the German infantry to a halt and the performance was repeated in the afternoon with the same result. A drizzling rain continued intermittently all the time.

The general object of the battle, generally called by the name of the village of Broodseinde, was to gain a foothold on the higher ground to the east of Ypres and to kill as many of the enemy in the process as could be done. It could never have been another Messines for the elaborate mining that had preceded that operation could not be repeated and the German position was a very strong one. Firms other than Monash & Anderson had been active in the field of ferro-concrete and the ridge was planted thick with pillboxes of a solidity capable of withstanding anything short of a direct hit from a heavy shell. In between lay the mud, churned and churned again by the never silent guns and traversable only by well-recognized tracks. The Anzac divisions had each been allotted a front of about a thousand yards with advances of between twelve hundred and two thousand paces to the portion of the ridge in face of them, though the New Zealanders, charged with capturing the Gravenstafel spur, were more widely extended.

Monash himself occupied a command post in the ramparts of the old city, hard by the Menin Gate itself. Once his brigades were in position there was no more for him to do but smoke pipe after pipe of Havelock tobacco and wait. The other divisional commanders were similarly tucked away near the Lille Gate. All of them kept an anxious watch on the grey clouds of a Flanders autumn.

The consensus of opinion amongst the generals was that it would be best for the attacking brigades to concentrate as far forward as practicable in order to be out of the way when the retaliatory German barrage came down. For the 3rd Division this was not possible, for their assembly area was just ahead of Zonnebeke village and narrower than the others. However, Cannan, now a brigadier, came to the conclusion that to spread out in rear of the village was to court casualties and he crammed his brigade together behind the leaders. The target thus presented was a tempting one, but he relied on the methodical German adhering to his habits and he was right.

At about 5.20 sheafs of German flares, looking dull and glazed through the drizzle, lit up the dawn and the enemy guns began to play upon the waiting lines. Many Australians, remembering Bullecourt, thought that the plan had been discovered and that they were going to have to attack without the needed artillery cover. Things like that did not happen in Sir Herbert Plumer's army. Precisely at 6 am the mighty British artillery went into action pulverizing everything in its target area. With the power of many more heavy guns its reach had increased to such an extent that the German army had had to revise the defensive tactics that had proved so successful in the recent past. The divisions of the Empire rose up and strode inexorably forward in the face of a gale and low, scudding clouds. Their own shells, bursting before them in a barrage so close that, as one present said, you could have toasted bread on it, raised clouds of smoke and steam from the wet earth.

Inevitably, the battle line broke up into an infinity of small fights. Captain Carrington, leading his company of the Royal Warwicks, described it as 'all-in wrestling in the mud' and, for all their grievous losses, the British soldiers everywhere attained their objectives. On the 3rd Division front, two pillboxes, fortuitously named 'Israel' and 'Judah', fell, the leading battalions halted and began to dig while the following ones passed through them and went on. German divisions, massing for the counterattack, were ripped to pieces by the guns before they could intervene in the fight. On their left, the New Zealanders pushed magnificently on to the Heights of Abraham—the Old Testament must have been in the front of the mind of whoever was responsible for naming the day's objectives—and after about an hour the first bound, known as the 'Red Line', had everywhere been reached. Here they halted for another hour to reorganize for the final push on to the ridge itself.

Regimental officers had their work cut out to keep their men in hand, for Germans in large numbers could be seen bolting out of their pillboxes and the Australians wanted to get after them. They had cause to be grateful to the men who had died on the Somme, for these had taken the shine off the old German army; von Kluck's men of 1914 would never have done this. It was not peculiar to the Australians, for down on the right the 2nd Gordons of the 7th Division would not be stopped and took many casualties from charging into their own barrage.

At 8.10 the second phase of the battle began. Pillbox after pillbox was eliminated by the intelligent use of Lewis gun, bomb and Stokes mortar, prisoners began to give themselves up in ever larger numbers, and by a little after 9 am the whole of the ridge, with one trifling exception, was in British hands. Another meticulous set-piece battle had been won, entirely in accordance with Plumer's plan. Airmen flying contact patrols picked up the signals of the triumphant infantry and relayed them back to the waiting headquarters. A jubilant Monash cabled to Melbourne: 'All well division again brilliantly victorious in greatest battle of the war.' It seems that he was not alone in using the expression, for in the letter to Mrs Monash that followed there occur the words 'I quote from a letter the Commander-in-Chief sent me yesterday.'

Three days later the 3rd Division was relieved by the British 66th and was taken out of the line to have a couple of days for rest and refitting before the next battle. It was to be called Passchendaele.

Whether this last battle should ever have been fought at all is a question far beyond the scope of this book. Everybody knows of the pressures exerted on Sir Douglas Haig. Admiral Jellicoe was insisting that if the Belgian coast could not be freed then the U-boats alone would win the war. Pétain had told him at least something of the mutinies in the French armies though his plans for the battle of Malmaison on 23 October indicated that their case was not hopeless. Lloyd George was threatening to move the seat of war to Italy on the eve of Caporetto. Something very disagreeable was happening in Russia, though nobody knew quite what it was. The armies of the United States did not yet exist in significant numbers. His own chief intelligence officer, Brigadier-General Charteris, was brimful of optimism. The sober and realistic Plumer favoured the attack to secure a tenable position for the winter. Only Hubert Gough, still under something of a cloud, opposed it. It may well be that the field marshal should have rejected the advice given him and contented himself with the gains already achieved but to write him down as a blundering, heartless incompetent in the prevailing fashion calls for considerable hardihood on the part of the critic. One fact remains that cannot be questioned: until the echo of the last shot had died away, no condemnation of Haig was ever voiced by the rank and file of the two million strong army under his command.

However, the battle of Passchendaele was fought and the 3rd Australian Division was very much involved in it. More than ever before, it was dominated by the weather. Even apart from this, however, it could not have been yet another copy of the three battles just over. There is a law of diminishing returns with artillery, for barrels wear out quickly when subjected to the use these had endured. They had to be moved forward into position, those that remained serviceable, and even light field-pieces on narrow wooden wheels need a road of some kind for the purpose. The 60-pounder medium gun and the really heavy howitzers demand something much more stable and the roads of the Ypres salient were drowned in mud. Add to this that every shell to be fed into them must be brought up by animal transport led by Indian drivers, under fire and in the same dreadful conditions, and one ceases to wonder that the great barrages of the Menin Road and Polygon Wood battles cannot be laid on at short notice like gas or electricity. The same applied to signals at a time when the main instrument of communication was the field telephone with its miles and miles of vulnerable cable. Even if the rain were to hold off, the Passchendaele battle must begin without the advantages of the earlier engagements and could hardly be successful if the enemy put up a stiff resistance. True, the Germans had had a terrible hammering and were showing signs of cracking, but it is never wise to underrate this brave, hardy and disciplined race. Few other armies could have held Passchendaele ridge in October, 1917; no army but the British would have had the fortitude to attack it. The head of the spear was to be II Anzac; the New Zealanders and the 3rd Division were to form its tip.

The distances to be covered by the attacking troops were far more ambitious than those of Broodseinde and demanded that the infantry move at a much quicker pace. The rain had been falling steadily and the quagmire between the armies would have been almost impassable even without the assistance of their artilleries. Most of the British divisions that had been fighting steadily since August were withdrawn and replaced by some very green formations whose staff work was amateurish in the extreme. Only I Anzac, weary beyond words, were retained of the original formations to endure the last round of the long fight.

It is only necessary here to deal with the dreadful events of 12 October in outline. The bombardment, by comparison with the earlier ones, was feeble. The raw British divisions plunged forward into thigh-deep mud sodden with old mustard-gas, excrement and decomposed bodies. Not surprisingly, they disintegrated in spite of much gallantry by individuals and small, isolated bands of men. Liquid mud effectively jammed the working parts of both Vickers and Lewis guns and the Royal Flying Corps was kept on the ground by the appalling weather. Worst of all, the diligent Germans, far from rushing home to Berlin, had constructed many more obstructions of double-apron wiring which the artillery had left uncut and their machine-gunners, unhampered by the mud below, showed that they at least had their fighting spirit unimpaired.

The 3rd Division attacked Passchendaele village at dawn, the timetable demanding that it reach the Red Line at 6.37, halt until 8.25, take the Blue Line at 9.21 and finally move to the assault of the ultimate Green Line at 11.29. The march out had started at 6 pm the previous evening in inky darkness and pouring rain under a steady bombardment of shrapnel and gas-shells. They reached their start line at 3.20 am and duly moved into the open at 5.20.

As soon as they broke cover the German machine-guns tore into them, men fell by the score and the programme went to pieces. Indomitably the Diggers pressed on and one small party actually set foot in the deserted church in the village, but the enemy fire was so intense, particularly from a redoubt known as Bellevue, that the advance could not be maintained.

Monash, from his post in the ramparts, asked the New Zealand division to help by turning every available gun on to this feature — it was then ten o'clock — under the impression that the hold-up was only temporary and that the advance elsewhere was going ahead. Shortly after noon, a pigeon flew in from his 9th Brigade bearing a message that a composite force of three battalions was on the Blue Line but that both flanks were in the air. Later still, at about 4.30, he ordered his last battalion in reserve, the 33rd, to work north but, in fact, the battle was completely outside his control. The New Zealanders had lost nearly three thousand men to no purpose, vainly trying to fight their way through thick wire between undamaged pillboxes. The 3rd Division, in no better case, had begun to fall back an hour earlier. To all intents and purposes, they were back where they had begun. The division had lost over three thousand men in order to achieve this. Much the same thing happened on the fronts of the other formations engaged and the battle of Passchendaele petered out in the filthy mud and rain.

Monash gave a full description of it from which his own feelings plainly emerge. 'It is bad to cultivate the habit of criticism of higher authority and, therefore, I do so now with some hesitation, but chiefly to enable you to get a correct picture of what the situation was. You will remember that the Division was relieved in the line by the 66th Division, and, from the point which we had reached, viz some 2300 yards from Zonnebeke towards Roulers on the Zonnebeke–Roulers railway, this division was to divide with us the further advance to and inclusive of Passchendaele; each division having about a mile to go in depth. Moreover, the plan was to steadily shorten the interval of time between the successive blows. As you know, the first blow was on 20 September, the second on 26 September, the third on 4 October. Then came the necessary pause while army and corps divisional boundaries were changed, leading to the fourth blow on 9 October, and a fifth and final blow on 12 October. I am inclined to believe that the plan was fully justified, and would have succeeded in normal weather conditions. It could only have succeeded, however, in the hands of first-class fighting divisions whose staff-work was accurate, scientific and speedy. My own division and the New Zealanders had proved their ability to march for five successive days, and then go into a complex battle with only three days preparation on the ground, and you must understand that each division has to make all its own preparations in regard to roads, tracks, pushing forward its guns, supplying its ammunition dumps, burying its telegraph cables, establishing its numerous headquarters, aid-posts and report centres, and a thousand and one other details. We did it, as you know, with complete success and perfect co-ordination in the period between 10 am on 1 October and daybreak on 4 October and the operation was a complete and perfect success. Under normal conditions we might, and probably would have, done it again in a period of forty-eight hours. But the Higher Command decided to allow us only twenty-four hours, and even under these circumstances with normal weather conditions, we might have succeeded.

'However, a number of vital factors intervened, and I personally used every endeavour to secure from the corps and army commander a twenty-four-hour postponement. The Chief, however, decided that every hour's postponement gave the enemy breathing time, and that it was worth taking the chance oı achieving the final objective for this stage of the Flanders battle.

'Considerable rain began to set in on 6 October. The ground was in a deplorable condition by the night of 8 October, and, in consequence, the 66th and 45th Divisions who had taken up the role of the 3rd Australian and the New Zealand Divisions, failed to accomplish more than about a quarter of a mile of their projected advance. Even in the face of this the Higher Command insisted on going on, and insisted, further, that the uncompleted objectives of this fourth phase should be added to the objectives of our fifth phase; so that it amounted to this that Russell and I were asked to make a total advance of 1¾ miles. The weather grew steadily worse on 10 and 11 October. There was no flying and no photographing, no definite information of the German redispositions, no effective bombardment, no opportunity of replenishing our ammunition dumps; and the whole of the country from Zonnebeke forward to the limits of our previous captures was literally a sea of mud, in most places waist deep. Even in spite of all these difficulties, I might have succeeded in accomplishing the goal aimed at, but, most unfortunately, the division on my left (the New Zealanders) had in the first stage of their advance to cross the Ravebeek, which not only proved physically impossible, but the banks of it had been strongly wired on the enemy's side. Consequently, the New Zealand Division could obtain no footing upon the Bellevue Spur, and the left flank of my advance was, therefore, fully exposed to the enfilade fire of a large number of concrete forts scattered over the spur. At the end of the day's operations we had accomplished only about another three-quarters of a mile of our advance, being pulled up by the exhaustion of our men within 1000 yards of the village. My casualties have been rather heavy, and will, I fear, exceed 2,000, but the display of gallantry and self-devotion of the troops was altogether beyond praise. We captured 351 prisoners and did a lot of successful bayonet fighting, but on this occasion I doubt if the Boche casualties were any severer than ours . . . The inability to achieve the objective set is not considered in the slightest degree as a reflection upon the division and I have had the most kindly and sympathetic letters from Haig and Plumer and Godley, all saying they are more than satisfied with the work of the division, and expressing the belief that what these two divisions could not achieve no other division in the army would have been able under similar circumstances to achieve . . .'

Canada relieved Australia and New Zealand on 22 October and the soldiers of yet another member of the Anglo-Saxon family were sent into the abomination of desolation. Monash was becoming more indignant about it all. 'Our men are being put into the hottest fighting and are being sacrificed in hare-brained ventures, like Bullecourt and Passchendaele, and there is no one in the War Cabinet to lift a voice in protest. It all arises from the fact that Australia is not represented in the War Cabinet, owing to Hughes, for political reasons, having been unable to come to England. So Australian interests are suffering badly, and Australia is not getting anything like the recognition it deserves.' This was not really quite fair. To write of Passchendaele as 'a hare-brained venture' three days after saying that 'I am inclined to believe that the plan was fully justified' was hardly consistent and the most controversial part of the long battle had not then started. The casualties in the divisions from the UK proclaim pretty eloquently that the islanders were not sheltering behind their cousins. As to 'Billy' Hughes — 'that little devil, Hughes', as the King called him — the War Cabinet could hardly be blamed if Australian politics kept him at home. On one point, however, Monash was absolutely right. Australia was not receiving, nor has since received, the recognition her soldiers merited. The object of this book is to try to make this good, however imperfectly and belatedly.

# CHAPTER NINE

## Interlude

THE winter of 1917–18 found the opposing armies in a condition like that of two heavyweight boxers during an interval between the last rounds of a world-title contest. Each was battered, tired and sapped of the strength that had gone with some of the wild swings of the earlier rounds but each knew the weak spots of his opponent and was seeking the opportunity of delivering the last blows that would finally crack the remainder of his endurance. The analogy breaks down, however, since there were no Queensberry Rules about it and if either boxer was able to increase the force of his punch by the use of a knuckleduster he was perfectly at liberty to do so. In the camp of the Allies, the knuckleduster was being made ready with the production of more and better tanks. The Central Powers relied more on the stimulant of knowing that, before the last bell sounded, the submergence of Imperial Russia would free vast numbers of men and quantities of guns. For the next few months, however, they were left to the care of their seconds.

During this period, it is possible to make some assessment of Monash's growing stature. He had shown up well at Messines and the series of battles compendiously known as Third Ypres, for these had been set-pieces of the kind at which he excelled. His past experience had fitted him for command as effectively as had the more conventional military education of most generals, for these had been planners' battles. A bridge is built by the consideration of many factors, some being accepted and others turned down, rather than by a *coup d'oeil* and the swift recognition of a course of action that will bring success. So it had been with the battles of

1917. The preparation had been lengthy and meticulous, the plan involving the actions of hundreds of thousands of men and their impedimenta unalterable once put into operation, and the lessons of all military history were largely irrelevant. The old, unchanging principles remained; how to achieve surprise, as Rawlinson had done by his night attack on the Somme, Plumer by his mines at Messines and Byng by the tanks at Cambrai, could still be a key question but the method of attaining such an object now was yet to be found. The secret moves of large bodies from one end of the line to another by which Marlborough had won Ramillies could not be carried out under the eyes of observers in aeroplanes. Poison gas and flame-throwers alike had proved to be *bruta fulmina*. The pessimists saw no alternative but to wait for 'The Yanks and the Tanks' but Douglas Haig was never numbered amongst these. Nor was the man who had 'erected optimism into a creed'.

By the beginning of the last year of the war, Monash was still no more than one of half a hundred good divisional generals. Birdwood and Godley had come to be looked upon as fixtures. White was a man never in the public eye and the Australian general most known to fame was Harry Chauvel, the leader of Allenby's Desert Mounted Corps. Monash's business was to maintain his 3rd Division as a fighting instrument as near to perfection as possible and not to look for advancement. There was some feeling in Australia against Godley, for he had steadfastly refused to replace the British officers at II Anzac HQ by Australians whose competence had now been well proved, but this affected the divisions little.

Monash, in whose veins was no drop of native English blood, had somehow absorbed the colour of his surroundings as does the chameleon. In his khaki service dress and red-banded cap, he was indistinguishable from any Imperial general, as the expression then went. This gentle, kindly man was writing fiercely home that he never allowed a man who had once failed him to have a second chance. Kitchener himself could not have put it more brutally. Yet at the same time he is found writing a letter to a strange young woman in Melbourne who had thrust a note of good wishes under the lid of a tin of Havelock tobacco given by the Comforts Fund. The general, weighed down by great responsibilities, replied in his own hand: 'Dear Miss Barton, I think you would like to receive a few lines from me, to convey to you my thanks for your share in this welcome gift, and to send you a message of greeting for Christmas. All we Australian men at the front appreciate most warmly all that our Australian womenfolk are doing for us, and the thought of all the girls we have left at home makes us very homesick. Can you realize what it is like for our boys not to have an Australian girl to talk to for months and months on end . . . our Australian girls are the finest girls in the world. We want no better.' The last sentence is a little confusing, but the warmth of feeling comes through.

It was at about this time that Monash began to take a personal interest in his divisional concert party. This now sadly forgotten institution was a well-established and popular form of entertainment, owing much to men such as Harry Pelissier and Davy Burnaby. Every division had its own troupe and some of them reached a very high standard of professionalism, 'The Roosters' in particular continuing for many years after the war. At No. 25 General Hospital near Hardelot Plage there was a notable one and Monash, on one of his visits to the wounded, was taken to a performance. 'You doubtless know the pretty duet out of *A Little Bit of Fluff*—"They'll Never Believe Me". This duet was beautifully rendered by our very pretty "leading lady" and his singing partner (who both have very sweet voices and act well), and was twice vociferously encored. At the third encore, instead of this handsome couple, there came on one of our three funny men—a woebegone spectacle of mud and battlestains, carrying a decrepit pack, with tin hat, rifle, respirator all complete—and delivered himself with the greatest unction and splendid character acting, of three verses of the same song but with novel words. The audience was simply convulsed, it was such an exquisite parody, exquisitely performed. The author of the parody let me have a copy of the words which I enclose. Try them to the tune and see how well they go.'

Mrs Monash seems to have been a little suspicious of concert parties and had to be reassured; all the performers took their turn in the line like everybody else and it was not a shameful refuge for aesthetes. Monash went to much trouble to see that his troupes – eventually increased to four, so that each brigade had its own, were cared for in the same way as his guns, transport or other services. In a few weeks he was writing that the principal company – at Divisional HQ – had a twenty-four-piece orchestra under 'a highly capable conductor, Lance-Corporal Pierce, who can perform even Wagner very creditably,' and, 'I recently sent [the two 'ladies'] to London to get a complete new outfit of wigs, gloves, shoes, hosiery, frocks, jewellery, etc, and the result is most startling. Both have beautiful clear soprano voices, and in the concerted numbers the combined effect of voice, bearing and gesture is all that could be desired.' It must have required fortitude out of the ordinary to be a soprano singer on Monday and to be carrying a fire-lock amongst a horde of ribald Diggers on the Tuesday, but volunteers seem to have been found without difficulty.

For once, Monash found himself with time on his hands. He set himself to read the works of O.Henry 'and like them very much, although my American friends who are now staying with me tell me that Texas is now highly civilized and that San Antonio is now as much up to date as New York, with electric trams, central heating and latest Paris fashions.' On New Year's Day, 1918, came this characteristic PS. 'I re-open my letter in order to send you my heartiest congratulations upon the news just received by phone from General Birdwood, that the honours list, published in London, this morning, confers on us the honour of knighthood. GHQ has just rung up to say that I have been created Knight Commander of the Bath.'

By the end of January nobody could be left in any doubt but that the greatest attack of all was soon to be made by the German army, now fighting on one front only. The Allies, on a count of heads, had long ago passed the peak of their strength and a large proportion of the numbers on the ration strength consisted of quasi-civilians who would be of no value when the battle began. Monash makes the general feeling clear. 'Things are very quiet, for the corps has a quiet sector and we do not fear an attack. Weather and ground make impossible any activity on our own account. On the other hand an attack is definitely expected further south, and all preparations are being made to meet it. In this, it is hoped that the American contingent, which is already large, will contribute powerful help.' The forecast of the place where the blow would fall was accurate enough but there it ends. 'All preparations' meant, for Sir Hubert Gough, the taking over of miles of ill-constructed trenches from the French, a denial of the labour needed to build a line that could hold out against an overwhelming artillery and a shortage of everything. General Pershing, determined on the creation of an all-American army, though practically every weapon it possessed had been provided by Britain or France, could not bring himself to move any of his huge divisions into a place where they might have to take orders from a British officer.

None of this concerned Monash. On 9 March he motored to Paris and four days later he began his leave again in Menton where his old room at the Hotel Regina was awaiting him. 'Yesterday I spent in absolute idleness, just lolling about in the sunshine on the sea-beach, not even reading.'

During the days of unwonted idleness and silence in the mediaeval setting of the old fortress of the Grimaldi, he devoted time to thinking about the future. The war could not endure for ever; though the loss of an ally on the Eastern Front must mean a great accretion of strength for the enemy in the West, it could not now be sufficient for them to avoid defeat. The American army, now flooding into France and becoming more battleworthy every day, would do more than merely redress the balance, even though the armies of the Allies were weaker and less full of fight than they had been a year ago.

As usual, he set it all down on paper. His letter of 15 March reads: 'I shall be senior Australian commander in the field (except Chauvel) and, if the war ends in a way that makes it necessary for Australia to maintain her ability to defend herself, they simply cannot, on my record, afford to pass me by—Of course I do not say that I should accept anything in the shape of a permanent post; I am too keen on preserving my independence, as I have written on a former occasion; and I have also my present business affairs to liquidate, even if I decided to retire altogether. There will be so many openings offering and so many public and semi-public positions which in the past I aspired to, that the difficulty will be what to choose and what to leave alone.

'Don't be amused—I merely write of it because I am in a frank humour—and that is a Governorship—The day when State Governors will be chosen from Australian citizens is rapidly approaching. When that day arrives, the field of choice will be very limited. There will not be a great supply of otherwise qualified men who are not disqualified by their political prejudices or careers, or by having been State officials and so lost their independence. It is therefore a quite legitimate ambition for a man in my position; and nothing like so difficult a job as that of commanding a Division in the field. Birdwood has been quite openly mentioned as Governor-General, and what could be more appropriate than for one of his Divisional Generals to serve under him as a State Governor. Now please don't laugh, but regard with equanimity the prospect of your, one day, becoming an Excellency. Of one thing I am very certain; that is that all those people are perfectly right who have told you that they feel sure you will worthily grace the position you have reached, and may still reach—for myself, I have never felt any doubt of it—and I have always thought you both clever and brilliant. Now this is a monstrously egotistical letter; but I suppose—like the male peacock before the pea-hen—one may be permitted to do a little strutting before one's own wife once in a while.' It is sometimes a great mercy to have the future hidden.

Birdwood was certainly staking a claim for consideration as the King's representative in the Dominion and nobody could say that it was unearned. Demands for the AIF in France to be put on a footing of equality with the Canadian corps, to become, in effect, a national army, had become too strong to be resisted. The man chiefly responsible for the consummation was the Australian journalist Keith Murdoch who had proved a good friend to the Australian soldier since Gallipoli days. He had both allies and enemies in high places, but even these last acknowledged that however unconventional his approach might sometimes be, it was always made for the entirely honourable reason of obtaining justice, or more than justice, for the force. Ever since Bullecourt he had been beavering away to get the authorities in both countries to constitute an Australian Corps of all the five divisions under an Australian commander and with an Australian staff. On 1 November, 1917, he achieved something near to success; Sir Douglas Haig agreed that the 1st, 2nd, 3rd and 5th Divisions should be grouped together, with the 4th Division retained as a draft-finding formation, under the title of the Australian corps. The 'Larkhill Lancers' promptly looped up their hat-brims. The victory was incomplete for Birdwood retained the chief command. What had been II Anzac became the XXII Corps, still under command of Sir Alexander Godley. The redoubtable New Zealanders remained with their old chief for the time being.

Monash made the most of his leave in spite of the drizzling weather. When, on 21 March, six thousand German guns on a front of nearly forty miles proclaimed that the great attacks had begun and while the shattered remains of Gough's Fifth Army were falling back over the old Somme battlefields, he was at the opera. We next hear of him on 24 March when he wrote home that 'I intended to stay here another week, but have just half an hour ago received a telegram from Jess to say that my division had received orders to move up from the back area to the front. This is doubtless in consequence of the great Boche attack which commenced on 21 March.'

CHAPTER TEN

## The Corps Commander

WHILE Monash was speeding back to his division at the best pace he could manage, the famous Conference was in session at Doullens. As Haig, Plumer, Horne, Byng and Rawlinson were in conclave with President Poincaré, Clemenceau, Pétain, Foch and the later arrivals Lord Milner and Sir Henry Wilson, now CIGS, the Australian corps was being subjected to the usual consequence of order and counter-order. Birdwood, too, had been enjoying a spell of leave and until he arrived back in a commandeered aeroplane the burden fell, as usual, on White. First, the 3rd Division was to make ready to move back to Ypres while the 4th was to go to the First Army area to back up the Portuguese corps. Colonel Jess had already arrived at Steenvorde when fresh orders greeted him from Plumer. Both divisions, instead of returning to the salient, were to march to St Omer and there entrain for the south. Nobody knew exactly where they were going but every furphy agreed that it must be back to the Somme where the fighting was the most fierce and the issue still in doubt. It was, in fact, a change made pursuant to Plumer's characteristically unselfish pledge to Haig that he would give him a fresh division in exchange for each one of those that had been used up in the course of the tremendous battle on the front of Gough's Fifth Army and the right wing of Byng's Third.

Unknown to everybody, including the grandees at Doullens, was that an extremely dangerous situation was developing in the last-mentioned sector. At the southern end of the Third Army front stood the VII Corps of Lieut-General Sir Walter Congreve VC, whose task was to hold the line between Albert and

Bray. Early in the morning of the 26th, Third Army, in accordance with the usual practice, had transmitted to him by telephone his next set of orders which would later be confirmed in writing. These orders contained a clause the sense of which was that, if withdrawal became necessary, he was to move two divisions from the extreme south to a position behind the River Ancre. The divisions concerned were the 9th (Scottish), which included the fine South African Brigade, and the 35th, now a conventional division since the supply of 'bantams' had been exhausted long ago. Both had fought hard for three days and suffered many casualties but their fighting spirit was quite unbroken and their line intact. Congreve erroneously took the telephoned order as requiring him to move them back whatever his own view might be and, at about 2.30 am, he passed it on to the divisions. By early afternoon, a gap ten miles wide between the Ancre on the north and the Somme on the south, had been opened up before the German Second Army. An attempt was made to send the 35th Division back when understanding dawned, but it was too late. Only a part of the 1st Cavalry Division and Cumming's scratch force of about two thousand reinforcements and stragglers could be thrust in to hold what had been the line as best they could.

During the early part of the morning Monash, all gubernatorial aspirations temporarily set aside, arrived at Frevent. There he reported himself to Lieut-General Sir Thomas Morland under whose X Corps he understood that he would be operating; he might well have said, as had General Humbert of the French Third Army, that he '*n'avait que son fanion*', but his division was near to joining him. Morland sent him on to Doullens, where Monash noted the assembling of the great men, and there he received his first coherent orders from Major-General Vaughan, Byng's Chief-of-Staff. He was to take his division to a concentration area around Mondicourt and place himself under the command of Congreve with the object of putting his men firmly in the way of von der Marwitz. As he left, he learnt that his leading brigade, Cannan's 11th, was at that moment detraining at Doullens station.

At about midnight Monash arrived at the Chateau de Montigny

to which Congreve had just moved his HQ. With his usual intelligent anticipation, he had brought with him a good deal more than his *fanion*, for he had an idea of what would be required of him and had come accompanied by a staff officer of each branch and a couple of motor-cycle dispatch riders. Congreve's relief was evident. 'Thank God, the Australians at last,' was his greeting. Monash, of course, kept a record of what passed between them. 'General Congreve was brief and to the point. What he said amounted to this: "At 4 o'clock to-day my Corps was holding a line from Albert to Bray when the line gave way. The enemy is now pushing westwards and, if not stopped to-morrow, will certainly secure all the heights overlooking Amiens. What you must try to do is get your Division deployed across his path. The valleys of the Ancre (to North) and Somme (to South) offer good points for your flanks to rest upon. You must, of course, get as far east as you can, but I know of a good line of old trenches, which I believe are still in good condition, running from Mericourt l'Abbé (on the Ancre) to Sailly-le-Sec (on the Somme). Occupy them if you can't get further east." '

Monash asked for a room to be put at his disposal and drafted the orders to his brigades. They are models of lucidity and give no excuse to anyone for failing to comprehend what he was to do. His staff officers took them, in note form, and wrote them out by the light of their torches at the road side. By 3 am the division had been aroused from such slumber as it could get outside Doullens and loaded into motor omnibuses, pre-war London buses, painted grey and with all their windows missing, and were lurching over the *pavé* in a generally easterly direction, towards the dawn. At about 6.30 am on 27 March the column stopped on the road between Franvilliers and Heilly where the 'Diggers' alighted. The staff officers handed over the written orders to the brigadiers and within the hour they were moving across country to the old French position of which Congreve had spoken. They met with little opposition, for Cummings and the cavalrymen, with powerful assistance from Third Army's artillery and from the pilots of the RFC (now in the last few days of its existence), had beaten off the only German attack made.

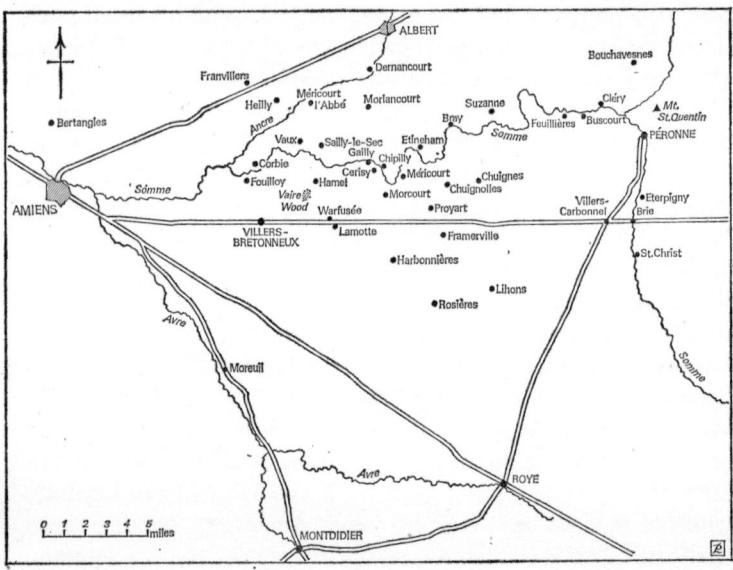

The Australians approved of Cummings, emerging from his breakfast dressed as if for a review in spite of the fact that he had been fighting hard all through the night. They approved, too, of the cavalry, the last vestige of the old regular army, as they watched mounted patrols riding down parties of the enemy and bringing in prisoners. Before noon the line from Albert to Bray had been re-established. The 4th Division was similarly ensconced beyond the 35th Division to the north, but the state of affairs south of the Somme was anything but clear. During the afternoon reports began to come in from Fifth Army that the Germans had crossed the river in unknown strength by the half-destroyed bridge at Chipilly and Congreve therefore ordered his horsemen to cross it also and find out what was happening. The 3rd Division had added to their burden the responsibility for guarding all bridges between Sailly-le-Sec and Aubigny. This took Monash's reserve brigade and all he had now with which to manœuvre, should it be necessary, was Cumming's people.

As things turned out, no great harm came of it. The 3rd Division was in the eye of the storm and was not called upon to endure the weight of metal and men that fell upon its neighbours. Maclagan's 4th Division was heavily attacked at Dernancourt but beat off its assailants, though at a heavy price. In two separate battles the division was compelled to yield up some ground to the two German divisions opposed to it but the line was nowhere penetrated. The Australian corps was now coalescing as the 2nd and 5th Divisions moved south, Plumer not yet having made good the whole of his generous promise, and their place by Messines being taken by the exhausted 9th and 35th Divisions. Before the formal relief of VII Corps was completed on 6 April the German tide reached its high-water mark in front of Villers Bretonneux. Monash was deprived of his 9th Brigade, Rosenthal's, for the duration of the battle and they were placed under command of the British 61st Division. Apart from that, the 3rd Division was not employed in this next great Australian battle though elements of the 2nd and 5th Divisions were involved. Rosenthal lost thirty officers and 635 other ranks, a large proportion of them coming from the 36th Battalion whose extremely gallant counterattack was prepared and carried out at the double when the line to the south of the town crumbled. The leading German troops could see the spires of Amiens hull-down on the horizon but with that they had to be content.

On the front of the 3rd Division and that of their adversaries, the German 13th Division, a new problem arose. The speed of the German advance had moved the fighting to a part of France that had remained, so far, quite unravaged. The people who lived there remained in their homes until the last moment possible and, when they moved out, their houses were left crammed with all but their most portable possessions. It is widely asserted, probably with truth, that one of the factors that inhibited any German move beyond Albert was the discovery of loot of every kind, much of it liquid, which distracted the attention of men whom the blockade had made strangers to all luxuries.

The Australians also were not slow to liberate commodities for which their owners would plainly have no further use. Monash, freed from the cares of immediate battle, took the situation in hand. Town majors were appointed for every inhabited locality and men were put to work gathering up the salvage. His division rescued ninety-four tons of precious wool (its value was given with the usual precion as £87,964), about 180,000 lbs of almost equally precious forage (£975 16s 6d), 214 head of cattle and wine to the cost of £667 17s 0d. In addition more than sixty cases of clocks, tableware, linen, curtains and furniture were turned over to the French Mission, the grand total in value being put at £94,472 13s 6d. The French Mission was understandably grateful, for such transactions are not common in time of war. It is doubtful whether such a thought would have entered the head of a general whose education had been of a more regularly military kind.

After the next hammer-stroke of Ludendorff had fallen upon Plumer's army, the 1st Australian Division was also on the road to the south. They brought with them shocked stories of the condition of some of the British battalions to whom they had handed over. Britain indeed was nearing the bottom of her well of manpower. Conscription had been effective for nearly two years and the age for service had been raised to 50 and even, in some cases, to 55. The new men filling the ranks were those returning after their second or third wound, men who had been upgraded in their medical categories to a flattering extent, grandfathers, and boys with the down still on their cheeks. Australian commanders had for some time past been complaining about the quality of their own new drafts, for a second referendum on conscription had shared the fate of the first and recruiting had fallen badly away; their newcomers were frequently men who fell far short of the earlier enlistments both in physique and in character but they had never found themselves in straits like this. The British divisions from April, 1918, onwards were largely composed of soldiers who might well have been still at school. Many of the disparaging opinions expressed by dominion troops at this time were caused by the sight of these children and by what they had seen in the rear areas of the Third and Fifth Armies. Apart from non-combatant units and those, such as heavy artillery, which were being deliberately withdrawn, there were certainly plenty of stragglers. What they did not see was the other side of the medal, the men who were doing the real fighting and being mown down in swathes. Dr Bean, ever a fair critic, readily avers that the mighty German offensive of March, 1918, was stopped by the British infantry, gunners and pilots. The men of Canada, Australia and New Zealand did not come into action until the battle had been won, though the South African contingent had fought all the way through and had gained praise from all sides.

From April onwards the dominion soldiers were to assume the dominant role on the British front; comparatively fresh, mature men with spirits higher than ever before at the prospect of an end to the vile trench-warfare and, possibly, of victory in 1918, these formations were now the head of Haig's spear. But spearheads are of little use without shafts and the infant British infantry of the last months merit recognition. They were not the valiant, Rupert Brooke legions who had gone over the top on that dreadful 1 July or even the less enthusiastic but more crafty warriors who had made the Ypres salient almost a part of the British Isles, but they were pathetically eager to learn, like the marines at Anzac, and they did their duty in full measure. The British divisions, though they had halted the German onrush, had so exhausted themselves in the process that a major counter-offensive in 1918 would have been beyond their strength. The same thing applied even more forcibly to the armies of France. The Germans and their Allies had shot their bolt and, even with what remained of the million men released by the disappearance of a front in the East they could no longer hope for military victory. The Americans were following closely to the precedent of the BEF of the early years; after their great fight at Belleau Wood it was remarked how their dead, especially the dead of the Marine Corps, lay in beautifully ordered lines where the traversing machine-guns had caught them. Their administrative arrangements also were very imperfect by the standard of the other combatants and, as a great national army, it was highly unlikely that they would exert much influence in bringing the war to a conclusion before the year was out. However, their presence in France and the speed with which General Pershing was adding to the number of US divisions provided a guarantee that it could not now be lost. The main weight of the

British army from now on would be felt in arms and services which, if they had existed at all, were only in the rudest form in 1914. The Royal Air Force was now the mightiest flying service in the world, the medium and heavy artillery was almost entirely the contribution of the United Kingdom, the Machine Gun Corps were troops of very fine quality and the Tank Corps had become something very different from the rather dubious adjunct that it had seemed a year or two ago. The Mark V and Whippet tanks were efficient weapons, far in advance of the older Mark IV and not to be compared with the mild-steel, under-powered and unmanageable Marks I and II of the Somme and Bullecourt. Except for two American battalions at the very end, the Tank Corps remained an entirely British unit and its value was out of all proportion to its ration strength. However, the remainder, the 'ordinary' divisions were fewer in numbers, reduced in size and made up largely of men who were the antithesis of veteran soldiers. Without the powerful help of the younger sons from Canada and Australasia the war must inevitably have dragged on into 1919 or even 1920. The two men who realized most clearly that a result could come in 1918, Sir Douglas Haig and Ferdinand Foch, have received as their reward the vilification of too many historians.

The remainder of the month of April passed relatively without event on the front held by the two brigades that were left to Monash. They were, however, by no means idle as the units began to clear their feet and to enlarge the area of occupation by the process of patrolling with great vigour and moving quietly into the enemy trenches whose occupants had withdrawn with the intention of coming back. They gave it the name of 'peaceful penetration', an expression that sounds as if it must have originated with some French liaison officer who recalled Lyautey in Morocco. The German attack on Villers Bretonneux, which gave them the satisfaction of briefly occupying the little town before they were driven out by the Australians, passed Monash by.

The lull gives an opportunity to take stock of the situation around Monash, for great events for the AIF were impending. To understand them some knowledge of the British military hierarchy and its organization is needed. Before the war, British officers had, for practical purposes, two types of commission open to them. The regular officer began his career by being appointed to the rank of second lieutenant and this important event was made public by an announcement in the *London Gazette*; thenceforward, every step in rank he received depended upon the existence of a vacancy to be filled and usually went by seniority. On promotion, the fact again appeared in the *Gazette,* together with the date from which the higher rank became effective. The same procedure was followed for officers of the Territorial force but with this difference: the TF officer, always subject to military law and invested with power of command over Regular and Territorial alike, was junior to every regular officer of his own rank irrespective of the dates of their gazettings. The Indian army was an entirely distinct organization; officers who had left Sandhurst together might find great differences in their respective advancements dependent upon which army they had joined.

The officers of the dominion forces also held King's Commissions but took place after regular British officers. When the New Armies came into being their leaders were granted, at Kitchener's behest, temporary commissions in the regular army for the duration of the war. By an army order all dominion officers who held non-regular commissions in their own forces were deemed to hold temporary commissions dating from 4 August, 1914, in whatever rank they enjoyed at that date. 'Temporary' rank, however, is susceptible of another meaning. On promotion and gazetting, the new rank was described as 'substantive'; the holder of a substantive rank cannot be deprived of it save by the sovereign revoking his commission or by sentence of a court-martial. In time of war this could lead to great inconvenience: the lieutenant-colonel commanding a battalion, for example, might have an enforced absence by reason of wounds or sickness and somebody else must fill the vacancy. On his return, the former CO would find another man in his chair and both would be of the same rank even after the locum tenens had returned to his former duty. To obviate this, a system had been devised whereby after the commencement of the war all substantive promotion ceased. When the filling of an appointment called for a step in rank for somebody, he was granted a temporary promotion in army orders which endured merely for so long as he occupied his specific position; should he be absent, no matter what the reason, for more than twenty-one days then he reverted to his earlier rank. There was a salutary provision that saved any officer from dropping more than one rank; thus, a lieutenant left in command of a company would be given the 'acting' rank of captain; if he retained it for twenty-one days, he became a 'temporary' captain. Should he go on to become a temporary major and then sustain a serious wound, he would at least have the satisfaction of knowing, as he lay in his stretcher, that he could not fall below captain again.

Sir Douglas Haig had been promoted field marshal (a rank that has its own rules) in 1917. All five army commanders held the rank of full general and they were all British regular officers. Birdwood, however, had his commission in the Indian army and had enjoyed a stroke of good fortune as a result. In the autumn of 1917 a number of senior Indian army officers had retired and Birdwood came to the top of the list. Thus, though only a corps commander and, at 53, younger than most, he became a full general. Canada had realized her ambition in obtaining command of her corps for a Canadian officer and Sir Arthur Currie had had the distinction of becoming the first non-professional, non-native-British officer to rise to such a height. Haig had never revised his opinion of Birdwood but he recognized that he was a good fighting general; he had made no major mistakes and a corps commander equal in rank with his army commander could be an embarrassment. In any event, the arrangement by which Rawlinson had taken over Gough's former Fifth Army had never been intended to last for longer than was necessary and the time was near when a substitute must be found. Birdwood had no serious competitor, but what was to happen to the Australian corps? Haig would have been pleased to see an Australian officer exercising this great command but he could not be expected to be in a position to judge the merits of all the Australian generals in the way that he could measure up men whom he had known for decades. In point of seniority, M'Cay stood first in the queue and was readily available in England. Haig knew that nobody wanted

M'Cay and his appointment would cause trouble. After him came Chauvel, a total stranger and without Western Front experience though, by repute, a fine soldier. Next in seniority, in accordance with the curious rules adumbrated above, was the non-permanent officer John Monash followed by the professional Brudenell White. Talbot Hobbs, commanding the Fifth Division, was actually in the middle but he was not really in the running. The choice lay between Monash and White, but the matter did not end there. Two senior divisional generals, Walker and Smyth, were British officers. They must be found appointments in the British army commensurate with their rank and high abilities with the consequential move up the ladder of Australian officers to command three divisions and three brigades.

There was also the factor that the Australian government must be consulted and approve the man chosen by Haig, though there was a refreshing lack of political interference about the whole matter. It was not the first time that Haig had had to exercise his mind upon the subject, for Dr Bean quotes 'from a private but completely reliable diary' a conversation in the previous July at Hazebrouck shortly after Currie had been given his corps. Sir Douglas: ' "Why don't you have a corps commander of your own? You know, you ought to be commanding this corps." White: "God forbid. General Birdwood has a position among Australians which is far too valuable to lose." Haig said he knew all that; Birdwood could have an administrative command. White replied that Birdwood's great reputation in Australia depended on his being the fighting commander of their troops. Haig turned away impatiently and since then has been very short with White.' No doubt the diary is completely reliable but Sir Douglas was too big a man to permit a moment of irritation resulting from a failure to be rid of Birdwood to feel any rancour against the man whose loyalty to his chief had foiled him. He knew perfectly well that White had been the effective commander of the corps many times during the absence of Birdwood and that he would make an admirable successor. On the other hand seniority meant a lot to Haig, though to nothing like the extent which it obsessed Kitchener, and there seemed no reason for Monash to be passed over. Haig had seen the man and admired his work; as a person the Antipodean Jew was surprisingly congenial to the Presbyterian Scot and Monash was unconcealedly Haig's man. According to Dr Bean, Monash took the firm view that the promotion of generals during a war was the business of the general-in-chief and not of governments or cabinets. No doubt his reading had included the experiences of the British army in America during the revolutionary war where the disastrous effect of political meddling in soldiers' business had been even plainer than on most other occasions.

The place where the proposed changes were most eagerly discussed was Brewery Farm, Querrieu where the Australian war correspondents had their headquarters. Keith Murdoch, who had risen rapidly from the obscure young journalist of Gallipoli and now was regularly exchanging confidential information with the prime minister, kept them well briefed about what was in the wind from his position of vantage in London. The correspondents, including Bean, were solidly behind the claims of White. The successive operations that he had planned with such ability between the landing and the most recent battles put him in a class entirely by himself amongst Australian staff officers. Neither he nor Monash had ever had the opportunity of distinguishing themselves by leading desperate charges, pistol in hand, or of rallying wavering men to get into the fight once more and stop the Germans from reaching Villers Bret. But no soldier wants to spend his entire career on the staff; why should White be denied the supreme appointment simply because, on 4 August, 1914, he had been the holder of a permanent commission as lieutenant-colonel whereas his rival was deemed to hold a temporary one as full colonel? Apart from that, Monash had his own detractors. He had not shown his face in the forward areas around Quinn's Post and such places as often as Bridges and Birdwood had done; he was a Jew and insisted on keeping Jewish ADCs and other personal staff; there remained some unexplained things about what had happened that night when his brigade did not get to the Asma Dere; he could not have White's ability to stand up to a superior and tell him why he was wrong; he was too ambitious;

even that he was too portly.[1] All recognized his splendid capacity as an organizer, but, if Birdwood really had to go, White was the man who should command the Australian corps and the AIF.

It was a strange contest, the strangest aspect of it being that all concerned come out of it with credit. Birdwood said that he would gladly give up all preferment if only he could stay with his beloved Diggers. Walker and Smyth readily agreed that they would waive their undoubted claims to the command in favour of an Australian officer, no matter who he might be. White followed the advice of his old chief Sir Edward Hutton; 'Go on as you have begun. Oblivious of yourself and of your own interests or your future, do what you know to be right and shame the devil.' As for John Monash, he had long ago said that he would never stoop to canvassing for his own advancement and he never did. The correspondents urged Murdoch to persuade his powerful friends to make sure that the corps went to White while Monash was compensated with the administrative command of the AIF. The honesty of the participants rubbed off on Bean who wrote in 1940 that 'Murdoch's cable [to the prime minister] painted a picture in much stronger colours than most writers would have considered justifiable' and adds a footnote; 'Murdoch was, however, doubtless misled by Bean and Dyson, who believed that their views represented those widely held in the AIF.' Certainly the correspondents then wanted something more than pastels, for Bean spoke for them all in saying that Monash 'had an almost Napoleonic skill in transmitting the impression of his capacity'. In due time they readily agreed that it was something more than an impression.

However, while all the lobbying was going on amongst the non-military men, the soldiers still had a war to fight. The Australian corps was at last brought together as a homogeneous formation and placed at the extreme south of the British line, from Morlancourt in the north to a point south of the Somme where the Diggers joined hands with General Debeney's First French Army.

A word about formations is called for; a division has already

---

[1] There might have been some truth in this at the beginning of the war when, according to army records, his modest 5 ft 8¾ in supported a weight of 14 st 10 lbs but he had fined down a lot.

been described and once created it remains unchanged unless some emergency demands that it be split up. A corps, on the other hand, is no more than a headquarters and some specialist units such as heavy artillery. Divisions come and go, being allotted to corps as needed and there is not the continuity that makes for the esprit that one might expect. Many a man would say that he belonged to the 7th Division and was proud of it but few would boast about their corps. The difference of reputation, however, was more than sentimental. Hearts rose when it was learnt that a division was going to, say, Jacob's II Corps, for men knew that operations would be carefully worked out and that it would be very rare for rations not to arrive on time; they remained unmoved on going to Haldane's VIth, for, although the staff work was good the general did not approve of alcohol and there would be no rum; their hearts sank rapidly when warned for the VIII Corps at the time it was commanded by Hunter-Weston and for which nobody had a good word. Only the Canadians maintained a permanent formation of four strong divisions always under the same commander. From a Canadian point of view it was right and sensible, for it was a small army in everything but name; from the standpoint of the C-in-C, however, it was less satisfactory, for an unbreakable force of this size is an unwieldy instrument. The Australian government and people naturally wished to see their soldiers grouped in the same way. They had loyally accepted a situation where divisions were placed under British corps for a time but now there seemed no excuse for dissipating them in this way any longer. British divisions would henceforth be placed under the command of the Australian corps from time to time but, except for a short time when the 1st Division was engaged in the defence of Hazebrouck, the AIF in France would now fight as an Australian body. Soon it would rise up out of its trenches and, fortified with every appliance of modern warfare, it would move inexorably forward until the enemies of Australia and her friends would sue for peace.

There was an incident during the last days of Monash's command of the 3rd Division which made a strong appeal to the romantic streak in him. Amongst the squalor of life in the trenches one form of warfare still seemed to be followed in accordance with the knightly tradition of an earlier age. The pilots of the flying services had the advantage of going into battle bathed and wearing clean shirts which alone lifted them above the level of their less fortunate brethren. The little single-seater scout aircraft fought each other year in and year out with superiority passing now to one side and now to the other according to the merits of the latest machines and armaments the factories could deliver. Prominent amongst the more famous of the German fliers was the former cavalryman Rittmeister Freiherr Manfred von Richtofen whose very large score of confirmed victories consisted of the shooting down of R.E.8 artillery-spotting aeroplanes whose poor performance gave them no chance against the later generation of Fokkers. Richtofen commanded a *Jagdstaffel* of Fokker triplanes, painted red and easily recognizable. The day came when the Rittmeister waxed overconfident and he drove one of these easy victims down to a low level above the lines of the 3rd Division. A couple of cooks from an artillery battery promptly turned a Lewis gun on him and had the satisfaction of seeing pieces fly from the fuselage of the triplane which crashed into a nearby field. Richtofen's riddled body was taken from the wreckage and he was buried with full military honours. The RAF dropped a wreath over the German positions and the chivalrous gesture was much appreciated. There was a rather sour note when a Canadian pilot claimed to have shot him down—possibly feeling that it would have been a more seemly end to a career of such distinction—but a diligent inquiry proved beyond doubt that the scalp belonged in the gunners' cookhouse. Monash secured his personal souvenirs, 'a tiny piece of the red fabric of Richtofen's machine, the Red Falcon... [and] a piece of the wooden propeller'. The former was dutifully sent home. A few days later another machine was brought down in the same neighbourhood and 'the pilot was slightly wounded but the officer observer was quite all right. He was brought into me; I gave him a glass of wine, and he talked freely. He told me that the German Flieger Corps much appreciated the action of our No. 3 Australian Flying Squadron in placing a wreath on Richtofen's grave.'

On the third Anzac day came the great victory of Villers Bretonneux; 'My 9th Brigade had securely kept the Boche out of the town for 3 weeks. They were then withdrawn for a rest on 23 April and the 8th British Division (regulars) took over from them. On 24 April the Boche attacked (with 4 divisions) and took the town. Late at night we had to organize a counter-attack. This was undertaken by the 13th and 15th Brigades in the early hours of Anzac Day. They advanced 3,000 yards in the dark without artillery support, completely restored the position, and captured over 1,000 prisoners. I can see the prisoners pouring past this château from the window of my office as I write this letter. It was a magnificent performance.' His last letter as a divisional general is dated 7 May, 1918, and tells of 'another brilliant success'. 'Seizing a sudden opportunity of a change in an enemy division opposite to me, I made arrangements for a surprise attack. This was carried out by Rosenthal's brigade and was completely successful. We captured 200 prisoners and 15 machine-guns and advanced our line half a mile over a frontage of $1\frac{1}{2}$ miles, or a greater gain of ground than at Messines.'

By the time of the next letter, 14 May, Haig had made his choice and it had been formally approved by the Australian government. 'I expect within a few days to be appointed to the command of the Australian Army Corps, in place of General Birdwood, who will be appointed to the command of a new army of which this corps will probably in the near future form part. This appointment will carry with it my promotion to the rank of lieutenant-general. The Australian Corps is much the largest of any of the twenty army corps in France, for it contains all the five Australian divisions, and a very large number of corps troops, comprising a regiment of cavalry, a cyclist battalion, many brigades of heavy and super-heavy artillery, several battalions of tanks, corps signal troops, ammunition parks, supply columns, mobile workshops, labour battalions, two squadrons of flying corps, and many other units. The total command, of course, fluctuates in accordance with locality and the military situation, but at present exceeds 166,000 officers and men. Moreover owing to the great prestige won by the corps during the last three months, it is much the finest corps command in the British Army. ... Cables have gone to Australia to-day to get the approval of the Government to the arrangement but I do not think that it will affect my own promotion to the corps because that is a matter in which Sir Douglas Haig will insist on making his own appointment and I am proud to say that he has selected me.'

The conclusion was perfectly correct for it had been to Haig alone that thanks were due. It is possible that the King had been consulted, for Haig maintained a regular confidential correspondence with the head of the armies and from that quarter approval might be taken for granted. Monash would not, in all probability, have been Birdwood's first choice. He fully appreciated the claims of his successor but there was another aspect of him which did not win Birdwood's entire approval. To him, the first duty of any officer was to lead his men and, by his presence amongst them when the shells were flying, to inspire them with the will to win. His own prestige amongst the highly critical Australians had been gained almost entirely by the fact that he was always to be found where the fight was hottest and shirked no danger to which the humblest of his followers was exposed. This was the British tradition of generalship; had not Wellington's men placed an exaggerated value upon the sight of their chief's long nose in a fight? Had not Marlborough's men performed seemingly impossible feats because they loved the man they called Corporal John? How could a leader command loyalty such as this from the safety of some remote headquarters? Monash might have replied that a very slight difference in the amount of foresight taken by the Turkish sniper who had 'creased' Birdwood would have deprived the corps of its leader at a time when he was most needed. When Birdwood's HQ at Hazebrouck had come under sporadic shellfire from a monster gun, he stayed defiantly where he was; when the same thing had happened to Monash at Bailleul, he moved out. An excellent case can be argued for either proposition but, to Birdwood, Monash had a little of the Plaza Toro in him though his motives were of the highest and he was certainly no coward. It has been mentioned before that one of the weaknesses in the 3rd Division was a disinclination by commanders to leave their headquarters and this is a most difficult matter on which to pontificate. Life being what it is, the only thing that is certain is that by leaving to go and see what is going on in front a commander will inevitably be absent when some vital signal comes in demanding an instant decision; if he stays put, nothing of the sort will happen but some part of his command will waver and he will not be there to inspire it by his example. The problem is incapable of short answer and calls for compromise between the two supported by a measure of luck.

However, the thing was done and on 31 May, 1918, at 11 am Birdwood and White left for the reconstituted Fifth Army and John Monash assumed command of a force twice the size of the BEF of 1914 and containing five times as many British soldiers as Wellington had had under him at Waterloo. Though he might not have been the unanimous choice of his countrymen the British corps commanders who knew him gave him a cordial welcome. The gallant General Congreve, alumnus of Sandhurst and Camberley, said that he was the best divisional general he had met on the Western Front and the view was shared by those who knew what had gone on before Amiens. All the same, from command of a single division to that of a great corps is a very long stride indeed and Monash had much to learn. Fortunately he was a swift learner.

He did not have to face the chilling task alone. As so often happens, an outstanding Chief-of-Staff appeared to serve an outstanding commander. Napoleon had had Berthier, Plumer had Harington and now Monash was to have Blamey. The pity of it was that no comparable figure ever emerged to perform the same office for Haig. Thomas Blamey was a professional soldier with all the advantages of a formal staff college education; above all he had been with the AIF in one capacity or another since the earliest days in Egypt and had learnt much of his business from White to whom he bore many resemblances. Birdwood had been true to his declared intention of making Corps HQ as nearly as possible all-Australian, for only two British officers remained. One was the commander of the heavy artillery which was entirely British and the other had an Australian understudy. He had chosen well for all the heads of departments were regular soldiers of more than common ability.

Far from being daunted by the magnitude of his new command, Monash revelled in it. 'For all practical purposes,' he wrote, 'I am now the supreme Australian commander, and thus at long last the Australian nation has achieved its ambition of having its own Commander-in-Chief, a native born Australian—for the first time in its history.' In sober truth the Australian Corps was still not by any means Australian for it included about fifty thousand British troops, mostly gunners, and one thousand US engineers. Nevertheless it was Australian commanded, Australian staffed and all its divisions were purely Australian. The weapon was delivered to Monash ready forged and now it was for him to wield it as best he could.

His articles of faith about the protection of advancing infantry by every possible mechanical means we already know. His experience of tanks was slight for he had been spared the debacle of Bullecourt and had had little to do with them at Third Ypres. At least this gave him the advantage of being able to preserve an open mind on a subject in which the common Australian opinion was very definite. Tanks were no good. Anybody who had been at Bullecourt would tell you that. They broke down before doing anything useful because their engines were no good; even small arms ammunition would go through them after the plates had been hit often enough; they could not steer nor could they reverse; even when they did move, they were so slow that they could not keep up with infantry and they only served to draw fire. True, they had a formidable weapon in the 6-pounder gun they had acquired from the navy; it could fire case-shot—small shrapnel balls joined by a thin wire—but it never had the chance of getting anywhere where it could be used.

Monash was not so sure. In his engineering experience he had seen compressors, mechanical drills and other tools which had been unimpressive enough in their early models but which had blossomed out into indispensable pieces of equipment. The reports that reached him led to the belief that something like that was happening with the tank. It was necessary to find out all about it for, all humanitarian reasons apart, the AIF could not now afford to be prodigal of its manpower. Drafts were becoming smaller and smaller, desertion was rampant and venereal disease was playing havoc with men who could never hope for a home leave. Bad though the crime figures were, Monash noted with satisfaction that those of the 3rd Division were by far the lowest of the corps. In the fine Rolls-Royce presented to Birdwood by admirers in London and which he had left behind, Monash drove for miles to acquaint himself better with the many developments that had been made in the science of armoured warfare. The Tank Corps, who had suffered much from sceptics and had even come within an ace of being disbanded, made him welcome and showed him all their secrets.

The Mark V and Mark V Star might look superficially like 'Mother' but there the resemblance ended; one man could drive, the much more powerful engines very seldom broke down now and the armour was proof against anything short of a direct hit from a field-gun. The Whippet tank was there to do the work that in an earlier age would have gone to the cavalry. Smaller and lighter than the others with a separate engine for each track, it could travel at eight miles an hour with invulnerability to most things and its four Hotchkiss light machine-guns could produce the firepower of a squadron of dismounted cavalry. There was still no settled doctrine of armoured war, for tanks existed in 1918 only as mobile shields for their infantry; even then plans were being drawn up for their much more ambitious use in 1919, for the carrying forward of the infiltration practice to unheard of extremes including raiding back areas and shattering the most important headquarters miles behind the lines. For the moment, however, the important thing was to work out the best combination of tank, gun, aeroplane and foot-soldier, for it is as fatal an error to try to fight a war with the weapons of the next as it is to employ only the weapons of the last. Monash and Blamey had much to think about.

In the midst of this, while the German attack on the Chemin des Dames was petering out and the thrust at Noyon was being countered, Monash heard rumours of an impending palace revolution. It was no news to him that the non-soldiers wished to see White in his place but he had assumed this to have passed into history. He had underrated the pertinacity of Murdoch who, for reasons entirely patriotic, was still doing what he could to achieve that happy conclusion by having Monash moved to the non-operational command of the AIF. He got no sympathy from White but stuck to his guns and arranged for the prime minister to meet him. Hughes demanded of White the name of the man who was, in his judgment, best fitted to command the Australian corps. White gave a direct answer; 'First Monash, next Hobbs'. 'And isn't there a man called White?' Hughes asked him. White waved it away with a smile. Nothing would persuade him to accept the command unless it was the consequence of a direct order and Monash had voluntarily relinquished it. Monash wrote of it, 'An intrigue is going on taking all sorts of subtle forms ... in order to persuade me to accept such a position (ie command of the AIF alone) they promise to try and win me with the offer of further promotion and emoluments ... they have started an attempt to attack my capacity to command the Corps, and are putting about propaganda that Brudenell White, being a permanent soldier, would be better fitted for this job, and that it would be in Australia's best future interests that he should get the appointment. These proceedings are being undertaken in London, in order to bring pressure on Mr Hughes. My own personal view is that I cannot relinquish the corps command until I have made a proved success of it without impairing my prestige and, further, without a certain amount of infidelity to B. I propose, therefore, to fight them on their own ground and to insist upon retaining command of the corps. In this battle I possess, of course, very many and very strong cards, and some of them are trump cards, amongst which is my undoubted belief that both Rawlinson and the Chief will see me through.' Had he known the whole story, he might have added the name of White at the end. What does shine out from this letter is the man's supreme self-confidence; there seems to be no question in his mind but that he would make a proved success of the command and it is wryly amusing to see a situation where the conspirators to dethrone a non-professional soldier from a high command find themselves opposed by British regular generals. The honourable behaviour of Brudenell White took all the steam out of the business and little more was heard of it.

Monash and Blamey had far more important things to do, for they were industriously planning the first modern battle, a battle that one feels would have been fought more naturally by Rommel or Montgomery a quarter of a century later. By itself it was not a particularly important battle but it was the military equivalent of the encounter in Hampton Roads between the *Merrimac* and the *Monitor*. It was to render all previous battles obsolete even though it would take time for this truth to become generally realized.

The battle of Hamel was a necessary one but, for a change, it was fought at a time and place of Australian choosing. During June the 2nd Division had made considerable progress at Morlancourt, to the north of the Australian line, with the result that a substantial part of it bulged out to the east. From their positions to the south of the bulge German guns could, and did, sweep the rear of that division (now under the command of Rosenthal) without serious molestation. At the same time German forces on the Western Front were reckoned with good reason to be anything but spent and there could be no certainty where they would strike next. The critical Arras bastion was strongly held by Canada, Plumer's Second Army had mauled its opponents sufficiently to make it unlikely that lightning would strike twice in Flanders and the prize of Amiens by way of Villiers Bretonneux was not beyond the aspirations of Ludendorff. The German tide was running its last hour of flood but there was, as yet, no real sign that slack water was near.

Quite apart from these considerations, Monash was anxious to put into practice certain theories of his own about the variations on the offensive which had been occupying his mind for some time past. The 4th Division, still under MacLagan, lay opposite the village of Hamel while Monash's old 3rd, now commanded by Gellibrand, neighboured them to the south, straddling the Roman road from Villers Bretonneux through the German-held village of Warfusée. Beyond Gellibrand was the French First Army of

Debeney whom Monash rightly judged to be less enthusiastic than some others about mounting an attack at this moment. The most potent ally of Australia on this occasion would be Brigadier-General Courage of the 5th Tank Brigade.

Monash and Blamey saw the necessity of making further proselytes to armoured warfare though they were under no illusions about the resistance they would meet. There was only one way by which this could be overcome; Courage and his men held open house to all the Diggers. Not only did they lay on demonstrations to be watched from a respectful distance as demonstrations usually are, they turned the whole business into a party. Individual tanks were adopted by sub-units; they gave rides to the infantrymen, showed them their capability by driving backward and forward over mock-up machine-gun nests which they flattened as if with a smoothing-iron. 'Like a man destroying a scorpion with his boot-heel' was another description. Men rode about on the roofs of the Mark Vs, got to know the people who drove them and each had intelligent suggestions to make about how to communicate with the other. The Australians were converted; tanks were now very different from what they had been in Bullecourt days. The burden must still fall on the infantry but from now on they could count on help of a new kind in overcoming strong points, flattening wire, mopping-up and consolidating. Not only would the tanks relieve them of some of the most costly of their work during the actual fight but others, called supply tanks, could take away the dreadful labour of transporting hundred upon hundreds of loads of tools, wire, ammunition and all the other things for which carrying parties had had to be found in the past.

At a higher level, Monash, Blamey and Courage set to work to hammer out a doctrine of armoured warfare. Plainly tanks could not be sent naked into battle for they remained vulnerable to artillery and the Germans now had also reasonably good weapons designed exclusively for the purpose. They needed to have moving before them a curtain of fire and this was not as easily achieved as it had been with infantry alone. The Mark V tank stood some ten feet high and Courage, naturally, was uneasy about the likelihood of shells from British batteries on the last lap of their downward course neatly decapitating them. Until the day of the Stuka only artillery could provide the protection needed and Courage eventually agreed that the risk must be taken.

Tanks were not to be the only novelty; large numbers of American troops were now in the back areas and many of them were being attached to British formations for training. The use of a few of them in the forthcoming battle was the idea of Rawlinson and of General Read, who commanded the US II Corps. Haig was enthusiastic; Pershing was less so. It may have been that he had not been kept fully informed of his subordinates arrangements; otherwise his subsequent action becomes hard to understand. It was agreed between the army commander and Read that ten strong American companies, drawn from the 33rd Division of National Guardsmen from Illinois, should be at Monash's disposal. Everybody was delighted. The Diggers took more kindly to the American youngsters than they had done to anybody but the New Zealanders. It was generally agreed that the newcomers had much in common with them; there were comments from seasoned Australians that these men seemed like the ghosts of the former comrades whom they had left behind at Gallipoli, big country boys with all the loose-limbed independence of outdoor men, not yet stunted by the dark satanic mills of the old country. It was not all that surprising, for the United States of 1918 was nearer both in time and in spirit to the men of Chancellorsville and Gettysburg than to those of Korea and Viet Nam. It seems true to say that the Doughboy was a better man and a keener soldier than his son or his grandson, an observation that is true of all the belligerent nations, for these were nothing like the popular conception of the brash, cuspidor-missing Yankees who had come to win the war. Quite on the contrary, their modesty, keenness and anxiety to learn made them the most agreeable of comrades and the two families of ex-colonials found a relationship that could not have been happier.

Lastly, airpower was going to play a role of the greatest importance, not just as a supporting actor but as one of the stars. Conference followed conference, ideas were put up and either accepted or knocked down; nobody who might have something original to contribute to the score was denied his opportunity to be heard and eventually the final and inflexible plan was approved. Every chance of a dummy-run compatible with secrecy was taken and eventually the date was fixed for the evocative 4 July. At the last moment two unheralded difficulties presented themselves; first Mr Hughes and some colleagues, quite unaware of what was in the wind, arrived on a sightseeing tour. Second, General Pershing suddenly appreciated what was afoot and refused to let his Doughboys play.

Monash was furious; he disposed of his prime minister easily enough by telling him frankly that he had come at a most inconvenient time and could not expect much attention from his military commander. Hughes was so pleased at the prospect of seeing a battle that he was unnaturally tractable. The business of the Americans was much more serious. Even if his orchestra was going to be deprived of no more than its second triangle, it still ruined the score and the conductor would not have it. At 4 pm on 3 July the news reached him that not a single American soldier would participate; earlier in the day he had been told that Read required six of the ten companies to be left behind, but this was the end. Monash managed to speak to Rawlinson on the telephone and practically demanded that the army commander come to him at once; Rawlinson, never a man to stand too much on his dignity, complied. Monash delivered his ultimatum; his troops were already moving into position and it was far too late to alter his plans. There were only two possible courses, either the attack must continue or it must be called off altogether; at 6.30 pm the infantry would be on their tapes and he must have an answer by then. Rawlinson, much upset, replied, 'But don't you realize what it means—do you want me to run the risk of being sent back to England? Do you mean it is worth that?' Monash began to feel that the visit of Mr Hughes was, perhaps, more opportune than it had at first seemed. With his prime minister in his pocket the Australian commander was invulnerable to Rawlinson or to Haig himself. 'Yes, I do,' he replied uncompromisingly. 'It is more important to keep the confidence of the Americans and Australians in each other than to preserve even an army commander.' Probably no subordinate had ever so addressed Sir Henry Rawlinson before; his sympathies were entirely with Monash and, after some thought, he went so far as to agree that if Haig did not countermand the order before 6 o'clock the attack might go on, Americans and all. Monash replied with a grin that he knew Haig to be in his motor somewhere between Paris and Montreuil and that he could not possibly be reached before seven. In fact, the message reached Lawrence just before seven and he passed it at once to the chief. Haig said that the operation was important for the improvement of positions in front of Amiens and must not be stopped just because a few American detachments could not be got out before zero hour. Nobody was better pleased than the Americans who were going into their first battle under such excellent chaperonage.

The night of 3 July was particularly quiet; at 6 pm the signal went out to the battalions, ten of them and drawn from the 2nd, 3rd and 4th Divisions for the occasion, telling them that zero hour would be 3.10 am. Eight minutes before zero the guns began a harassing bombardment; they had done exactly the same thing at the same hour every day for the past fortnight, firing a 'mix' of high-explosive, smoke and gas shells. This time the gas was omitted but force of habit compelled the enemy to hamper their vision and movements by putting on respirators. At the same time exactly, sixty of Courage's tanks started at full speed on the last half-mile to the front line; to drown the unmistakable tank noises, the RAF kept up an incessant patrol of low-flying aircraft, even bringing out old F.E.2s from retirement because their engines were noisier than any other; they also made themselves useful by dropping 25lb bombs in likely looking places. The guns gradually shortened their ranges until at 3.10 their shells were falling on the line from which the creeping barrage was to start, the 18-pounders firing two-hundred yards in advance of the infantry, the 4·5 howitzers two hundred yards further ahead still and the big guns, eighty 6-inch and twenty 8-inch and 9·2 howitzers, the same distance ahead yet again. The machine-guns of all four Australian divisions plus some borrowed British ones covered the entire front in enfilade. Exactly at zero the infantry moved out, rifles slung and cigarettes drooping, and as they walked forward the barrage lifted every four minutes providing a curtain-wall of steel between them and the defenders. Certain men had been given the congenial task of confusing the German gunners; as the German infantry fired, say, two red flares, these marplots promptly fired two green and so on. The artillery could hardly be blamed for not producing the fire expected of them.

The German position was not a particularly strong one—there were few such on either side at this time—but it was well supplied with machine-guns and fairly well wired. It was divided into three sectors, from Hamel village in the north through a pear-shaped redoubt known as Pear Trench in the centre to Vaire Wood in the south. In length it totalled about six thousand yards, and for much of the way the infantry had to go through the growing corn now three feet or so in height. The dawn was warm and dry, so much so that the dust clouds produced by the shells would have served the purpose of concealment without the need for smoke. As the barrage lifted, so the tanks lumbered through the fog of war. At first they found it difficult to see where they were going (Monash had refused their request for another five minutes of daylight) but as the sun's light began to break through each headed for its designated objective. The barrage, mostly shrapnel now, bothered them not at all and the targets were found with little trouble. All along the line the story was much the same, machine-gun posts being crushed out of existence or blasted with case-shot as the infantry continued to amble onwards. Well within the hour the first stage was over and most of the few casualties had been caused by friendly but unregistered artillery firing short. The aeroplanes came back, this time tooting their Klaxon horns as a signal to the infantry for flares to be lit for identification. As the flares appeared observers marked them in on their maps which they then dropped at the HQ of 4th Division. At the consolidation stage there arrived four specially equipped carrier-tanks, one of which disgorged 134 coils of barbed wire, 180 long and 234 short screw-pickets, 45 sheets of corrugated iron, 50 petrol tins of water, 150 trench mortar bombs, 10,000 rounds of small arms ammunition and 20 boxes of grenades. In all the four tanks delivered loads that would otherwise have demanded carrying parties of about one thousand two hundred men. Nor was this the total of mechanized bounty. The Vickers machine-gun has a gargantuan appetite and one of the heaviest crosses infantrymen had had to bear during advances on other occasions had been the carriage of boxes of belts through mud, swamp, wire or anywhere else and under shellfire of varying degrees of severity. This time there appeared yet more relays of aeroplanes and, at the invitation of the Klaxon, the machine-gunners unrolled a canvas sheet in the shape of a letter V and down came small brown parachutes from which depended the precious boxes. The raven had done something of the same sort for Elijah, as Monash would have been taught long ago. One last refinement that must be mentioned was used in a feint attack; a number of papier-maché Diggers were issued to one unit and from time to time were held up for German inspection; they cost the Kaiser a substantial amount of ammunition before the trick was realized and perhaps kept men busy at shooting them when they might have been engaged in something more lethal. It was rather unmilitary but by mid-1918 people had got past caring about such things.

The battle was over in less than an hour and a half and, with a few minor exceptions, everything had happened exactly as it had been planned. The casualties amounted to about one thousand four hundred, a tenth of them American, and many of these were only lightly wounded. It produced lessons so far without precedent. Because of the availability of the sixty tanks from the 8th and 13th Battalions of the Tank Corps it had been possible to effect great economies in the numbers of infantry needed. The artillery strength amounted to 432 guns, some lent by Fourth Army, and more than a hundred machine-guns had laid down their deadly carpet of fire in addition. Trench mortars, including the new, heavier Newton mortar, had proved invaluable as a supplement to the tanks and, thanks to their lightness and mobility, they had been able to go forward with the attackers. Comprehensive aerial photography using the new and superior technique of the oblique picture had given to all concerned an excellent idea of the details of the German positions and the most painstaking arrangements compatible with the equipment then available had been made for communications.

For Monash nothing remained to be done after he had issued his orders; he spent most of the time while the battle was raging in making a sketch of the head of a poilu, one of the chauffeurs who happened to be waiting at his HQ. The fruits of victory, apart from the captured ground and the strengthening of the position before Amiens, amounted to 1600 prisoners, 177 machine-guns, 32 trench-mortars and a number of novel anti-tank weapons.

The success of Hamel was so great and so deserved that it is easy to see in Monash some new genius of war sprung fully armed to the battlefield like a middle-aged Pallas Athene. It was, of course, his victory and that of his beloved Diggers but one must look a little below the surface. Tactics such as these could hardly be bettered in 1918 but there is no reason to suppose that their adoption, even had the means been available, would have altered the outcome of the battles of 1917. The German position was nothing like as strong as the Flanders Line and many at this time were struck by the youth and puny physique of the enemy. On more than one occasion, according to diarists, Australian soldiers had not the heart to shoot children and preferred to apply a stout boot instead of a bayonet. The ground, open cornland slanting gently uphill in most places, was perfect tank country with no more resemblance to the brown porridge of the Ypres Salient than to the Sahara. But the lessons of Second Army had not been wasted on an apt pupil; the long conferences, (one alone dealt with 133 items), the aerial photographs, the Tanks 'at home' and the dummy-runs all bear the hallmark of Sir Herbert Plumer. The precepts that Monash enunciated were those on which Harington worked and they were none the worse for that. The real novelty, novel because the equipment and the circumstances were novel, was the co-operation that worked itself out between tanks and infantry, each dealing with the foes of the other and, in concert, achieving objects beyond the dreams of 1917. This was war of movement, the first since the autumn of 1914, but with such a difference that the lessons of the battle of the Aisne now had no more to teach than had the tactics of Salamanca. Fortunately for the Allies, there were men, including, but not only, Rawlinson and Monash, who had still enough elasticity of mind to digest them. Henceforth what would be exposed to the enemy's fire would be *les machines* rather than *les poitrines*.

Hamel secured not only the Villers Bretonneux ridge but Monash's personal position. The prime minister of Australia, the Minister for the Navy and, not least, the ubiquitous Murdoch had all been witnesses of his triumph. Congratulations poured in, from Rawlinson, from Haig, and from that well-known admirer of military men, Mr Lloyd George. Georges Clemenceau, the Tiger burning brighter than ever, visited the 4th Division. Standing in the midst of a ring of Diggers, he spoke to them in English: 'When the Australians came to France, the French people expected a great deal of you . . . We knew that you would fight a real fight, but we did not know that, from the very beginning, you would astonish the whole continent. I shall go back to-morrow and say to my countrymen: "I have seen the Australians; I have looked in their faces . . . I know that these men will fight alongside of us again until the cause for which we are all fighting is safe for us and for our children." ' Even the King came to decorate with his own hand some of the Americans, thereby doing something to mollify 'Black Jack' Pershing. Not only could Monash now say with his hand on his heart that he had made a proved success of his command; when the war ended, as now seemed a not too remote possibility, it would be hard to resist his claim to the governorship for which he so hankered.

Rawlinson, their tiff over the Americans quite forgotten, was now his enthusiastic co-adjutor. If more and greater Hamels could be devised the tide would not merely have turned but the ebb would set in and, in the way of ebbtides, it would run faster than the flood.

On 18 July all observers could see that the waters were indeed beginning to reverse their course. The ferocious Mangin, once discredited but now back at Foch's insistence in command of the Tenth Army, struck violently towards Soissons aided by two hundred and twenty-five Renault tanks and two of the double-sized

American divisions. Ludendorff at last grudgingly accepted that for Germany there could be no more great attacks and that all that remained was for his armies to go back to the defensive. It need not yet mean that the war was lost, for there still remained between the Allies and the German homeland the tremendous strength of the mighty fortifications known to Germany's enemies as the Hindenburg Line.

# CHAPTER ELEVEN

## A New Doctrine of Warfare

WHATEVER impression he may have given at the head of smaller formations, Monash as a corps commander was the most aggressive of men. Before the dust had settled over the mid-summer cornfields around Hamel he was importuning Rawlinson for permission to strike again. From every report that came into his HQ in the lovely Château de Bertangles there were references to the apparent disorganization and demoralization of the enemy facing the Australians. With memories of the disastrous results of giving away time that he had acquired at and after Messines he was burning to hit them again before they could have recovered their balance and his feelings were shared by every man under his command. With Rawlinson he was pushing on an open door but the commander-in-chief, whose lofty gaze ranged the whole front from the Australian corps to the Channel, would have none of it. His attitude was anything but negative, for he and Foch were maturing great plans, but it was exasperating for the Diggers. Even so, there was no need for them to remain idle; peaceful penetration had paid useful dividends in the past and there was no reason why it should not do so again.

Throughout the remainder of July, Monash's divisional generals turned their attention to this nibbling form of warfare and their line was advanced and improved with the inevitability of gradualness. Within the week two brigades had quietly taken over an area of France nearly three miles long by half a mile deep at the cost of only 437 casualties. It was no wonder that the adjutant of the 265th Reserve Infantry Regiment wrote glumly in his diary that 'this sort of warfare cost us more than a regular attack'.

# A NEW DOCTRINE OF WARFARE

The 1st Division, still under Plumer around Hazebrouck, was no less enterprising. When, at the beginning of August, the time came for them to leave Second Army and rejoin their 'cobbers', Plumer spoke to a small gathering of officers. 'You know, gentlemen, that it is not my practice to make eulogistic speeches — there will be plenty of time for that after the war. At the same time I would like to tell you that there is no division, certainly in my army, perhaps in the whole British army, which has done more to destroy the morale of the enemy than the 1st Australian Division.' Dr Bean adds a footnote. 'On Plumer's visits to the 1st Division he would ask, "What's this your fellows have been doing?" and would depart without comment, but his shoulders shaking with suppressed chuckles.'

Monash seized the opportunity of catching up with his interrupted leave. Time did not permit him to go back to Menton but he managed five days in London.[1] Arrangements were made for messages to reach him at the War Office 'and a destroyer would stand by at Dover to rush me across if necessary, as I was not quite prepared for the alternative proposition of flying across'. Birdwood had flown back in March, but Monash saw no reason to risk his life for the sake of a few hours. His presence would be needed at Flixécourt where Rawlinson had summoned a conference to discuss the next moves which he had in mind.

Monash, of course, was well aware that a further offensive, this time on the grandest scale, was in the offing and there was one aspect of it that he was determined to ventilate. On his right there was still the XXXI Corps of Debeney's army and Monash had come to the conclusion that these men were lacking in aggressive spirit and were far from being ideal neighbours. The Canadian corps, which had as yet taken little part in the year's fighting, was resting in a back area and these would be comrades far more to the Australians' liking. As it happened, Rawlinson gave him even more than he had asked for; the Canadians, whose corps commander, Currie, was also a part-time soldier, were moved

---

[1] During the journey he is said to have carried a card on which were punctiliously listed not only the articles in his baggage but also everything about his person, pocket by pocket.

south to form a buffer between Monash and the French, his own front was reduced from eleven miles to a little over four and, best of all, the 1st Australian Division was to be returned to its parent body. The British III Corps was still on his left; this was a pity, for it consisted of worn-out divisions brought up to establishment with some low-category troops and it was not to be spoken of in the same breath as the corps of the two dominions. The final battles of the war, the battles of the hundred days, were about to begin and Rawlinson, upon whose shoulders was to fall the greatest responsibility, would have need of the best soldiers left to the Empire.

In the plan for the battle of 8 August one can perceive the hand of Monash; in the Hamel formula he had fabricated the most efficient use of all the weapons at the army's disposal and, in particular, he had adumbrated a doctrine for the employment of the sovereign arm of 1918. The Hamel approach never was, nor was ever intended to be, a panacea against all difficulties; it was, however, the recipe for the most efficient use of the weapons of the day at a time when cavalry had outlived its usefulness as a mobile arm (though, as has been seen, there remained a place on the battlefield for mounted riflemen) and the tank had not yet acquired the speed and range that would enable it to do as much as, or more than, the traditional shock weapon had done for ages past. Attacks would still go forward only at the pace at which a man could walk but it is not difficult to see that Monash had grasped the pattern on which battles would be fought a score of years later.

Sir Robert Menzies, a good many years afterwards, heard Monash speak at a function held by their common university. At the close of the speech, Menzies, one of the most experienced men at the Bar, turned to his neighbour and said, 'You know, whatever else in his favour may be said about John Monash, he is the finest advocate I have ever listened to.' In another speech he said, 'He was a great advocate who knew how to think, who worked out his thoughts and who could then present them to other people with such compulsion, such persuasion that they began to wonder why they hadn't thought of it themselves.' Rawlinson was, even

## A NEW DOCTRINE OF WARFARE

more than Plumer, an essentially approachable man and a great arguer; the memory of the misuse of the earliest tanks of 1916, always charged to him, and the fiasco of Bullecourt, was not to be expunged by one small and, perhaps, idiosyncratic battle. Exactly what passed at the seemingly interminable conferences will probably never now be known but it seems reasonable to suppose that it gave Monash an opportunity to put his case and that he seized it. He would no more have considered fighting a battle without most of the exposure to fire being apportioned to the tanks than he would have set about building a bridge with no mechanical aids other than pick, shovel and wheelbarrow; his relationship with Courage's people can be deduced from their gift to him after Hamel, a model Mark V tank beautifully made out of the gunmetal of German shell-cases and the copper of their driving bands. It went to join the fragments of Richtofen's aeroplane, with strict instructions to 'take this little model to a jeweller and have the whole of the metal work polished to a bright polish, and then carefully lacquered so as to preserve it from corrosion'. The same letter contains this passage: 'The tactics of the employment of this new type of tank was [sic] my own invention and has now been adopted throughout the armies.'

The army commander convened a conference at his château at Flixécourt on 21 July and there Monash became acquainted with his Canadian opposite number. Sir Arthur Currie was a man for whom one must feel as much sympathy as admiration. Like Monash, he had passed his boyhood in straitened circumstances, so much so that he had been denied the opportunity of qualifying for a profession. His first job was as a schoolmaster and during this time he obtained a commission in his country's militia. Later on, he turned his attention to land agency in Victoria BC and was making a success of his affairs when the great slump of 1913 overtook him. Ill fortune, possibly coupled with unwise speculation, left Currie up to the neck in debt and he was forced to borrow money from some of those who were his militia subordinates. The war did nothing to ease his situation and the unhappy man has left it on record that throughout the entire conflict his last thought on closing his eyes and his first on opening them was of his hopeless financial situation. If this were not enough, he had powerful enemies in his own government, prominent amongst them being Sam Hughes.[1] Hughes never let pass any opportunity of publicly attacking Currie both as a commander and as a man; charges of incompetence were laced with others and doubt was even cast upon his personal courage. The worst and most scurrilous of these will be related in due time but it is eloquent of Currie's greatness of heart that he rose above these torments and was deservedly known as one of the most skilful and popular of all Haig's senior commanders. Certainly the two citizen-generals each had a full appreciation of the fine qualities of the other and the mutual liking and respect permeated to the lowest ranks of their commands.

There was much to be discussed at Flixécourt and none of those present was too stiff-necked to learn from German experience of the spring. First and foremost, secrecy must at all costs be preserved and the enemy must be kept in ignorance of the presence of the Canadians in face of him. If news were to leak out that the two strongest contingents on the Western Front were assembling in front of Amiens then Ludendorff would of a certainty move every available reserve to oppose them.

It was quite as important to keep the intelligence secret from friends as from enemy, for one careless sentence picked up by a seemingly innocent French peasant might swiftly find its way to the wrong quarter and all the advantages gained by the tedious night movements and the endless patrolling by police aircraft would be lost. For that reason, a nucleus of the Canadian corps, lavishly equipped with wireless, was left in their old territory and an immensity of signal traffic proclaimed to eavesdroppers that everything was going on as usual.

Monash, on the whole, was pleased with the task allotted to his corps; his front was to be reduced by a half and the last remaining Australian division, the 1st, was to come home after its splendid work before Hazebrouck. On some points, however,

---

[1] Birdwood in a letter (now at the Imperial War Museum) to his friend Colonel Rintoul, wrote that 'Having shown himself so very pleased with the world in general and himself in particular, he has been called "Le Roi Sam-Use".'

his powers o advocacy had to be employed to their full extent and they did not always sway the army commander. In one important particular Monash had his way. Rawlinson, grown wary over the years, proposed to set a limit to the objectives of only a mile or two; this was not nearly enough for Sir John. 'Rarely had any previous set-piece attack succeeded in reaching the enemy's line of field-guns. The result had been that the bulk of his artillery had been withdrawn at his leisure, and that his losses had been confined to a few hundred acres of shattered territory. But the task I had set myself was not only to reach, at the first onslaught, the whole of the enemy's artillery positions, but greatly to over-run them, with a view to obliterating, by destruction or capture, the whole of his defensive organizations and the whole of the fighting resources which they contained, along the whole of my corps front.' This was a highly ambitious project, for the German gun line was comfortably housed in the valley running from Cerisy to a point near Warfusée-Abancourt, an average distance ahead of the present Australian line of something over four miles. Rawlinson, knowing his man, let Monash have his way; he did not, however, have it in all respects. Sir John had all the engineer's insistence on the strength of joints and he did not at all care for the dictum of Field Service Regulations that decreed such features as roads, rivers and railways to make admirable boundaries. Within his own command junctions were firmly made by each battalion putting its flanking section within the territory of its neighbour and, as the size of units increased, the process was elaborated so as to make of each overlap the strongest and not the weakest part of the line. He was particularly uneasy about the arrangements north of the river. In its middle reaches, the Somme meanders from east to west by a series of wide loops through a valley that had been swamp before Napoleon's engineers had straitjacketed it into a canal running between banks of masonry. Along its course there are great stagnant ponds, impassable save to a swimmer, and the peninsulas inside the bends which extend from the higher ground to the north are, for the most part, high and wooded. Biggest and most formidable is the great tooth of Chipilly that sinks into the flat land opposite and on which the Germans were known to have strong battery positions. If Chipilly remained in enemy hands, these guns could and would take the Australian corps first in enfilade and then from the rear as it pressed forward.

Rawlinson would not be swayed. The Somme was to be the boundary and Chipilly must be stormed by Butler's III Corps. The effect of this was to entrust the most difficult task of all to the troops least fitted to carry it out, but there was no help for it. Butler had been deputy to Kiggell at GHQ and lacked the hard experience of other officers of his rank. His troops consisted of two divisions, the 58th and 18th, both of which had been ground down to bedrock and made up to something like their war establishment only by filling the ranks with such drafts of boys and middle-aged men as it had been possible to scrape together. These would have to fight one of the most difficult battles of the war to guard the flank to the north whilst the overseas infantry romped ahead. Nobody liked the idea but it would have been absurd to expect Butler's men to carry out a great advance with the drive of either the Canadians or the Australians and they must simply make the best of it. Their task would have taxed the eager young volunteers of 1916; Kitchener was dead and the young conscripts of two years later were to find the task beyond their powers.

In the interplay of ideas at conferences, when experienced and highly intelligent men strike sparks off each other, plans are made for which no particular individual can claim credit. Monash, however, was never the man to reap where others had sowed and if he is correct in his assertion about 'the tactics of the employment of this new type of tank' being his own invention, the credit for one step forward into the era of mechanized warfare is rightly his. The Mark V Star tank had been lengthened in order to give it the capacity to cross trenches too wide for its forerunners. This gave a certain amount of unused space inside and from this appeared the first armoured personnel carrier. The men upon whom the greatest reliance was placed for the consolidation of newly won positions were the machine-gunners; why should they walk to the place where they would be most needed, at the considerable risk that they

# A NEW DOCTRINE OF WARFARE

would never arrive at all, when they could be carried there behind a layer of armour plate? Experiments at Vaux-en-Amienois showed that no less than eighteen men could be crammed inside but the conditions then were so appalling that the number was reduced to two complete Lewis gun sections. The thirty-six Mark Vs at Monash's disposal would be used with his exploitation brigades and so could decant seventy-two light automatics to thicken up the attenuated lines of infantry over the ten thousand yards of open arable land that they would have to hold. It was the technique of the 1940's but it worked well enough in 1918.

Next was the problem of how to protect the tanks themselves. They had long ceased to be a novelty — there could never be another Cambrai — and the German army had anti-tank weapons at least as good as those of the BEF of 1940. There were two ways of eliminating these; if they could be reached by infantry firing Lewis guns from the hip — a standard practice amongst the Australians — or blotted out by the guns, so much the better. If not, then it must be made as difficult as possible for the defenders to get a decent target and that meant smoke. In addition to the normal smoke-shells carried by the artillery, some of the patrolling aircraft were supplied with smoke bombs and charged with the single duty of watching over the tanks and obscuring them behind a cloak of invisibility whenever they seemed to be in trouble. Attempts were made to equip each tank with the means of making its own smoke but the necessary gadgetry did not yet exist.

Additional guns of all sizes, many of them good modern pieces of a quality not seen since the pre-1914 weapons had been replaced by the ill-made products of a crash programme, were quietly eased into their positions and the advanced techniques of flash-spotting and sound-ranging marked down the position of every known German battery. Great pains were taken to see that the ranging of the newcomers was carried out in a fashion that would raise no suspicion that these were additional to those already known to be present, the railway engineers performed prodigies of track-laying and repairing. Also the Canadians began to arrive. They were to take over the line of the French XXXI Corps as far south as Morisel but it was highly undesirable that this should be done until the news of their presence no longer mattered. Accordingly it was arranged that the 4th Australian Division, technically resting, should relieve the French and no attempt was made to conceal the fact. The natural deduction would be that the Australians, by widening their front, could not be contemplating offensive action and the French would be going to rejoin Pétain in his battle for Soissons.

Another arrival was the American 65th Brigade, placed under Monash for the battle, and no troops ever received a warmer welcome. There was an ugly moment on the night of 4 August when a German raiding party captured an Australian sergeant and four men, for there was no knowing how much they might have learnt or guessed of what was going on. Nobody imagined that they would talk voluntarily but the use of 'pigeons' — bogus prisoners-of-war — was common to both sides and something might be wormed out of them. There was no cause for alarm; the German Intelligence officers got no change from the 'Diggers', only ribaldry.

Monash and Blamey had not exhausted their talents for a mechanical invention. They had always set great store by sparing their infantry from needless physical effort and devoted much thought to the problem of getting them to the place where they must be without imposing more strain than could be avoided. The usual course of an attack was something like this; the first wave would get up out of its trenches and follow the barrage until it had reached its prescribed objective; once there, the attackers would be at their most vulnerable, tired, disorganized, spread out and reduced in numbers and in no sort of posture to beat off an immediate counterattack. Their job, then, was to dig themselves in as best they could and strengthen the position they held while other men, not so far engaged, passed through them to keep up the impetus of the assault. This process, 'leap-frogging', had one major defect: the second wave would have had a long march, heavily laden, from their billets several miles away to the front line and then over the freshly captured ground. In the nature of things, much virtue would have gone out of them before their battle had even started. There must be a better way than this. Monash decided that there was one, but it involved taking a considerable risk. He divided his front into a right- and left-hand sector, each under the senior general of the two divisions which would be operating there, whether as first or second wave. The 4th Division, relieved by the Canadians, was on the north side, teamed up with the 3rd, and the 5th and 2nd in the south. They had in support a brigade of field artillery to each brigade of infantry and the divisional commander had at his disposal three more brigades and a battery of 60-pounders. Three days before the battle, the two divisions in the line thinned out leaving only one brigade to hold the entire front. The two brigades remaining thus became available for carrying out the first phase of the attack with its complement of tanks. Reduced to a basic simplicity, the scheme meant that the divisions to be employed in the second phase held the line immediately before the battle and the first-phase divisions, bivouacked nearby, passed through them at the beginning. When these were on their objective, the divisions from the line carried out a second leap-frog and moved onwards. Bearing in mind the numbers of men, guns, horses and equipment involved, one can see the enormous intricacy of the staff work demanded to prevent the plan from degenerating into confusion; only the best of troops, confident in their leaders and well-served by their staff officers, could have attempted it. It had never before been considered, let alone tried, and it carried with it risks commensurate with the rewards.

Though the German infantry had been badly shaken, their artillery was almost untouched and was well stocked with gas-shells, a commodity which the British army lacked. If they had had any inkling that the attackers were so thickly massed in such a small space, a deluge of mustard gas would have come indiscriminately down and a great disaster would have been possible. Monash, applying his wonted psychology, considered the risk remote after so much care had been taken to preserve the illusion of normality; his counter was to arrange that the moment the first gas-shell dropped, all his medium and heavy artillery would instantly open up and smother the German batteries in a deluge of high-explosive. Happily, it never had to be put to the test.

When Sir John came to write of the battle after the war he

seemed to give some evidence of hubris or even smugness. 'In a well-planned battle of this nature, fully organized, powerfully covered by artillery and machine-gun barrages, given a resolute infantry and that the enemy's guns are kept successfully silenced by our own counter-battery artillery, nothing happens, nothing can happen, except the regular progress of the advance according to the plan arranged. The whole battle sweeps relentlessly and methodically across the ground until it reaches the line laid down as the final objective. Such a set-piece battle lasts usually, from first to last, for 80 to 100 minutes; seldom for more. When the artillery programme is ended the battle is either completely won or to all intents and purposes completely lost. If the barrage for any reason gets away from our infantry, and they are relegated to hand-to-hand fighting in order to complete their advance, the battle immediately assumes a totally different character, and is no longer a set-piece affair. It will be obvious, therefore, that the more nearly a battle proceeds according to plan, the more free it is from any incidents awakening any human interest. Only the externals and only the large aspects of such battles can be successfully recorded. It is for this reason that no stirring accounts exist of the more intimate details of such great set-pieces as Messines, Vimy, Hamel, and many others. They will never be written, for there is no material upon which to base them. The story of what did take place on the day of the battle would be a mere paraphrase of the battle orders prescribing all that was to take place.' It might have been written by Montgomery.

Taken in the round, the averments are well founded but battles, even set-piece battles, do not always proceed with the reliability of a railway timetable. On the evening before 8 August something happened entirely by chance that might have upset the arrangements very seriously. In a small plantation just to the north of Villers-Bretonneux, eighteen carrying tanks of the 4th and 5th Divisions were parked, loaded to the gunwales with food, water and ammunition of all kinds together with their own store of No. 1 aviation spirit. A random shell fell neatly in the middle of this mass of combustibles and set it on fire; the pillar of smoke which resulted drew the attention of the German gunners who

# A NEW DOCTRINE OF WARFARE 233

promptly 'strafed' the area with such a volume of high-explosive that fifteen of the tanks blew up; did this mean that they knew what was lurking there and, if so, how much more did they know? As things turned out it was no more than a fluke and the losses were soon made good.

Launching a great attack is rather like lighting a bonfire; the paper and the wood are craftily laid and when they are satisfactorily in place the match is applied. In some places the fire will catch at once and roar away; in others, a flaw of wind or some inexplicable cause will blow the flame out or prevent it catching at all. So it was on 8 August. All along the Australian front between the river and the railway the blaze sprang up splendidly and the orders foretell what happened. On Butler's end, however, it blew out almost at once and all his attempts on the Chipilly spur were driven back. Monash was scathing about it. 'What were the reasons for the failure of the III Corps to complete its allotted task may have been the subject of internal enquiry, but the result of any such was not made known. The official report for the day was to the effect that "the enemy on this front had resisted strongly", that fighting had been fierce, and that no progress could be made. But one is compelled to recognise that such language is often an euphemistic method of describing faulty staff co-ordination, or faulty local leadership.' He was probably right; in terms of Sherriff's *Journey's End*, the Stanhopes and Osbornes were all dead and only the Trotters and Hibberts, with an occasional Jimmy Raleigh, still remained. Many of the junior commanders would not have been regarded as 'officer material' even six months before. The result was that Maclagan had to refuse his north flank with a brigade of the 4th Division until the spur was taken on the following day by an American regiment, the 131st. Before it fell, German guns on the spur had knocked out six of the nine tanks attached to 4th Brigade.

Everywhere else success was complete. Monash records it in the signals to Fourth Army which 'on a point of responsibility, I made it an invariable rule to draft myself'. They include these:

Sent at 7 am. 'Everything going well at 6.45 am. Heavy ground mist facilitating our advance, but delaying information. Infantry and tanks got away punctually. Our attack was a complete surprise. Gailly village (on the South bank of the river) and Accroche Wood (a mile south-east of Hamel) captured. Enemy artillery has ceased along my whole front. Flank Corps apparently doing well.'

Sent at 8.30 am. 'Although not definitely confirmed, no doubt that our first objective green line captured along whole corps front including Gailly, Warfusée Lamotte and whole Cerisy Valley. Many guns and prisoners taken. Infantry and artillery for second phase moving up to green line.'

Sent at 1.15 pm. 'Australian flag hoisted over Harbonnières at mid-day to-day. Should be glad if Chief would cable this to our Governor-General on behalf of Australian Corps.'

Sent at 4.40 pm. 'Captured enemy Corps HQ near Framerville shortly after noon to-day.' (This was the 51st German Corps.)

Sent at 8 pm. 'Corps captures will greatly exceed 6,000 prisoners, 100 guns, including heavy and railway guns, thousands of machine-guns, a railway train and hundreds of vehicles and teams of regimental transport. Total casualties for whole corps will not exceed 1200.'

In fact, the figures for booty were an underestimate. One hundred and seventy-two guns, including the enormous affair that had been constructed for the sole purpose of ruining Amiens, had fallen into Australian hands with machine-guns and mortars in such numbers that no attempt was made to put even an approximate figure on them. A fatigue-man who had been furnished, in addition to his battle kit, with a brush and pot of white paint with instructions to put 'Captured by the 41st Battalion AIF' on every piece, ran out of paint long before his task was finished. The engineer stores taken at Rosières and La Flaque were sufficient to make the Australian corps independent of all other sources of supply for the rest of the war. It does scant justice to the Canadians to say baldly that much the same thing happened on their front but their story is well told elsewhere. The Canadians were in an ugly mood for they had just learnt of the sinking by a U-boat of the hospital ship *Llandovery Castle* and the drowning of 234 people, including some Canadian

# A NEW DOCTRINE OF WARFARE

nurses and a number of wounded. Before the afternoon was over they had reached the old defences of Amiens between Hangest and Quesnel, penetrated fourteen miles, captured 9,131 prisoners, taken 190 pieces of artillery and machine-guns beyond counting. In the process they had freed twenty-seven distinct towns and villages of France.

Now at last the axe was at the foot of the tree. 8 August was not the first battle of the final closing of the ring—that had been fought on 28 June when two British divisions of First Army had gained a mile of ground in front of the Forêt de Nieppe without benefit of tanks—but this was a victory on an incomparably greater scale. Though hard men remained in the German army, as they have always done in every army, who would fight on to the end without hope of victory, the bulk of the soldiers knew now that they must continue the war conscious that it could only end in defeat. Most of these hard men could be found in the ranks of the artillery and machine-gunners and there remained plenty of fight in them.

While the battle still raged, Monash pondered on what should happen next. Would Haig allow Fourth Army to continue exploiting its massive victory by allotting it the extra troops that it would need to keep up the pursuit or did his plans envisage the transference of the weight of the blow to some other part of his front? During the afternoon, while the big twin-engined Handley-Page 0/400 bombers, designed to lunge at Berlin, were pounding the retreating enemy and the armoured cars were creating havoc ten miles behind the morning's front, the answer came from Rawlinson. 'While the whole situation was being considered, and troops movements were in progress to enable the necessary concentrations to be made elsewhere, the Fourth Army would continue its advance forthwith; but that, instead of driving due east, the thrust was to be made in a south-easterly direction.' Haig was after the important railway town of Roye whose possession was essential to the Germans if they were to be able to continue to supply their forces in the great salient on the French front opposite Montdidier and Moreuil which they had taken in the advances of April and May. This would be a job for the

Canadians, advancing between the Amiens–Roye road and the railway line, with the Australian corps only having the task of forming a defensive flank to the north. It would mean that they would have to stand firm on the left and swing the right-hand division forward along the railway line, a feat that could hardly be productive of great results. Monash described the order as 'unpalatable' for it 'condemned me to leaving the whole of the great bend of the Somme, on which lay Bray, Peronne and Brie, in the undisturbed possession of the enemy' and that at a time when he was gasping for breath.

Five or six miles ahead of him lay the wilderness of the old Somme battlefield but those few miles consisted of unravaged farmland which could easily be taken by the 'open warfare' tactics with which the Diggers were now becoming familiar and, with that done, the enemy would have to carry out his reorganization amid the devastation left behind by the earlier battles. Not all the advocacy in the world, however, could alter the fact that this was a definite order and not a mere basis for discussion; Monash could do nothing but comply. He fed in his 1st Division, only a part of which had been so far engaged, and after a stiff fight in which they were given the powerful help of three battalions of tanks, they stormed the Lihons ridge in the course of the 9th and joined up with the Canadians on the railway a mile east of Rosières.

The unpalatable orders at least gave him the opportunity to rest those of his troops who had been the most tried and the 4th Division was relieved by the 3rd. One of Monash's less spectacular but most appreciated characteristics was the manner in which he always went to considerable trouble to make sure that hardship and fatigue were shared equally; no division of his ever had cause to complain that it was being 'put upon' and the knowledge did much to endear him to the fighting men of Australia. The only initiative left to him was to perform some tidying-up operations consequent upon the capture of Chipilly which strengthened his left flank and brought in a small haul of three hundred prisoners to swell the numbers in the Fourth Army cage at Abbeville.

The enforced lull gave time also for another letter home, dated

11 August. 'I snatch a few minutes late in the evening to give you brief particulars of an exceptionally interesting day ... During this forenoon I was busy at Bertangles ... all the morning preparing plans for a further advance. I was much interrupted by visitors. Quite early I had a call from Mr Winston Churchill, Minister of Munitions, and at 11 o'clock, according to arrangements, I received a call from Field-Marshal Sir Douglas Haig, who came formally to thank me for the work done. He brought with him the chief of the general staff, Sir Herbert Lawrence, and while they were still with me I received a further call from General Sir Julian Byng, the Commander of the Third Army. The Chief thereupon seized the opportunity to have a conference with General Byng on certain contemplated operations and would not hear of my withdrawing, so that I was present during the whole conference and was frequently asked for my opinion. I had earlier in the morning arranged to meet my own five divisional commanders at Villers Bretonneux, so that I might have a conference dealing with the contemplated programme of operations tomorrow. This conference was to have been at 2.30 pm and I mentioned the fact to the Commander-in-Chief. He said at once that he would very much like to come up, so as to be able to meet the five divisional commanders personally. About noon Sir Henry Rawlinson ... rang me up to say that there had been important developments and that Marshal Foch was coming up this afternoon to give fresh orders about the tactical policy of the next few days. He said the Commander-in-Chief "could not be found" and that, therefore, it was necessary for him to take matters in hand without delay, and that he had arranged for an Army Conference at Bertangles at 3 o'clock. I told him at once about the arrangements for the Chief to meet me and my five divisional commanders at Villers Bretonneux at 2.30 pm and he at once said that in those circumstances he would arrange for his own Army Conference to be at Villers Bretonneux also at 3 o'clock. He said, however, that as he did not want to interfere with my own Corps Conference he would have his in the open fields just west of the village. Shortly after this had been fixed up, I received word by telephone that Sir Henry Wilson, Chief of the Imperial General Staff, was in

France and wished to call on me to congratulate me. I had to send a message to say that I was unable to receive him here, but would be at Villers Bretonneux between 2.30 and 3.30 pm. In due course I proceeded with . . . Blamey . . . and selected a place on the outskirts of the town, suitable for the Conference under a bunch of trees . . . On one side of the main road was a large wired-in prisoners cage in which were over 3,000 prisoners captured during the last 24 hours, and many small parties of prisoners, captured this morning, were being marched down the road. An immense stream of traffic was pouring up the road towards the front, guns, troops, strings of horses and mules, hundreds of motor lorries, ambulance wagons, and the usual motley traffic of war. On the other side of the road ran the main railway, and a swarm of Canadian Railway Battalion men, together with two of my own Pioneer Battalions, were busy relaying the rails and reopening the line and the first railway train which had succeeded in getting through Amiens since the battle was actually steaming through the cutting at 2.30 pm. At the appointed hour my five divisional commanders, each in his own car, arrived . . . We had scarcely assembled and sat down with our general staffs, when another car drove up, bringing General Sir Henry Wilson. Shortly after him came the Commander-in-Chief in his two cars and with him Sir Herbert Lawrence . . . The Field-Marshal made a little speech to us and was very complimentary to me, saying that, as always, my plan was perfectly worked out and deserving of the greatest credit etc. In the middle of it all arrived Sir Henry Rawlinson for his Conference . . . There followed in quick succession Lieutenant-General Sir Arthur Currie, commanding the Canadian Corps, Lieutenant-General Kavanagh, commanding the Cavalry Corps, Lieutenant-General Sir A. J. Godley, temporarily commanding the IIIrd Corps, Major-General Elles, commanding the Tank Corps and Major-General Charlton, commanding the 5th Brigade Royal Air Force . . . we all squatted down on the grass while great maps were spread out and Rawlinson commenced to expound the situation and ask for our views. We had scarcely started when still three more motor-cars arrived, out of which hopped Monsieur Clemenceau, Prime Minister of France,

# A NEW DOCTRINE OF WARFARE

Marshal Foch, and the French Minister for Finance. This completed the gathering, met literally by chance on the actual battlefield and on a site which will live for ever in Australian history. I suppose that it rarely happens that such a distinguished gathering should so meet under such stirring surroundings, with the guns thundering all around.' It was fortunate that another distinguished person did not join in: Hauptmann Herman Goering, whatever his subsequent backslidings, was at that moment commanding Richtofen's old Jagdstaffel and was probably not very far away. Adjoining the Château de Bertangles was one of the biggest aerodromes of the RAF. One of the squadrons there was commanded by Major Sholto Douglas, who learnt to admire both the Australians and their commander. Amongst the pilots were a New Zealander named Keith Park and an American lieutenant named John G. Winant.

The following day a gentleman whose distinction surpassed them all came as a visitor to Bertangles. In the presence of a detachment of one hundred men from each Australian division and amidst avenues of captured guns, the King dubbed John Monash knight. The solemn occasion was nearly spoilt: when a sword was called for none could be found, for they were not commonly worn in 1918. Happily a staff officer remembered that a friend of his in Abbeville still had the one he had brought to France in 1914 and His Majesty's attention was diverted to other matters while a car was dispatched at break-neck speed to collect it. All was well. 'A square of carpet had been arranged in the centre of the piazza and on it stood a small table, a footstool and a drawn sword. The King then had my name called and I stepped up before him and, at his behest, knelt and received the accolade of knighthood, and, when he had bidden me rise, he presented me with the insignia of a Knight Commander of the Bath. He shook hands most warmly and made me a little speech, commending my work and that of the Australian troops ... the whole ceremony lasted only half an hour and took place amid brilliant sunshine, and with our Australian Squadron aeroplanes circling overhead.'

With some regret, it is necessary to differ from the two writers of monographs about Sir John who suggest that the circumstances of the ceremony might have given him the status of a knight-banneret. The banneret (or ban-rent) was a kind of brevet promotion invented by Edward III to single out knights or squires who had particularly distinguished themselves in battle. Froissart has a description of the ceremony when the Black Prince so honoured Sir John Chandos before the battle outside Vittoria against Henry of Trastamare. At the end of it, the swallow-tails were cut from the knight's forked pennon, thus converting it into a square banner. Camden avers that, by the reign of Henry IV, it had fallen into desuetude. In any case, Monash had been a knight since the publication of the gazette containing the New Year Honours. Sir Arthur Currie was dubbed at the same time. There were other honours of a less formal nature. 'Among the spoil gathered up (in the capture of 51 German Corps HQ) was a box containing 100 Iron Crosses, all ready for issue. They were in due course "issued" to our own "Biljims" who came back from the battle wearing Iron Crosses all over their anatomy.'

## CHAPTER TWELVE

## Australia Victrix

THE conference with Haig and Byng presumably brought to John Monash a good deal of information that, had he possessed it earlier, might have altered his judgment about the wisdom of pressing on along the Somme. The enemy's resistance was hardening as he fell back – Lihons, fought with half the number of troops engaged on 8 August had cost twice as many casualties – and, equally significantly, the machines were melting away. Of the 415 fighting tanks that had gone into battle on that day only 145 remained serviceable on its morrow; though the repair shops (manned largely by very competent Chinese coolie mechanics, Monash says) worked day and night and new tanks were dribbling in from England, they were going to be very thin on the ground from now on.

The RAF also had suffered heavily; throughout the war air superiority had passed from one side to the other as the designers produced new and better machines. By mid-1918 the RAF was on top but the enemy was still extremely formidable; the Fokker D VII, with a top speed of 125 mph and a remarkable rate of climb, could be fought on terms of equality only by the British SE5A or the Sopwith Camel. When these excellent aircraft were not about, the Fokkers made hay with most other designs and it was in a large part their depredations that cost the British ninety-six aircraft destroyed or damaged beyond local repair in the fighting on 8 August. Losses on this scale cannot be made good overnight and it was clearly somebody else's turn to 'give it a go'.

Foch, as we now know, was anxious to keep the attack going along the Somme with the aid, such as it was, of Debeney's First

Army. He persuaded Haig to comply and it was only after the famous meeting at which Rawlinson spoke to the chief as no army commander had ever done before that he abandoned the idea. Mangin and Byng went into battle instead and won their victories on the Chemin des Dames and at Bapaume during the last ten days of this *mensis mirabilis*.

On the Somme, friendships came to an end when, on 22 August, Currie handed over the front of his corps to Monash and the Canadians began to move back north to the country in front of Arras which they knew so well. In exchange Monash was given the 32nd Division from GHQ reserve, one of those peripatetic formations whose misfortune it was never to stay long enough under any corps commander to get to know his foibles. Monash had no intention of remaining idle, even though he could now only fight battles on a moderate scale with no resources but his own. He put it to Rawlinson that the straightening of his line south of the Somme was a practicable proposition and that it might produce a bonus by driving the enemy across the river where it alters course to a north-south axis above Peronne. Rawlinson agreed. For Monash and Blamey the preparation was more arduous than usual for the formations earmarked for the attack, Glasgow's 1st Australian Division and Lambert's 32nd, had not been educated in the ways of the Australian corps under its present management. The pre-battle conference (at Fouilloy, where the great Australian memorial now stands) was a long one. It deserves attention, for nothing illustrates more clearly the methods of working adopted by Corps HQ. Monash himself tells of it: 'The conference of that day was of special interest in that I had to deal with two divisions which had not participated in any of those corps conferences previously held, which had initiated a fully organized corps operation. The commanders and staff were strangers to each other and, some of them, to me and my staff. Nearly all of them were yet unfamiliar with the special methods of the corps. The conference was, therefore, a lengthy one, for many problems of tactical mechanism which had been settled in connection with the preceding battles of Hamel and 8 August had to be re-opened and elucidated. These regular battle conferences were in the Australian Corps an innovation from the time the command of it devolved upon me. They proved a powerful instrument for the moulding of a uniformity of tactical thought and method throughout the command. They brought together men who met face to face but seldom, and they permitted of an exhaustive and educative interchange of views. They led to a development of team work of a very high order of efficiency ... they more than repaid me for the effort entailed. They enabled me to apply the requisite driving force to all subordinates collectively instead of individually and thereby created a responsive spirit which was competitive ... The senior representative of the heavy artillery, tank and air services invariably attended, and listened to all the points discussed with the divisions, and the divisional commanders heard all matters arranged with these services. In this way, each arm acquired in the most direct manner a steadily expanding knowledge of the technology of all the other arms.'

Nobody will suggest that Monash invented the conference; but one gains a strong impression that in the Australian Corps it did not take quite the same shape as in British formations. Monash was not a man with whom any would dare to take a liberty but the habit of subordination in the army undoubtedly fosters a tendency for many conferences to be simply the giving and receiving of orders. After all, the officer convening the conference has usually made his plan after much hard work and juniors who suggest ways in which it can be improved do not always receive the acclaim they might expect. Monash saw himself not so much as the chief handing down the tablets of stone but as the man in overall charge of a great engineering project consulting with his most important subcontractors. Of a certainty he did not suffer fools, but any that there may once have been had long since vanished. His old Gallipoli brigadier, Cox, now Director of Military Intelligence at the War Office, says that he used to attend Monash's conferences whenever he could, simply as an academic exercise. It is a great tribute to the uninitiated Generals Glasgow and Lambert that they were in all respects ready to march on to their tapes within thirty-six hours.

If the battle of Chuignes had been fought at any other time or in any other circumstances, it would have been accounted a great and glorious victory. In August, 1918, it was just a two-division attack on a three-mile front which completely succeeded. Each objective fell as the timetable prescribed, twenty-one guns and more than three thousand prisoners were swept up. The casualties show that it was no bloodless walk-over, for the 1st Division lost 70 officers and 1,354 men killed and wounded while the 32nd, very much the junior partner, suffered 19 and 358. The reward was that the town of Bray on the north side of the Somme fell to the 3rd Division and the enemy began his withdrawal from the entire bend in the river.

These were not the only matters to demand the corps commander's undivided attention. 'Quinn the artist has been over again in France, and has been working here at the replica picture which is destined for you. It is not really a replica as he is practically painting a fresh picture, and it is very much better, in my opinion, than the one which he painted for the Commonwealth Parliament House. Longstaff is also going to pursue a similar course and paint an entirely fresh picture, and not a replica of the one he has painted for the Australian War Museum. He will also paint a third in a different pose for the Sydney National Gallery. It is very trying work indeed sitting for these artists. I can only give them from ten minutes to half an hour at a time, and it is an extremely tiring process.'

Albert, Albert of the Leaning Virgin (then, alas, no more, as a shell had finally destroyed her without bringing the war to an end), the town with ties of emotion to the British army second only to those of unconquered Ypres, fell to III Corps in the early hours of the 23rd, the day of Chuignes. The tonic effect of this was out of all proportion to the military value of a heap of rubble and hearts all along the front felt somehow lightened.

For Monash, the next target was the sister town of Peronne, eight miles away across the Somme. Peronne, too, was more than just another small French town. English soldiers had passed this way before when 443 years ago, almost to the day, Edward IV, in alliance with Charles the Bold, Duke of Burgundy, had encamped around it. In the fields around St Christ he had entered into the treaty with Louis XI which, for all practical purposes, had put an end to the Hundred Years War. Long after that bowman army had passed away, English soldiers were there again. Sir Walter Scott described it in *Quentin Durward*: 'Situated upon a deep river, in a flat country and surrounded by strong bulwarks and profound moats, [Peronne] was accounted in ancient as in modern times one of the strongest fortresses in France. Indeed, though lying on an exposed and warlike frontier it was never taken by an enemy but preserved the proud name of Peronne-la-Pucelle until the Duke of Wellington, a great destroyer of that sort of reputation, took the place in the memorable advance upon Paris in 1815.' Since her virginity had been once lost, Peronne had been regularly violated. Goeben took her by force in January, 1871, von Kluck had seized her again in 1914, until her release in May, 1917, and von der Marwitz had torn her from the protection of Sir Hubert Gough in March, 1918. Most of the population had then escaped to the west but those who remained were waiting anxiously for the sound of British bugles in her streets once more. This time, they would be blown by a kind of Englishman of which Duke Charles and his eternal and crafty enemy King Louis had never dreamt.

Rawlinson, however, acting on peremptory orders from Haig, had firmly forbidden any more battles for the time being. Monash found this extremely irksome for he was now filled with the lust for pursuit. Though he never said so, he plainly felt that Rawlinson was letting him down by not standing up to the chief and that he did not appreciate the golden opportunities immediately before him. The Australians were tired, of course, but they were far from being exhausted and nothing could be more galling than to see the Germans slipping away under their noses and taking all their impedimenta with them. The tanks had gone and the heavy guns were experiencing the usual difficulties of movement forward over roads that were both bad and choked with traffic, but much could be achieved at this time without their aid.

Monash read his orders carefully; they contained a paragraph of a purely routine kind which observed, without conspicuous originality, that 'Touch must be kept with the enemy'. Monash decided that he would interpret this in a manner that suited his own feelings and disposed his divisions for an immediate move forward. If this were to impel the enemy to speed up his withdrawal and to travel lighter than he might otherwise have done, then clearly it was the duty of the Australian corps, consonant with Rawlinson's commands, to tread on their coat tails. It was neither peaceful penetration nor a set-piece battle but rather something between the two. He placed four divisions in the line, each with one brigade forward and two in support, with orders to follow up any movement the enemy might make until the leading brigades had reached the limits of their endurance whereupon they would be rotated with the others which would have been following at a more leisurely pace. By this expedient, and on the assumption that they would meet no great resistance, he reckoned that he could maintain the impetus for twelve days while the other formation got some rest. Vigorous patrolling began all along the line and, when it revealed that many of the German positions had been abandoned, a regular general advance followed. Within three days, by 29 August, not an enemy soldier remained west of the Somme between Brie and Peronne who was not in the prisoner-of-war cage or on his way there.

The novel situation called for novel tactics and Monash provided them. In a reversion to eighteenth-century practice, he split up many of his field batteries and placed sections, two guns, under the direct orders of infantry battalion commanders; furthermore, he insisted that they carried with them 20 per cent of their ammunition in smoke shells. The gunners protested, for to a gunner a shell that did not lash the enemy with high explosive or shrapnel was a shell wasted. Monash, however, knew what he was doing. A few rounds of smoke usually served to blind the German machine-gunners and made it possible for his dexterous infantry to get to grips with them. The inventor remarked blandly that he expected this to bring about a change in gunnery school doctrine. By nightfall on the 29th the three divisions south of the river were looking down the gentle slopes that fringe it from points opposite Clery in the north, past Peronne to St Christ. Even more important was the fact that his parish now extended without interference well to the north where his old 3rd Division stood on a line from Curlu to a point beyond the last of the great bends.

The topography is of importance. At Peronne the river makes a sharp turn to the right and flowed directly across the path of the

Australian advance. It remains wide and swampy with its main course canalized and can only be crossed by two bridges, at Brie and St Christ. These had, of course, been destroyed with a thoroughness not achieved in the previous March. Here the importance of owning the east–west reaches became apparent, for it would be perfectly feasible to cross to the north bank and move on Peronne from that direction. All this had been obvious to Monash before the advance even began and every possible resource was already in use to repair the bridges on this stretch of the river while the divisions were contemplating the awesome remains of the old Somme battlefields and reckoning up the vast amount of booty abandoned by the Germans in their headlong withdrawal.

Peronne is dominated by a feature to the north, Mont St Quentin, and this had, by some means or another, to be seized. The heavy guns were still making their ponderous way forward aided by pioneers and more Chinese coolies who painstakingly filled in craters, carted roadstone and levelled out some sort of roadway. What remained of the tanks were still employed with Byng. The Diggers were now really tired and the German position was a strong one. The longer they were left in possession of it, the stronger it would become.

The battle for Mont St Quentin is the true measure of the greatness of John Monash as a general; if he were to fight it now, as every instinct told him he must, it meant throwing to the winds all those articles of faith about 'advancing under the greatest possible protection' and not exposing the soft bodies of men to the lead and steel of the defenders. It could only be attacked in the old way, by a soldiers' battle after the fashion of Oudenarde, where the highest commanders could hardly influence events at all and everything must be left to the individual private and subaltern to do what seemed best at the moment. It was obvious that such a fight, whatever its outcome, must present a very large bill for killed and wounded and in the Australian corps every casualty was more felt as a personal loss by the commander than could be the case with troops from more populous countries. Monash faced this knowledge and accepted the inevitable with the fortitude of Ulysses Grant. His plan, however, was inspired by another master of war of the same period. 'I am sure', he wrote, 'it will live to become a classic in military literature. It followed a swift turning movement at night, on the lines of some of Stonewall Jackson's sudden onslaughts, but, of course, on a very much larger scale.' There is another comparison that occurs; Monash, who made almost a fetish of sparing his men from needless exertion, was to drive his tired brigades as relentlessly as Napoleon had driven his troops over the Somosierra in pursuit of Moore; appeals for relief, this once, fell on deaf ears and were answered only with appeals to Australian pride. This touched the Diggers as nothing else could have done and men half-dead with fatigue returned to the charge again and again.

Monash took comfort, however, from the fact that he did not have to rely on any other troops to perform any task at all for him ('I had had some experience of the futility of relying too much upon the sympathetic action of flank corps') and that, come what might, it would be an all-Australian operation. This was more than mere nationalistic pride for in all probability there remained no body of troops in the entire army capable of carrying out the exacting task he was going to set them. The kernel of Monash's plan was speed, speed that would keep the pressure on his enemy maintained from beginning to end and that would permit him no moment in which to draw breath or to reorganize himself.

There was also a factor which gives the plan all the hallmarks of a Monash design. He had always fancied himself as a conjuror and, even if he fell a little short on the actual legerdemain, he appreciated the mystique of the art; the conjuror must force his audience to devote all his attention to something unimportant while the vital moves are being made. The unimportant thing here was the 32nd Division, which Monash ranked far below any of the others. Their job would be to demonstrate noisily and obviously along the river line on the north-south axis while the men who would do the bayonet work were slipped across as circumspectly as possible by the bridges available. First, however, there were certain decencies that had to be observed. By no stretching of language could the operation Monash had in mind be described as 'keeping touch with the enemy' and Rawlinson's blessing must be obtained. It happened that the army commander paid a routine visit to the Australian corps during the afternoon of 30 August. 'I have already referred to the pleasant and attractive personality of this distinguished soldier. His qualities of broad outlook, searching insight, great sagacity and strong determination, tempered by a wise restraint, never failed to impress me deeply... On this occasion he was pleased to be pleasantly satirical. "And so you think you're going to take Mont St Quentin with three battalions. What presumption! However, I don't think I ought to stop you. So, go ahead and try—and I wish you luck!" '

The 3rd, 2nd and 5th Divisions, in that order from north to south, were charged with the main task. The 3rd, being already north of the river, had no bridging problems and were ordered to make for the high ground north-east of Cléry and then on to the Bouchavesnes spur. The 2nd were to make for the bridge at Halle, right in the bend of the river with the object of storming Mont St Quentin with a proviso that, if the crossing proved impossible, they were to follow the 3rd by the footbridge at Ommiécourt and the recently repaired one at Feuilleres and press on with whatever could be got over with such limited means. The 5th was to go straight at Peronne, over the bridges if it could be done, but if not then by the same circuitous way as their neighbours. Their eventual object was the wooded spur to the east of the town. It will be seen at once that these orders are riddled with 'ifs' and 'buts' in a way that makes them appear almost indecently amateurish. The decisions that must be left to divisional and brigade commanders were of the utmost importance and any miscalculation by any one of them could precipitate a disaster worse than Fromelles. Monash, however, knew his men. Gellibrand, Rosenthal and Hobbs were commanders of great skill and experience; more to the point, they could be relied upon to help each other unselfishly, a thing that does not always happen with general officers. Even taking all this into account, however, Monash was risking everything, for, once the battle had started, he would have little control over events. It was the brigadiers, the battalion commanders and even lesser men who would have to plan and fight this battle and the essence of it would be speed. To describe in detail what happened during the next four days would be beyond the scope of this book; even Dr Bean, dutifully following every move of each formation as far as one man could do it, admits that the hundred pages of the Official History are inadequate for the purpose.

The 3rd Division did everything demanded of it and fought its way against fierce opposition to the heap of brick-rubble that had borne until recently the notice saying that 'This was Bouchavesnes'. The bridge at Ommiécourt, an obvious target, came under such a volume of fire that it could not be used and the 2nd Division was compelled to move back a mile and a half to the west and cross by a newly established one at Buscourt. As the 5th Division could find no bridge at all opposite Peronne itself, Monash ordered Hobbs to send his reserve brigade, the 14th, back to Buscourt also and, having crossed there, to move against the town from the north while the 15th Brigade kept up its efforts to find a crossing place. The 14th arrived at Buscourt simultaneously with the 7th Brigade of Rosenthal's division. His brigadier sensibly conceded right of way to the 14th who had a long fight ahead of them. The 6th Brigade, three weak battalions and a few machine-gunners, stormed the hill of Mont St Quentin against the toughest opposition the AIF had yet encountered. These were no exhausted conscripts but the Kaiser Franz, Kaiser Alexander and Kaiserin Augusta regiments of the Guard Corps. After bitter fighting the Mont passed into Australian hands on 1 September.

Thanks to the progress made in the north, it was not too difficult for 15th Brigade to scramble over a footbridge into a town almost empty of defenders. The only complication was a break in signal traffic when the brigadier, the fire-eating 'Pompey' Elliott, missed his footing and cascaded into the river. The battle had to wait whilst delighted signallers informed their friends that 'Pompey's fallen in the Somme'. The honours of the day went, above all, to Rosenthal and his men. Rawlinson spoke for the whole army: 'The capture of Mont St Quentin by the 2nd Division is a feat of arms worthy of the highest praise. The natural strength of the position is immense, and the tactical value of it, in reference to Peronne and the whole of the Somme defences, cannot be over-estimated. I am filled with admiration at the gallantry and surpassing daring of the 2nd Division in winning this important fortress and I congratulate them with all my heart.'

It had been a near-run thing and Monash had come near to biting off more than he could chew. He had told his generals before the battle began that he required their men to continue to the limit of human endurance and the cord had been stretched near to breaking. More than once he had had to reject pleas that the men were exhausted beyond words and could go no further; each time, with a harshness that he did not feel, he ordered them to keep going. In one battalion there was something very much like a mutiny by three platoons led by their officers, but an appeal to Australian pride set them stumbling forward again. This is the quintessence of true discipline, which the AIF never lacked whatever scrapes some of its members got into during the off-season. Their casualties totalled 3,047 (191 of them being officers), not counting a further 1,200 sustained by the 3rd Division during the earlier advance.

The taking of Peronne was the apogee of the many feats of the AIF. If one is tempted to criticize Monash by reason of the things that might have happened, he would be perfectly entitled to reply: 'But they did not happen, and I knew that they would not happen. The Australian Corps at this point of the war was an instrument so perfect that it could be trusted to carry out the task I gave it without undue risk. And that is what it did.' It demands great hardihood on the part of any man, more than half a century later, to assert that he knows better. Most of all, it proves beyond doubt that Monash was not a one-talent man. He was known already as a planner of set-pieces second to none but this was something utterly different; quite a number of generals, before and since, have mastered the composition of the battle-symphony but few could have produced an impromptu on this scale. Lee might have done it; Grant probably could not have done; Wellington achieved something like it at Vittoria but he kept the main battle under his own hand. If he had no other claim to consideration, Mont St Quentin assures John Monash of a place amongst the great captains. If Lieut-General the Hon Sir Frederick Stopford had possessed a tithe of his audacity the war might have been over long ago.

However, the long hard fight had put a strain upon the corps sufficient to keep it out of battle for some time. The 1st Division was enjoying a well-deserved rest in the lovely Somme valley around Chipilly, silent again now and reminiscent of a Claude landscape; the less fortunate 4th were billeted in and around the battered city of Amiens. The divisions that had been so mauled in the recent fighting needed rest and, above all, reinforcements before more could be expected of them and drafts were becoming smaller and smaller. Meantime there was much work for the engineers in rebuilding the railways needed to keep the corps supplied with the every-day essentials of life and to bring forward the lumbering heavy guns against the day when they would be needed again. All the indications were that the series of blows recently delivered by Byng's Third Army and now the unexpected side-swipe by the Australians whom their propaganda machine had assured them to be worn away almost to vanishing point were driving the Germans into the series of neglected fortifications known to them by the splendidly Wagnerian names of Wotan, Hunding, Freya, Hagen, Brunnhilde, Siegfried and the rest. The Allies knew it by the less romantic name of the Hindenburg Line but either would have suited Monash. He was well aware that the cycle ended with *Götterdammerung* and the twilight was beginning to close in. However, Valhalla would not be seized by a *coup-de-main* as Peronne had been and the old, sound method of playing with full orchestra rather than a series of woodwind solos was going to be the only way of ending the long concert.

Haig and Monash did not see exactly eye-to-eye on what should be the immediate consequence of the victory. Monash was all for pressing hard on the heels of the retreating Germans but, in order to carry this out, he would need a large body of fresh troops. Haig, while naturally delighted that the Australians had done it again, would not be diverted from his own grand design, worked out painstakingly with Foch, and his attention was turned to the fronts in the north where Currie's men, part of Horne's First Army, were smashing their way into the supposedly inexpugnable Drocourt-Queant Switch and Byng was lunging forward on Rawlinson's left.

Monash was left to watch impotently from the heights above Biaches and to observe the enemy withdrawal across the eight miles of undamaged country that lay between his new positions and the formidable Hindenburg defences. As the clouds of smoke from burning dumps ascended gently into the skies of high summer he had much work to do in improving the communications over the country behind him and in entertaining his guests. There were plenty of these 'Schlactenbummlers', as the Prussians had called them in 1870. Apart from Haig, his callers included Winston Churchill and Lord Milner, Ian Hay and Sir Arthur Conan Doyle, together with a profusion of artists, attachés and journalists. One feels that of all these Sir Arthur Conan Doyle must have been one of the most congenial; his strong Imperial feelings were well known and the creator of Sir Nigel Loring, Samkin Aylward and Hordle John would have felt himself thoroughly at home in the company of their dispersed descendants. Indeed, under steel helmets akin to those of the Black Prince's men and against a background of the changeless fields of France, they might have come from an illustration to Froissart.

Sir Arthur, for his part, found much of interest. He writes of Monash as 'an excellent soldier who had done really splendid work, especially since the advance began ... He showed that the long line of fighting Jews which began with Joshua still carries on. One of the Australian Divisional Generals, Rosenthal, was also a Jew, and the Head-quarters Staff was full of eagle-nosed, black-haired warriors.'[1] (Sir Arthur deceived himself, for Sir Charles Rosenthal was not a Jew but a Wesleyan Methodist of Scandinavian antecedents.) Though he went on to visit the French he would have found little of Brigadier Gerard in General Debeney.

Birdwood, still the nominal commander of the AIF, was also a frequent and welcome visitor. Monash had almost surpassed his old chief, for his corps, which had at one time numbered eight full divisions, was a force of a strength at least equal to the Fifth Army. Another old acquaintance was Godley, still commanding III Corps in Butler's absence, and now almost subordinate to Monash. Godley was not among the great captains, for Hankey, now

---

[1] Sir Arthur took the opportunity of addressing some twelve hundred Diggers and 'I ventured to remind them that 72% of the men engaged and 76% of the casualties were Englishmen of England'.

secretary to the Cabinet, says that he enjoyed the reputation of being no more than second-rate. Certainly, after Chipilly, Monash had no great opinion of the capacity of his corps. It is a pity that he had not known it six months earlier, for of the men who had fought so valiantly during the retreat little trace now remained beyond the same old names and flags.

During the lull Monash was by no means idle. 'There were medals and ribbons to be distributed to the gallant winners; addresses to be delivered; and the work of re-organizing and refitting the resting units to be supervised. Still farther in rear, demonstrations of new experiments in tactics or in weapons, or in mechanical warfare, had frequently to be attended for study and criticism.'

These last were of major importance. There would never again be another 8 August, for tanks and their crews were being destroyed at a greater rate than they could be replaced. Even in support of Byng's battles it had proved necessary to bring out obsolete Mark IVs and no more could the infantry expect to move out under cover of armour in great quantity. Those which remained must be preserved for the work which only tanks could do satisfactorily, the crushing of pathways through the vast belts of wire; but some other means must be devised from the tools available to put the infantry on to their objectives with the least possible loss on the way. The events of late 1917 had proved that the big gun was not the answer; aerial bombing, now a considerable factor since the new Handley Page machines could carry bombs weighing 1,600 lbs, was an improvement but accuracy depended entirely on weather conditions.

One weapon remained whose possibilities had, perhaps, not been exploited to the full. The Vickers machine-gun is no mere automatic rifle; firing from a tripod it sweeps a beaten zone at a range of one thousand yards which is long and narrow, one hundred and fifty yards by fifteen, and it can be directed by instruments which do away with the need for the gunner to see his target. Given a number of guns far more than used on previous occasions and reducing their consumption of ammunition by keeping the rate of fire to about two hundred rounds to the minute, it could be possible so to interlock these zones that nothing could live in a wide expanse of front. Monash put his machine-gunners, conspicuous amongst whom was the almost legendary Harry Murray, to work on the problem. Meantime he must pacify some of the exalted visitors who, since Corps HQ was now in small huts which had to double as offices and bed-chambers, did not feel that their dignity was sufficiently studied by the provision of a blanket and six feet of bare floor. When Corps HQ had been housed in palatial châteaux it had been fashionable to pay visits to 'the front'. Australian messes had always had the reputation for being a thought rough and ready when compared with the British ones but this was too much for some of the tourists. Monash bore their departure with composure.

It might be expedient to glance at the AIF on the eve of its last battles. The voluntary system had broken down and willing horses were being flogged to death. The officers were now nearly all a generation younger than the middle-aged men who had carried out the landing. All had come from the ranks and the boyish Australian colonels came probably nearer to Cromwell's ideal than any body of men since the New Model Army took the field: 'Plain, russet-coated captains who knew what they fought for and loved what they knew.' The men, though still excellent, were nonetheless becoming what would later be known as 'browned-off'. The principal reason for this was the lack of publicity given to their exploits or, even worse, their wrongful attribution to others. Certainly perusal of the account given in *The Times* of the Battle of Amiens would leave the reader unaware that any Australian troops had been engaged there at all. They were understandably bitter. The reasons behind it were not necessarily ignoble for the newspapers did not want to back up the German propaganda machine which was working hard to give the populations at home in Canada and Australia the impression that their men were being given all the hard and bloody work while the native English were spared. It would be hard to understand this from a hole in the ground around Morlancourt and there was often heard a grumble like, 'Whatever we do, they'll say they won the battle. Next time we'll let them win it.' Monash, in concert with 'Billy' Hughes, took the matter in hand. He approached every influential British newspaper and put the grievance squarely before them. The Australian, he explained, was a sportsman and he would refuse to play if his score was not displayed on the board. Bean says that the best of his men would have detested the analogy but it achieved its end. The tone of the newspapers changed immediately.

Hughes, unfortunately, would not be satisfied. Like others, he was beginning to understand the importance of the contributions made by the dominions and he had his eye, as a result, on a chair at the peace conference. It would be ungenerous to assert that he was influenced by future vote-catching considerations but the fact remains that it was at this point of the war that he suddenly began to interest himself in home leave for the Diggers and their preservation from casualties during the last round. Shipping, of course, was the factor that prevented the first part of the proposal from being carried out but, as a second best, Hughes began to insist that the AIF be taken out of the line by 15 October and thoroughly rested until the campaigns of 1919 demanded its return. Monash, aghast at the idea of giving up when victory seemed to be in sight, protested. Hughes told him quite bluntly that his job depended upon his carrying out the orders of his government. To Sir Henry Wilson he said that 'if the Belgian Government wants its troops withdrawn from the line it does not ask anyone's leave. It simply says they are to be withdrawn.' The King of Australia does not seem to have been consulted. Hughes assured Wilson that he intended to remain in London until the order had been executed.

For Monash it could not have happened at a worse moment. He had just been having a conversation with a German battalion commander in the cage at Abbeville during which he had been told, in reply to his enquiry why so many men had surrendered so readily, 'Well, you see, they are dreadfully afraid of the Australians. So they are of the tanks. But when they saw both of them coming at them together, they thought it was high time to throw up their hands.' Such an ascendancy had been won over their enemy and now there remained only a month in which to crown the work.

The order of battle had been rearranged; one of Godley's divisions, the 74th, whose device was the Broken Spur to indicate that they were dismounted Yeomanry, had come from Palestine, and they were allotted the area of the 3rd Australian Division. It was, in fact, already in III Corps area, for the drive up the Bouchavesnes Spur had taken Gellibrand out of his own area. The 32nd moved forward across the river, the 5th remained on their right and the 2nd was taken out for a well-deserved rest. The 3rd, however, had to be kept in the line for a few more days and so the formations stood, from north to south, in the order 3rd, 5th and 32nd each on a front of one brigade. Each division was given a squadron of light horse, who thus found an agreeable change from the dull and menial tasks of corps cavalry, and a body of cyclists. They both came in very useful for the purpose of maintaining touch with the enemy and saved the feet of the infantry. An inexorable pressure was kept up all along the line.

In the Australian tradition, frequent and vigorous patrolling continued and appreciable amounts of ground were stolen back from their occupiers. Monash had driven his men so hard that in one operation on 6 September the commander of 32nd Division felt himself obliged to interfere. As the Australian 6th Brigade arrived near Mont St Quentin in order to pass through the British 14th, their condition of utter exhaustion was so manifest that Lambert sought and obtained leave to finish the task with his own Englishmen and thus give the Diggers twenty-four hours' respite from fighting and marching. The Diggers must have been very tired indeed to have accepted so kindly an offer but they did and they were grateful. Dr Bean, who went everywhere and conversed with everybody, insists that Monash did not know as much as he believed about the state of his troops and he may well be right; obviously in the rarefied air of Corps HQ the commander would only rely upon what he was told from below — his concern with the next battle kept him far too busy to allow many excursions to see for himself — and no Australian subordinate general would say that his men were unequal to their task; certainly they told Monash bluntly that their men were tired beyond words but when he demanded one more effort they could hardly refuse. In truth things were so desperate in some formations that Pioneer battalions were doing duty as infantry and fighting their way towards the outposts of the Hindenburg Line shoulder to shoulder with the rest.

Like almost every other commander, Monash sometimes carried

optimism to extremes. However, by 8 September the line divisions had made such progress that they stood in a position a little northwest of St Quentin and within sight of belt upon belt of wire, some with the blue sheen of newness and some with the rust of two winters upon it, that proclaimed the presence of the German army's last and strongest bastion. Two days later the 1st and 4th Divisions, refreshed by their spell of summer sunshine in the Somme valley, took over from their sister formations. The 32nd left them to join a new corps, the IX, which moved into position on their right. Its commander was Lieut-General Braithwaite, his penance for Gallipoli completed; he might have been spared the irony of seeing attached to his new command the number which had been borne by Stopford's men at Suvla. However, there was something appropriate about the last fights of the AIF being neighboured by him and Godley, especially as there could now be no question as to the identity of the senior partner.

For the last few miles they had been moving over the wreckage of the old battlefields and their position was more or less that of the British support line of March, 1918. There would be no more cheap victories and a new set-piece was coming up.

It was worked out over a cup of tea at Australian Corps HQ by Rawlinson and his corps commanders. The task before them was nothing less than the breaking of the strongest fortified line ever built by man and defended by every modern weapon. Two years ago it would have been reckoned impossible, but the German army of 1918 was no longer, save for its machine-gunners and artillerymen, the force it had been in 1916. There was good ground for a quiet confidence in the outcome but, in the then state of Allied manpower, the job could not afford to be scamped.

When the German engineers had designed the works in 1916 they had naturally taken advantage of whatever existed already on the ground. The most useful artifact was the canal, in this part known by the name of St Quentin. It had been started in the middle of the eighteenth century with the object of producing an uninterrupted route from the Somme to the Scheldt, but in between lay the watershed of the Le Catelet plateau. The only possible means of joining the two river systems was by driving a tunnel underneath the

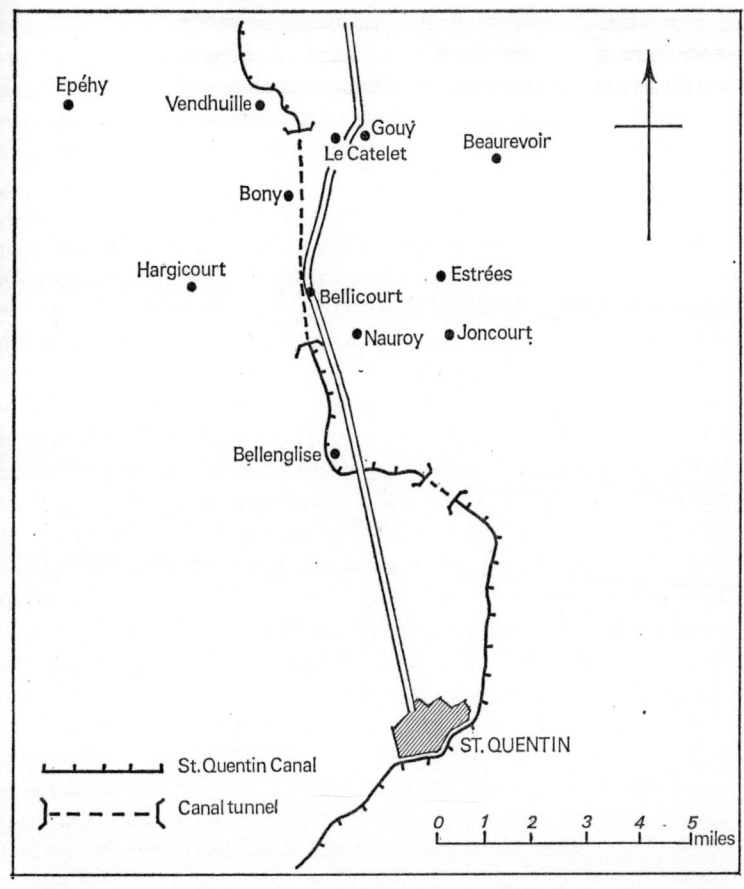

plateau, and the inadequate technical resources of Louis XV, coupled with his usual shortage of cash, had compelled him to abandon it. His successor, Napoleon I, had taken up the scheme again and his engineers had driven their shaft with such exquisite skill that, although it is more than six thousand yards long, from either end a pinpoint of light reveals the exit. Vendhuille marks the point where it emerges to the north and Bellenglise to the south. On top of the workings stand the villages of Bellicourt and, fortuitously, Bony. The existence of the tunnel was convenient in that it provided immense cover for men and installations but the absence here of the 'open cut' militated against its usefulness especially as a defence against tanks. The engineers, therefore, sited their main line of outposts a mile or so to the west and connected it to the tunnel by many and complicated passages and adits. Inside it, well lit by electricity, moored barges provided comfortable quarters, concrete dams were built at both ends and a movable wooden shutter concealed the whole from inquisitive eyes. The spoil from the original works had been brought to the surface through the many air-shafts and still lay in a bank along the top.

At the time of the conference, the line of the Australian corps was roughly four miles west of the outpost position (a misnomer, since additions during 1917 had made it as strong as the main one) and approached nearer to it in the south than in the north. Between the two lay the old British front line and this was to be the first objective. The second would be the former outpost line, half a mile further on, and there was included, in case it should be needed, a zone of exploitation. Monash described it as 'a normal advance with a normal very limited objective, a very simple form of advance'. He was equally plain that the final 'blue line' was 'a line for exploitation only ... it is not intended that a large body of troops should be detailed to capture this line'.

It was not going to be anything like a walk-over. The resistance had been perceptibly hardening for some time past and one Australian brigadier said later that the prospect had given him more anxiety than had any other operation. To add to Monash's difficulties, there were only eight tanks available for the whole corps and he had just received a cable from Birdwood. Hughes had scraped up the transport and 60 officers and 740 men, all 'originals', were to be sent off that instant for their leave. Inevitably, most would belong to the two divisions about to move into battle. Monash signalled that 'it was quite impossible in inadequate time to provide quota for embarkation' but Birdwood overruled him. The result was that the 1st and 4th Divisions had to lose more than five hundred of their best men. Battalions, already weak enough, were down to about 19 officers and 400 rifles. Many a British colonel would have felt this to be uncommonly strong but it was not so by

Australian standards. A reduction to three companies of three platoons was hurriedly carried out.

18 September is another of those dates that live on for ever in survivors' memories. Promptly at 5.20 am came the familiar aubade of the barrage; many experts thought it to be the heaviest they had ever heard, though it seemed to have an unusual timbre. This was not surprising; 256 Vickers guns opened up with a single roar, a sound never heard before or since, and kept up a steady lift three hundred yards ahead of the infantry. A German colonel said feelingly when it was all over 'the small arms fire was absolutely too terrible for words. There was nothing to be done but to crouch down in our trenches and wait for you to come and take us.' The other, less dramatic, novelty was the appearance of a number of dummy tanks which, though they lacked wire-crushing ability, had a moral effect as good as the real thing. The artillery start line was dead straight, the guns having been carefully trained beforehand by instruments, and, beginning two hundred yards ahead of the infantry, it moved relentlessly on in jumps of one hundred yards. It was of this advance that Monash wrote his sentence, already quoted, about the impossibility of set-piece plans (by inference, plans prepared by John Monash & Co) going wrong and the pointlessness of trying to describe the fighting. In this instance, he cannot be gainsaid, however pot-valiant the sentiment may sound as a generality. The battle commonly known by the name of one of the villages over which it swept, Hargicourt, went exactly as it had been planned. The old British front line was in Australian possession by 10 am. By the end of the day the entire Hindenburg outpost line along the fronts of both Divisions had gone the same way. Total casualties were less than one thousand whereas the prisoners exceeded that number more than fourfold.

After their relief the 1st and 4th Australian Divisions sloped arms, formed fours and marched out of history. They had fought their last battle and Hargicourt was a worthy climax to their unprecedented careers.

## CHAPTER THIRTEEN

## The Last Battle

THE marching away of these two veteran divisions created a serious difficulty for Monash. After Mont St Quentin he had tried to make some amends for his overtaxing of the 2nd Division by giving a firm promise that it would not be used again until the end of September and he could not renege on this even had he wished to do so. The 3rd and 5th also stood in need of rest though their case was not so strong as that of the 2nd. The result was that he had no troops at all with which to keep up the pressure in the way he judged to be essential. Monash took his problem to Rawlinson who, as usual, came up with an answer.

As a consequence of one of Haig's agreements with Foch and Pershing, there were two American divisions on their way to join Fourth Army; Rawlinson offered the use of them to the Australian corps and Monash accepted the gift with alacrity. Since Hamel and Chipilly he had felt an admiration for these troops which probably exceeded their real merits. People had naturally gone out of their way to praise the newcomers for their behaviour on those occasions and had been inclined to gloss over their many defects because of their fine spirit and willingness. Monash, who had had no opportunity of seeing these things for himself, did not realize how far their organization and individual skills lagged behind those of the more experienced formations and he began work on a plan which would have extended the best of the Australian formations to the limit.

The divisions concerned were the 27th from New York and the 30th from Tennessee, both made up almost entirely of National Guardsmen. They had spent about ten weeks in the rear areas of

Second Army to gain some experience but had never been seriously engaged. Major-General O'Ryan, commanding the New York men, however, had seen a good deal of war on the Western Front for he had been attached to the 29th Division during the autumn of 1917 and had watched the battles in the Salient under the expert guidance of Sir Beauvoir de L'Isle. He had also done a spell with the French army on the Chemin des Dames and had, deservedly, won the reputation of being a level-headed and teachable man.

The American army, thanks partly to its chivalrous conduct in rushing forward infantry and machine-gunners during the March retreat, got into serious straits with its supplies. It was entirely dependent upon the British and French armies for its guns, except for the platoon of 37 mm pop-guns that formed part of the battalion establishment, and also had to endure grave shortages of almost all war material. In consequence the two formations on the British front had been partially re-equipped with British weapons. The riflemen carried the short Lee-Enfield and the Lewis gun, the Stokes mortar appeared inside the battalions and the Vickers machine-gun replaced the Browning. Many men even had to endure the indignity of wearing British khaki, though their buttons still proudly bore the bald eagle and they retained their canvas gaiters. Monash noted that, in these, men could move through wire in half the time demanded by woollen puttees.

Their organization was quite different from that of the British. An American division was composed of two brigades, each of one regiment of three battalions. As their battalions numbered nearly one thousand men apiece, the total, on a count of heads, was double that of other divisions. They had, however, very limited technical arms and no artillery at all. A tank battalion, the 301st, was forming under Major Roger Harrison who was given forty-nine of the precious Mark Vs and a few light Renault two-man vehicles.

The most severe weakness of the Americans, however, was the shortage of regimental officers actually with their units. Very large numbers were absent on courses of all kinds and not nearly enough remained in the ranks to lead their platoons and companies in their first battle. When the time arrived for them to attack one battalion was commanded by the Judge Advocate who had insisted to O'Ryan that he had been an officer in the 106th Infantry before he took to the law and was allowed to have his way. He proved to be one of the best COs in the entire corps.

Before there could be any question of them taking on a major role, the Americans had to be taught many things, including the idiosyncratic brand of English spoken in the army, incomprehensible enough to a British civilian. Monash gave the task to Major-General Sinclair Maclagan who formed an Australian mission with advisers down to company level. 'It is not necessary to indulge in either a panegyric or a condemnation of these American divisions. Neither would be deserved nor appropriate. They showed a fine spirit, a keen desire to learn, magnificent individual bravery and splendid comradeship. But they were lacking in war experience, in training and in knowledge of technique. They had not yet learnt the virtues of unquestioning obedience, of punctuality, of quick initiative, of anticipating the next action. They were, many of them, unfamiliar with the weapons and instruments of fighting, with the numerous kinds of explosive materials or with the routine of preparing and promulgating clear orders. They seriously under-rated the necessity for a well-organized system of supply, particularly of food and water, to the battle troops. They hardly, as yet, appreciated the tactical expedients available for reducing losses in battle.' Nor were they allowed any time for improvement. Godley's corps, on the Australian left, had fallen short of the final line by about one thousand yards and Rawlinson wanted this made good before the main battle was joined. The Americans—correctly designated the II US Corps—arrived in the Australian sector on 22 and 23 September. Part of the 27th Division was locked in battle on the 27th.

On the afternoon of the 23rd Monash held his first conference with the American generals; General Read, the corps commander, modestly took a back seat and the two divisional commanders—O'Ryan and Lewis—with their staffs were the only participants.

The Australian advisers were deliberately excluded. Monash wanted the Americans to have the chance to make a name for themselves as Australia had had to do years before. Accounts of what took place differ. Monash reduced matters to the utmost simplicity. It was to be a perfectly straightforward trench-to-trench attack, from a straight line to a straight line for a distance of about one thousand yards 'under a dense artillery and machine-gun barrage and with the assistance of a large contingent of tanks'. A new wire-destroying instrument was to be used, the heavy artillery shell equipped with a fuse, the 106, which would explode the charge the moment it struck anything. This, experiments had shown, shattered wire without making any crater.

The knowledge that III Corps had made several unavailing efforts to secure the same ground did not weigh with Monash. The barrage maps for the artillery were already printing, based on a start line that the Americans were going to make available. These would need to be distributed at the larger conference held on the 26th, at which orders would be given for their part in the greatest, possibly the last, battles of the war and any last-minute adjustment to this would be an operation of the utmost difficulty and danger. He explained all this to the American generals. 'I began to realise that I was now confronted with quite a different proposition from that to which I had been accustomed... the exposition of the plan itself was brief and simple, but it elicited such a rain of questions that in the end I found myself compelled to embark upon a very detailed exposition of the fundamental principles of my battle practice. With blackboard and chalk, maps and diagrams, I had to speak for more than 3 hours in an endeavour to explain methods and reasons, mistakes and remedies, precautions, procedures and expedients.' O'Ryan, reading this some years later, expressed disagreement. No more than five or six questions were put because the disquisition to which Monash treated his hearers was so lucid and comprehensive that there remained nothing about which any of them needed to be better informed. Though the officers present had clearly profited from the experience, Monash had grave misgivings as to how much of it percolated down to the troops. The conference of the

26th, by far the biggest he had ever conducted, followed on much the same lines.

The morning of the 27th broke in rain. At the usual hour of 5.30 the three battalions which made up the 106th Infantry rose up out of their trenches and strode forward under cover of a barrage which included, for the first and last time, thirty thousand rounds of British-made mustard-gas shells. The concentration of smoke put down by nine field brigades was even heavier than usual and the Doughboys led by a dozen tanks disappeared into the murk. For a time encouraging reports began to come in and a few prisoners dribbled back. The signals became fewer and fewer until, at about 10.30, there arrived an ominous one saying that the situation was obscure: 'Chief trouble is shortage of officers forward. Some companies apparently have no officers at all.' This was the blunt truth. The twelve companies had contained between them no more than eighteen officers; their task was beyond the powers of any men and, before the day was out, all but one had become casualties. Patrols sent out into the summer dusk failed to find anything of the 106th and the only certainty was that the attack had failed. Somewhere in front of the start line for the battle of the 29th, exactly where the barrage was to begin, 2,000 American soldiers lay unaccounted for.

An instant and terrible decision was required. Either the barrage must be brought back to begin from a line in front of the present position of the attacking divisions, in which case it would fall on what was left of the 106th, or it must start as planned, a full one thousand yards too far in front to do any good. Discussion was brought to an end when an air observer's report (subsequently found to be wrong) was handed to Monash. American soldiers could be seen well into the Hindenburg Line. O'Ryan, naturally enough, was firm that he could not consent to the deliberate shelling of his own men.

Monash, horrified at the way things had turned out and wishing fervently that he had never agreed to the operation, went hot-foot to seek out Rawlinson. Could the army commander agree to the main attack being put back by twenty-four hours? Rawlinson was sympathetic but could not agree. Monash's corps was only a piece in the great battle. Such great issues were at stake that the timetable could not be disrupted at any cost. The most he could do was to release a few tanks from army reserve to give the main body of the 27th a better chance of covering the vulnerable one thousand yards before the guns opened up. At that moment Sir Douglas Haig called and found Monash 'in a state of despair'. This he strongly deprecated. The incident is awkwardly reminiscent of that bad moment at Sari Bair but, as on the former occasion, Monash seems to have shaken it off. He returned to his HQ and pronounced his orders. The barrage would continue as planned and Rawlinson's additional tanks must do their best to protect the New Yorkers during the first stage.

At the appointed hour on the morning of 29 September, thirty brigades of artillery, thirteen of them 'heavies', and battery upon battery of the big Newton mortars roared out in unison with the guns of the neighbouring corps. The entire First Army and the northern half of the Third were already on the offensive to the north and now they were being joined by Byng's southern half and the entire Fourth Army. Plumer's Second Army, in company with the Belgians, all under the command of the gallant King Albert, had lunged out the day before, Debeney's Frenchmen were striking out in co-ordination with Rawlinson and the Franco-American armies were on the move towards Rheims. While these great forces were shaking the pillars of Valhalla, General Franchet D'Esperey, far away in the Balkans, delivered his blow and the tradesmen's entrance swung slowly open. Twilight was thickening around the Nibelungs but there was plenty of fight left in them.

In the sector for which Sir John Monash was responsible plans began to break down at an early stage. O'Ryan's New Yorkers had been given a task which no troops in the world could have carried out. In addition to the long, unprotected approach march they were assigned objectives far more distant than anything attempted before by the most veteran troops. The intention was that the American divisions should advance under a barrage for about three thousand five hundred yards to a line which included the villages of Bellicourt (on top of the Tunnel), Nauroy,

Bony and Gouy. When they had accomplished this, an Australian division would leap-frog through each and move on, in open-warfare formation for a further four thousand yards to Joncourt, Estrées and Beaurevoir. A cavalry brigade would then be available for exploitation. All this was to be completed by 30 September. The American divisions, once the Australians had passed through, were to form defensive flanks to north and south while adjacent Corps moved forward. As it fell out these objectives were not taken until the morning of 5 October.

Only the briefest account of the battle is possible. The tanks sent to aid the 27th Division were caught in an old British minefield, laid by some unknown strategist in the previous year, and achieved little or nothing. The New Yorkers, coming under heavy fire and hopelessly lost in the smoke and mist, disintegrated into small parties, wandering aimlessly about the battlefield looking for somebody who could tell them what they ought to be doing. The Tennessee men on the right did rather better, though their task was less difficult, and got into Bellicourt even if their grip on the village was shaky.

The situation was saved by a wonderful feat of arms by British troops on the right. The 46th Division, Territorials from the Midlands, had been assigned the unenviable task of crossing the open-cut of the canal at Bellenglise where it runs deep and extends for about thirty yards. The 137th Brigade, on rafts, lifejackets from Channel packets and anything else that would float, stormed across it in the dawn mist and gained a strong bridgehead on the east bank. There has been no finer exploit in the long history of British arms; it took much of the weight off the 30th Division but the fact remained that Monash's meticulous plan had gone whistling down the wind. The first objective ought to have been taken by 9 o'clock with the Australians taking over at 11. Instead of that, messages were coming in after that hour saying that the Germans were counterattacking Bellicourt from the north, the 5th Division was hung up behind the 30th and the 3rd was digging in west of the Tunnel.

The crisis brought out all that was best in General Monash. He went instantly forward to find out things for himself and, having been satisfied that the accounts were basically true, he deliberately tore up the plan on which he had spent so long and formulated another. The information disclosed that his troops were now astride the Hindenburg Line, one division to the east and the other to the west. He held the southern entrance to the Tunnel but the Germans were still firmly in possession of the other. The weight of the attack must therefore be switched in direction, no longer from west to east but from south to north. Cables to his two commanders, Gellibrand and Hobbs, were cut and there was nothing for it but to produce written orders and send them by dispatch rider. Before this had been finished something happened that proclaims clearly the perfection which the Australian forces had attained. The two divisional generals had already sized up the situation for themselves, had met and decided to do exactly as Monash would have wished. Signals came in from each of them telling of what they had done before the written orders were even finished.

It has now become an entirely Australian battle though many parties of baffled Americans had attached themselves to the fourteen Digger battalions and fought manfully beside them. They were, however, a considerable embarrassment, for lack of knowledge of where they were made it impossible to use the powerful artillery that might otherwise have supported the infantry. Those that could be rounded up were withdrawn during the first night of the battle. In their place the 2nd Australian Division was brought back from its rest area around Peronne by bus and moved up in close support of the other two. From that time on the great attack became another soldier's battle, fought out by battalions and companies in a hundred disparate skirmishes. By nightfall on 1 October the entire Tunnel was in the Australian grip and the line ran west of Le Catelet and a little east of Estrées and Joncourt. Next day it was over and the enemy were in precipitate retreat to their last ditch known as the Beaurevoir Line.

Monash summed up the situation in his congratulatory message. 'Please convey to all commanders, staffs and troops of the 3rd and 5th Australian Divisions my sincere appreciation of and thanks for their fine work of the past 3 days. Confronted at the outset of the operations with a critical situation of great difficulty, and hampered by inability to make full use of our artillery resources, these divisions succeeded in completely overwhelming a stubborn defence in the most strongly fortified sector of the Western Front. This was due to the determination and resource of the leaders and the grit, endurance and fighting spirit of the troops. Nothing more praiseworthy has been done by Australian troops in this war.'

The 3rd and 5th Divisions followed the 1st and 4th away from the battlefield and into the books, their work done and their repute safe for all time. Their old friends the 32nd came back again to the corps.

The storming of the Hindenburg Line had shown Monash both at his best and at his worst. Bean has always been severe with him for deluding himself into believing that he knew more about the condition and morale of his men than the facts justified. He seems to have shared with Haig a readiness to believe that the Germans were cracking long before such thoughts were warranted. It is the less easy to comprehend in a man whose blood was the purest Polish and who might have been expected better to comprehend the strength of that brave and hardy people.

The use of the untrained American troops also was a grave error. It is entirely understandable that he wished them to have the chance to make a high name for themselves, as they would have done after more tuition, but it should have been plain after the first conference, if not before, that they were as yet totally unfit to discharge the heavy responsibility he placed upon them. It is greatly to their credit that they attempted the task at all and their courage can be judged from the fact that they endured more than five thousand casualties, about the same as the Australians at Fromelles. O'Ryan was magnanimous, describing the Australians as 'probably the most effective troops employed in the war by either side'.

The spectacle of a corps commander being rebuked by the commander-in-chief for giving way to despair (the account of the incident is given by Bean) is not an edifying one and the same writer has said, rather caustically, that it is just as well that Monash was never seriously tested by adversity. Nevertheless, the fact remains that, when all his plans had gone astray, he showed himself ready and able to make fresh ones on the spur of the moment and not to cling to the original idea. It is reminiscent of Wellington: 'They planned their campaigns just as you might make a splendid set of harness. It looks very well and answers very well until it gets broken and then you are done for. Now I made my campaigns of ropes. If anything went wrong, I tied a knot and went on.' There was no despair about Monash then.

All the same, one cannot help sometimes wondering whether his psychology was not on a par with his conjuring. It did, however, shine out on one occasion. A few days before the battle of Hargicourt a peremptory order had come that eight battalions must be disbanded because of the manpower shortage. When the luckless units were designated feeling ran so high that all but one staged what was a technical mutiny. They simply refused to disband, saying with one voice that they would rather go into their last battle and be wiped out than amalgamate with some inferior mob. Monash, wholly sympathetic, pleaded with Rawlinson who pleaded with Haig. Eventually the latter agreed to a fortnight's stay of execution and the AIF broke their section of the Hinbenburg Line under the numerals that they had come to love.

There were still some days to go before the expiration of Hughes's ultimatum. Only the 2nd Division and the two Americans now remained in the corps but some ground to the north had been handed over to the rugged 50th Division of North Country Territorials. It would be a pity to leave the Beaurevoir Line unbroken and to have once more to overcome the inertia of attacking a rested enemy. Between 2 and 4 October Monash directed his last battle in the course of which the 2nd Australian Division with no artillery but its own, and helped by what remained of the 5th Tank Brigade, fought their way through to Montbrehain. Three weak brigades took more than two thousand prisoners and at the end of the fight they stood on a line six miles to the east of the Bellicourt Tunnel with the Hindenburg Line behind them. It was a worthy climax to the battles fought by Australia in France and it was the last. On 5 October General Read, restored to the exercise of his command, took over what had been the Australian corps front and the 2nd Division in its turn marched away westwards. On the same day Prince Max of Baden, on behalf of the Imperial German Government, asked the President of the United States for an armistice. This did not, of course, mean that the war was over; another 125,000 casualties were to be incurred by the British armies alone during October and November and the last 'furphies' about going in for 'one more show' were very nearly true.

Monash was, in fact, on his way to Le Cateau and the 1st and 4th Divisions were making ready to move again when news of the armistice reached them. The AIF were more fortunate than the Canadians. The Canadian corps fought the last battle of the war and liberated the town of Mons, still heavy with memories of 1914. Sir Arthur Currie's reward was a savage attack made upon him in his own homeland by his political enemies who claimed that he had deliberately thrown away the lives of his soldiers in mounting a needless operation in order to satisfy his own vanity by claiming its capture. When he returned home his reception was glacial. Nine long years passed before a provincial newspaper had the courage to print openly what ill-wishers had been saying behind the general's back; he brought an action for libel and, at the famous trial which followed, he was completely vindicated.

Monash was criticized by Bean for something of the same reasons, the allegation being that Montbrehain should either not have been fought at all or that it should have been left to others. The charge, which did not have many supporters, was at least made in a spirit of honest appraisal free from spite and was never pressed very hard.

The Australian Imperial Force was not employed again and did not send troops to the army of occupation. In six months' fighting it had taken just under 30,000 prisoners and 338 guns. The amount of war material seized by the corps was vast beyond counting. One hundred and sixteen towns and villages of France had been restored to Frenchmen, every one of them after a fight of some kind, and four hundred square miles of country had been liberated. The five Australian divisions, with the British and American ones that had at various times belonged to the corps, had engaged thirty-nine divisions of the German army, some of them several times over. As a result of the hammering received at Australian hands at least six complete divisions had been disbanded. Monash worked it out that his corps had made up $9\frac{1}{2}$ per cent of the British forces on the Western Front and that their captures in prisoners, territory and guns averaged about 22 per cent of the seizures by the entire army. The price paid between 8 August and 5 October was 4,998 Australians killed or died of wounds, 16,166 wounded and a mere 79 missing. It comes out at about seventy casualties a day to each division; when one remembers that divisions occupied only in sedentary trench warfare reckoned on losing forty a day these victories cannot be said to have been excessively costly. The reason was not accidental. Scientific war scientifically waged costs far less than does the spectacular gallantry of the valiant but inexperienced. The Australian figures are more comparable with those of the 1940's than with other times between 1914 and 1918.

Much of the credit for all these things must go to the men at the head of affairs. Monash, thanks to his exceptional powers of mind and to the training he had undergone in earlier days, was a general of the new model. He was, perhaps, fortunate in that he began with little to unlearn and his ability to grasp the potentialities and the limitations of the new weapons of war that had appeared since 1914 surpassed that of most officers of his rank. Even Rawlinson began to doubt the value of the tank, and at the end of August he seriously considered the winding up of the corps. Monash never wavered; to him it was apparent that this was the genesis of a new fashion of war. The Mark V tank, twenty-seven tons in weight and powered by an engine of little over one hundred horsepower, was plainly only a beginning and the question as to what was its use demanded Faraday's counter-question 'Of what use is a baby?' The Mark VIII tank, which would have come into service in 1919, was as superior to the Mark V as that machine had been to the original 'Mother'. If the campaign of 1919 had been fought Monash would inevitably have played a very important part and possibly there would have been no campaign of 1940. Were the span of human life twice its allotted length, one can easily see Monash as a commander of the

Eighth Army in the Second War. The name of no other First War general of whom this could be said comes immediately to the mind. He was not an innovator, in the sense that he invented nothing; his talent was rather for developing the inventions of other men and demonstrating that they had the power to achieve results beyond the dreams of the creators. The machine-gun barrage was not a novelty but never was it carried to perfection until Monash took it in hand. The air-dropping of supplies was, no doubt, considered long before Hamel but it took an Australian officer, working under Monash's orders, to demonstrate that it could be done.

His greatest gift, however, was an extraordinary versatility. One who could discuss on terms of equality the building of harbours and railways with Weetman Pearson, the subtleties of the Beethoven symphonies with Klemperer, highly advanced chess with Bottvinik, sketching with Augustus John or the art of the pianist with Paderewski could hardly be expected to be narrowly trammelled when it came to war. A man of little more than average ability, given sufficient experience and a good staff, could compose a set-piece battle for a formation. It calls for skill and resolution far removed from the commonplace to design a battle like Mont St Quentin or to snatch victory from possible defeat as on 29 September, 1918.

Curiously enough, it was on the matter in which he most exercised his mind, the psychology of man management, in which he had the least success. His care for his men cannot be questioned but now and then he did things that jarred on them. A small instance was the business of the 3rd Division's hat brims, but a bigger one was the manner in which he tried to counter the feeling of being 'put upon' during the last months. Bean makes a fair point. The Diggers did not need nor want flattering banner headlines; their resentment would have vanished at once had they demonstrated to them the efforts of the people of the United Kingdom. Battalions of 17-year-olds waiting at Étaples for the birthdays that would send one more boy up the line; middle-aged bank managers, twice rejected for myopia, scraping through a not very exacting medical, coming joyously to France and being killed within twenty-four hours, the ships that were strangling the Central Powers by their blockade, the endless casualty lists in local newspapers, the food queues and the mobilization of the women of the country to do unheard of jobs. Told of these things by men whom they could trust, the Diggers would have dropped their sullenness at once. Monash never seems quite to have realized this. The contempt in which many Australian soldiers held most British troops, except the 7th and 46th Divisions, might have been mitigated by the knowledge that during the five weeks between the beginning of September and 9 October more than 200,000 men had fallen and that the breaking of the Hindenburg Line had cost 6,500 officers and 133,700 men. The propaganda claim that England was climbing to victory over a mountain of dominion corpses would not stand much examination.

It is not necessary to take too seriously his moments of despondency. They do no more than remind us that the man was human. The strain on the high commanders during the First World War greatly exceeded that imposed during the shorter periods of the Second—within ten years most of them were dead at early ages—and subsequent vigorous actions must expiate the crime of allowing private feelings to manifest themselves for an instant. If the test of greatness in a commander is his success in battle, there were few greater men than John Monash in the field when the cycle came to its end.

## CHAPTER FOURTEEN

# Australia Goes Home

In spite of all the straws that had been in the wind since early October, the war ended with a suddenness that caught most people unprepared. Monash, in common with most other generals, had been giving serious thought to the spring offensive of 1919 and he now found himself face to face with problems of an entirely different kind. As long ago as December, 1916, perhaps as a heartening exercise after the apparent failure of the Somme battles, an Empire Demobilization Committee had been set up. Its main concern was with the allocation of shipping to the members of the family who had sent their men to fight in France and all concerned were invited to inform the committee what policy they intended to adopt in dealing with the novel situation of returning millions of men to their homes and continuing their civilian education during the period that must elapse before this could be completed. The Australian government replied that it would notify its intentions as soon as it could but there the matter rested.

Birdwood, with the demise of his Fifth Army, came back into the saddle as commander-in-chief of the AIF with Brudenell White as his chief coadjutor. It was extremely awkward for them not to be able to tell their men of the principles to be adopted which would determine the speed of their release and they took their troubles to Hughes who was in London for the peace conference. White advised that in the AIF there was a man whose military achievements were matched by his considerable knowledge of the world outside the army and, as a result, Hughes invited Monash to accept the post of Director General of Repatriation and Demobilization, working from London.

It was a good deal to ask of a man who had not seen his family since December, 1914, for the general estimate was that the task would take all of a year to complete. Monash, however, accepted his duty without demur and at the end of November he was installed in offices at 54 Victoria Street charged with the execution of a formidable task for which there was no precedent. It is unfortunate at this point that his private papers remain private and his thoughts and his actions outside the public sphere have to be the subject of conjecture. It will be remembered that, early in 1917, he had seriously considered asking Lady Monash to join him in England but had rejected the idea as being too dangerous. With the war finished and the certainty that he would be in England for a long time, one may surmise that he might have now suggested that she come and join him. If indeed he did so, then Lady Monash must have found a reason for declining to make the journey. As will presently appear, she was quite unfit to travel but plainly she continued at pains not to let her husband know the reason why.

Naturally the greatest victory in all history was marked by celebrations and Monash was for a time at the apex of affairs. The Prince of Wales did a tour of duty as GSO2 at Australian Corps HQ and the honours showered down. The Croix de Guerre of France and the Order of the Crown of Belgium were added to Sir John's tally of decorations and he found himself moving in the most exalted company. At the finals of the British Empire Boxing Tournament 'while I was sitting in the Australian private box with a number of senior Australian officers, one of Prince Albert's equerries came into my box and told me that the Prince wanted me to come to him in the Royal box, which I did, and sat beside him for the remainder of the evening. With him was the Marquis of Milford Haven (formerly Prince Louis of Battenburg). Prince Albert is a real jolly boy, full of fun.' This was only the beginning.

'I should like to tell you something of the State Banquet last night at Buckingham Palace, to which I was invited. Apart from

the Royal Family, President and Mrs Wilson and their suite, the
members of the King's and Queen's Households, and the
Ambassadors, the guests numbered in all about 68 persons. It
was a very special privilege to be present, particularly in view of
the historic occasion ... I arrived at the Palace when about half
the guests had assembled in a spacious corridor leading to the
State Rooms, and there met for the first time the Marquis of
Crewe, Earl Reading (Sir Rufus Isaacs) and Lady Reading, Lord
Milner ... Sir Derek Keppel and the Archbishop of Canterbury
... we were conducted singly each by an officer of the Household, with his wand of office, into the White drawing room, where
the Royal Household, consisting of the King, Queen, Princes
Henry and George, Princesses Mary, Christian and Patricia, and
the Duke of Connaught were assembled. There was no formal
announcement of names. Each guest was first welcomed by the
King, and by him presented to President Wilson, who stood on his
right; then welcomed by the Queen, and presented to Mrs Wilson.
When each guest had passed, he was ushered along a brilliantly
lighted corridor, full of beautiful paintings, into the Banquet
Hall, which was a blaze of splendour such as, I imagine, has
seldom been seen before. In size it was about as wide and half as
long as the Ball Room of our Government House in Melbourne;
richly decorated in white and gold, with 6 great crystal electroliers
spreading a magnificent illumination. At one end was the dais
and Throne (which remained unoccupied throughout the evening)
and at the other end an organ gallery, accommodating the band of
the Royal Regiment of Artillery. The whole corridor and the whole
of the Banqueting Hall were lined on all sides with bearded Yeomen
of the Guard, in their traditional Tudor black, gold and crimson,
standing at attention, with their pikes and halberds, throughout
the whole banquet. In addition all the table attendants were in the
Royal livery, scarlet and gold, there being one to each guest,
standing stiffly to attention behind his chair. The chairs were
crimson damask with white and gold frames. The Royal gold plate
had been brought from Windsor Castle, and made a most
amazingly magnificent display. The table appointments, including
plates, knife-handles, forks, spoons, salt-cellars, flower-bowls,

vases and dishes were all of solid gold, highly polished and brilliantly scintillating. Each flower-bowl was a beautiful specimen of delicate modelling, and most of them were large and imposing. The flowers throughout were scarlet and crimson, comprising chiefly azaleas and ranunculi. Around 3 sides of the hall were displayed great high trophies of the remainder of the Royal gold plate, trays, dishes, vases and salvers, each most exquisitely modelled and chased, and each specially illuminated by concealed electric globes so that their polished surfaces reflected a blaze of golden light in all directions. On the walls were also 3 of the famous Royal Tapestries. Except the small handful of naval and military officers, the guests were in evening dress (not Court dress) all wearing the stars and ribbons of their orders and miniatures of their badges. The ladies were in full evening toilette, with diamond coronets and necklaces. As soon as all the guests had taken their appointed places at the table, which was arranged in one great horse-shoe, the Royal party entered, ushered in by the Officers of the Household, walking backwards and waving their hands. The President led in the Queen, and the King followed with Mrs Wilson, and then came the rest of the Royal family. As the small procession entered the Hall the band played a fanfare, followed by 'The Star-Spangled Banner' and 'God Save the King'. It was a most impressive and historic moment . . . I had on my right Rudyard Kipling; and beyond him Sir Joseph Thomson (President of the Royal Society), and on my left Lord Burnham (proprietor of the *Daily Telegraph*), whom I had entertained at my headquarters in France last September, and beyond him Sir Henry Wilson. Opposite to me were Louis Botha, J. S. Sargent (the painter) and Winston Churchill. The meal passed amid a loud buzz of conversation and laughter and without restraint of any kind . . . Cigars and cigarettes were served at the table, but the ladies did not leave alone, being conducted by their cavaliers straight into the Red Drawing Room, all the guests following. All the men smoked there and coffee was served . . . I had just 5 minutes with the King and the President; but over 10 minutes with the Queen, who talked about her son now at Australian Corps Headquarters, and was most enthusiastic in praise of Australia and her soldiers, many of whom she had met at

Windsor Castle... the Queen wore cloth of gold and many magnificent diamonds, especially on the corsage, including the Koh-i-Noor and the great Cullinan.'

Less magnificent but, in its own way, no less impressive was the farewell dinner to the AIF at the Connaught Rooms. The Prince of Wales was there together with Birdwood, 'Light Horse Harry' Chauvel and a figure from the past, Ian Hamilton. Modestly in the background was a future Governor-General, Major R. G. Casey.

The repatriation and demobilization of 180,000 men, however, was a task that left little enough time for leisure. From the start, Monash applied himself to it with enthusiasm. Nothing was going to be too good for his Diggers and, since they could not all be sent home at once, each would be given every possible opportunity to train for the civilian career of his choice. It presented some difficulty with two of the more exotic characters who desired instruction in deep-sea diving and wild-beast training. Monash inherited an education scheme devised some time before but, though good, it was not sufficient. Until the government could make up its mind about the method of bringing home its men he could only tinker with the scheme.

Opinion was divided. A strong school of thought wanted to bring home complete battalions or even brigades and give them the heroes welcome that the Americans were affording to their Doughboys. It was soon made clear that, although obviously attractive in many ways, such a plan would wreak appalling injustice on individuals. 'Billy' Hughes agreed that 'first in, first out' was the only possible method. Australian industry was not in the same case as that in Britain and it could manage perfectly well for another year without invidious tests being made for what the jargon of the hour called 'pivotal men'. It was not until the end of the year that the government agreed, though with some inevitable modifications. The colourless return of anonymous drafts was overcome with Monash ingenuity. Each division was ordered to reorganize itself in groups of one thousand men, that being the approximate capacity of a train and a ship. Each should, so far as possible, be officered as would be a battalion, the whole being of the same precedence for going home. It did not matter from what arms of the service the men came but they must have a band; so the AIF was able to march through the streets of home as formed bodies even though they were not in the old units. It was a great deal better than just arriving with a party of details belonging to nobody. He himself took time off from his desk, to lead the AIF contingent on the Anzac Day triumphal march through the City of London. For the first and probably the last time, the old walls gave back the brazen proclamation that 'Australia Will Be There' as the tall men in faded green uniform and slouch hats marched proudly to Guildhall through crowds of cheering Londoners. None, indeed, needed reminding that Australia had been there and that her deeds would not soon be forgotten.

Those who remained were kept in good spirits by the invention of 'Extra Military Employment'. This meant that everybody was free to profit from whatever facilities were available though remaining, technically, a soldier. Oxford and Cambridge opened their doors as widely as they could to all who had a mind to enter them; farms and factories welcomed Diggers and readily initiated them into their mysteries. Even the trade unions, suspicious as always of anything they did not understand, gave some sort of help. Australian soldiers went to Denmark to study the pig, to Yorkshire to see what happened to their wool at the other end, a school for training surveyors was opened at Southampton and an Agricultural Training College at Sutton Veney Camp. Excellent schools were set up by Australian education officers with all the British aid for which they asked, together with the Corps Central School at the mouth of the Somme. Here men were prepared for, and subjected to, a matriculation examination acceptable to the universities of Australia in addition to receiving instruction in the subjects needed for the civil service and professional examinations. The transfiguration of the AIF from being one of the toughest fighting formations on the Western Front into a vast technical college-cum-university was one of the most valuable services that Monash and his many helpers could have rendered their country. Not only did it improve the chances of the returning soldier of getting a worthy job, it provided Australia with a pool of extremely useful citizens; it also avoided the very considerable amount of mischief into which many would undoubtedly have got themselves if they had been sentenced to month after month of boredom. The credit must be divided amongst many people, but always at the heart of it, making the most important decisions, was John Monash. One who worked with him remembered that he was frequently being told at his conferences that something or other could not be done. 'But, gentlemen, it can,' was the invariable answer. It was nearly always so.

It was during this period that Sir John wrote his book *The Australian Victories in France* which was submitted as the thesis upon which his old university conferred on him the Doctorate of Engineering. He is said to have written it in thirty days and this may well be true. It is a most un-Monash piece of work, bearing all the signs of having been written in haste and not very carefully checked. Dates and names are frequently wrong, and the whole tone is that of a piece of unashamed propaganda. For example, writing about the aftermath of Hamel (p. 45), we are told that 'it was the first offensive operation on any substantial scale that had been fought by any of the Allies since the previous autumn. Its effect was electric, and it stimulated many men to the realization that the enemy was after all, not invulnerable ... It marked the termination, once for all, of the purely defensive attitude of the British front. It incited in many quarters an examination of the possibilities of offensive action on similar lines by similar means — a changed attitude of mind, which bore a rich harvest only a very few weeks later.' Nobody would seek to deny that the battle had been an important one, well deserving the staff pamphlet that described the methods employed for the benefit of other formations. But it was not the first move in the counter-offensive; that honour must go to the French army which, in the sector commanded by Mangin, had struck the first blow on 11 June and it had been preceded also by the attack of the First Army at Nieppe on the 28th. It is also hard to accept that, had Hamel never been fought, Mangin would not have made his attack towards Soissons on 18 July. Monash, however, was firmly persuaded of the correctness of his statement, for he had written home on 8 November that 'there is no doubt at all that it was the success of this battle which induced Marshal Foch to undertake a counter-blow on 18 July, which had the effect of arresting the German rush on Paris'. The book also conveys the impression that, after the writer had assumed command, nothing but success attended Australian arms. The 10th Brigade had failed badly in the attack on Etinehem on 10 August, largely as a result of the brigadier misunderstanding his orders; according to Monash, all that happened was that 'a sudden onslaught by a flight of enemy bombing planes threw the head of the 10th Brigade column into confusion and its Brigadier was killed'. He can seldom resist the opportunity of a dig at III Corps, particularly during the period of Godley's command, and one is tempted to wonder whether his relations with the 'fine, dapper little chap' were as good as they had been at the beginning of their acquaintance.

Now and then there is a palpable lapse of memory; writing of the sudden demand by the War Office on the eve of Hargicourt that six thousand men with four years' service were to be granted six months home leave and to be held in readiness to entrain at forty-eight hours' notice, he writes (p. 247) that 'I could not, obviously, take up any attitude which would postpone the well-earned furlough of these veterans; nor had I the smallest inclination to do so'. Yet his signal in reply asserted, with reason, that it was 'quite impossible'. It was Birdwood's message that 'it would be wrong to miss this opportunity and allow the ship to sail empty' that secured their departure.

Monash also, very understandably, shared the popular error about the fate of the US 106th Regiment on 27 September. The legend was, and still is, that the gallant New Yorkers pressed vigorously on into the Hindenburg Line, failed to mop up the enemy in the Tunnels and that these emerged as a kind of lethal sandwich-filling between the Americans and the Australians. In fact, few, if any, of the 106th got anywhere near the Hindenburg Line. Under-officered and over-extended, they made very little headway before breaking up into small parties many of which were swept up during the main assault.

However, one must remember the purpose of the book. Australia in 1914 was a group of six colonies, recently united but uncertain of its position in the world; by 1919, thanks entirely to the valour and skill of her soldiers, Australia had become a real power. Lacking a Washington or a War of Independence, she had no earlier experiences or personalities that would quicken the heartbeats of the most fervent patriot. The events of the last four years had changed all that and the Australian citizen now had the right to chuck a chest as much as any man and more than most. If the story of how this was achieved is a little imperfect it can be written down to the proper pride of the author.

By the autumn of 1919 the work of John Monash the general was done and he sailed at last for home with a GCMG added to his decorations. When he disembarked at Melbourne on Boxing Day he was received by a great and enthusiastic crowd. Lady Monash was not on the quayside to greet him. Her health had not been too robust during the years before the war but she had made light of it. What she had never told her husband was that before the year 1914 had run out, her doctors had diagnosed that she was suffering from cancer. With consummate courage, at least the equal of that which had gained many a Digger his Victoria Cross, she had concealed the dreadful truth from her husband and kept up her flow of chatty and inquisitive letters with no hint that anything serious might be wrong with her. On 27 February, 1920, having maintained strength enough to see her husband home victorious and laden with honour, this very gallant lady died at the early age of fifty. A state governorship might well be a real possibility, but what would be the point of it now? Sir John's grief must be left to the imagination.

## CHAPTER FIFTEEN

## Back to Concrete

Sir John, strengthened by an ancient faith, bore his bereavement with fortitude. He was not yet 55 and by all the ordinary canons of experience he should have many years of working life left to him. The question of how he could best employ them did not present itself with any obvious answer. The small forces that Australia might be expected to maintain in peacetime offered no scope to his talents; Chauvel was appointed inspector-general and, although he accepted a seat on the committee formed to advise on the future shape of the forces and also on the Commonwealth Council of Defence, Monash had come to the end of his military career.

Long ago he had said firmly that nothing would induce him to become a paid servant of the state but the premise upon which he had based his assertion was no longer valid. The man who had been honoured with the friendship of his King and who had walked on terms of equality with the great men of the world could hardly be expected to go back to practise a profession and disappear into a private station. Somewhere there must be useful work for him to do in the development of the new and greater Australia. He had the advantage of being without enemies in the political field and so would be spared the fates of Haig and Currie. The latter, having been studiously ignored by his government for some time, was offered no public situation of any kind; eventually he considered himself fortunate to be offered the post of Principal of McGill University through the good offices of friends. His debts remained. Monash was, at least, now free from anxiety on that score. Some of the great war leaders achieved their hearts' desires while others, for no obvious reason, did not.

Rawlinson went to India as commander-in-chief and died almost literally in the saddle—he had just finished a hard game of polo at the age of 65—and Byng became Governor-General of Canada. Birdwood, however, never received the appointment that he had so coveted (and many would say deserved); the governorship-general of Australia was never offered to him. All touch between the Australian corps and the King's vice-gerent was not, however, lost for ever; in the flickering candlelight in the Château de Montigny during that March night when Major-General Monash was reporting to VII Corps HQ that his 3rd Division was coming up to plug the hole, General Congreve's Chief-of-Staff, Brigadier-General Hore-Ruthven VC, had been present. Under his later style of Lord Gowrie, he became governor of South Australia and governor-general of the Commonwealth throughout the Second War.

Monash, one may imagine, spent a good part of the year 1920 in organizing his enormous collection of records and papers; the 'In' messages which came to him during the attack on the Hindenburg Line alone amounted to thirty closely typed pages. Then, in his own words, he 'went back to concrete'. The expression is a modest one for what actually happened was this. The city of Melbourne was growing fast and its demands for electric power far exceeded supply. All the necessary fuel had to be imported at great cost. It was known that there existed large supplies of brown coal at Yallourn, one hundred and twenty miles away, and a commission had been set up to investigate its possibilities. The chairman, Sir Thomas Lyle, and the other members were all appointed on a part-time footing and, by 1920, it was plain that something much less leisurely was urgently needed if Melbourne was not to grind to a halt for lack of power. The man at the head would need to be an experienced engineer who could handle men of all degrees, from labourers to cabinet ministers, and enforce his will on them all. It was not difficult for the State Electricity Commission to find such a man.

In October, 1920, Sir John Monash was appointed general manager of the State Electricity Scheme at a salary more than twice as great as that of the head of any of the Departments of

State. A few months later he became its first chairman. Here was the task to which he could bring that massive intellect, that lucidity of thought and exposition which had done his country such good service in war; it was employment in every way worthy of his gifts and position and it provided the anodyne he needed. His prodigious energy made itself felt at once; in 1921 the brown coal, buried for countless ages, was uncovered and work began on winning it. Swimming against the tide of anti-German feeling, he insisted on the hiring of experts from the Ruhr, about the only place in the world where the problems peculiar to brown coal (which is entirely different from the black variety) were understood. The powerhouse began to rise, one hundred and twenty miles of railway was cut through the forest and the transmission line went through. In three years the first electric energy from the project reached the city, though even before that Sir John had been driven to an expedient. Melbourne could not wait that long and, at Sir John's instigation, the railways department was pressed into service to help out. Their power house at Newport was increased in size and for a time Melbourne received its power by courtesy of the railway.

The work did not stop there. Australia was moving at such a pace that even a second power-house at Yallourn was not enough. Sir John bent his mind to sources other than coal. The result was the great hydro-electric stations in the Rubicon district; the coal deposits proved to be more extensive than the demands of electricity supply needed and they could not be permitted to lie idle. Sir John experimented with coal briquettes. The experiment succeeded and a large new industry came into being.

Things did not always run smoothly. In the early days of the Electricity Commission strident voices both in politics and the press demanded to know why results did not appear more quickly. Sir John decided that the time had come for another conference; he was given the unprecedented privilege of addressing Parliament on the subject. The critics went meekly away deflated.

Sir Robert Menzies, speaking at the Monash Commemoration Service on 11 April, 1965, gave a personal recollection. '[He] has a secure position in the industrial development of this State. His work for the Electricity Commission, his utter command of it, his lively capacity for telling politicians where they "got off" and where they "got on" contributed so much to the ultimate development of the Electricity Commission, now spreading or spread all over the State of Victoria that I'm perfectly certain that in that field alone he would never be forgotten.' Sir Robert went on to tell a story that perfectly describes Monash in his latter years. At the time, Sir Robert was Junior Honorary Minister in the McPherson government. 'Up came a proposal from the Electricity Commission, from Sir John himself, about some extension, about some trifling expenditure of a million pounds or something of that kind, which was, in those days, quite a lot of money. And we rejected it, it was knocked out by the chairman ... Sir John put his hat on ... arrived at the outer doors of the Cabinet Room and, if I know anything about him, demanded admittance ... the Premier, that most delightful and amiable of men, Sir William McPherson, said "Oh, yes, bring him in", and he came in and we all stood up instinctively, we all stood up, we were all in the presence of a man we knew was a greater man than we would ever be ... He looked around towards the Premier and he said "Well, Mr Premier, I gather that the Cabinet has rejected my proposal." "Well, yes, yes, I think that's right, Sir John." "Well", he said, "that can only be because they've utterly failed to understand it. I will now explain it." And he sat there, with that rock-like look, and he explained it, and one by one we shrivelled in our places, one by one we became convinced, or, at any rate, felt we were convinced, of the error of our ways. And for half an hour he went on; he explained the thing step by step. And we were left silent ... And that settled it, there was no more, not another word came out and so Sir John said, looking at the Premier, "Well, sir, I take it that your decision is reversed. Indeed, anticipating your approval of my proposal, and so that there will be no delay, I have brought with me (and he pulled it out of his breast pocket) the Order-in-Council that will be necessary for this purpose." And he passed it around and it was signed, and he went out.'

Sir John's horizon was not limited by coal and electricity. In 1923 he became chancellor of his old university and he did not regard the post as a sinecure. He was chairman of the commission appointed in the same year to enquire into the strike of the police and in all probability the associations of the Monash name had much to do with a settlement being reached. He took a lively interest also in the question of the future of the Jewish people. In 1918 he had met Arthur Balfour and it is reasonable to suppose that a topic so obviously of mutual interest as the declaration would have formed a large part of their conversation; he gave his support to the aspirations of Zion—his Sam Browne belt by some means found its way to a kibbutz where it is still preserved—and they named a grove of woodland after him. If a different posting had been made in 1916, Chauvel might have gone to France and Jerusalem might have been delivered from the Ottoman Empire by a Jewish general.

His main interest, however, was still in matters that touched the army. Cutlack, once his intelligence officer and later the editor of his *War Letters*, says that he 'lamented the decay of Australian national defences however plausible the political reasons for retrenchment'. He was one of the assessors who chose the design of Victoria's war memorial, the Shrine of Remembrance, and he led the Anzac Day parade every year of his life. In 1930 he was promoted to the rank of general, on the reserve list, the first of his countrymen to achieve the rank. (His old Chief-of-Staff, Blamey, was to become the first Australian field-marshal.) In his later years, while keeping up with his beloved music, chess and sketching, he found his interests insufficiently wide and became a keen amateur astronomer.

The war and the shock which followed it had, however, taken a heavy toll of his powers and in his last years he aged fast. On 8 October, 1931, after a short illness, John Monash died. Four battalions of slouch-hatted infantry, six squadrons of Light Horse and a great multitude of Diggers escorted his coffin through lines of sorrowing Victorians from the Parliament House, where he had lain in state, to the Jewish section of Brighton Cemetery. The inscription on his tombstone appears both in English and in Hebrew.

## CHAPTER SIXTEEN

# Envoi

To assess John Monash as a military commander it is necessary to take into account not only what actually happened but what the near future might have held. It was well within the bounds of possibility that the German army, falling back on its reserves of men and munitions and with an almost intact artillery and machine-gun corps, might have clung on to some sort of winter line even if it had been on the Rhine itself. Had that happened, the campaign of 1919 would have been something radically different from anything that had previously happened and new men would have come to the fore. Lloyd George might well have achieved his ambition of bringing down the commander-in-chief and a very interesting situation would have developed. It is doubtful whether any of the existing army commanders would have had much enthusiasm for accepting the seat made vacant by political assassination; Sir Henry Wilson would undoubtedly have fancied his chances but the army could not be expected to welcome the arrival of a man whose only field command had been at the head of a corps two years previously and whose tenure even of that had demonstrated his unfitness for preferment. Also, with the power of Britain and France on the wane and that of the United States growing daily, the man chosen would have to be a general with whom Pershing could work. There is no name that immediately springs to the mind. Monash would certainly have continued on his upward course. In all but name he was already an army commander — the title could hardly be denied to the man who had under him four times as many troops as had Wellington at Waterloo — and he would for a certainty have been given this extra status. Whether, as some have suggested, he might have achieved the supreme office is another matter but undoubtedly he possessed the capacity for it.

He was, above all things, the first twentieth-century general, a man with petrol in his veins and a computer in his head. All the other high commanders, one feels, were men who regarded Western Front conditions as something alien and freakish, to be jettisoned as soon as possible. They rather resemble sea officers who, after a lifetime in sail, are put in command of great liners; they learn the technique of steam but it does not come naturally and they have no wish to sign on for a second voyage. Even Sir Henry Rawlinson when translated to India seemed quite content to put the clock back to 1913; admittedly in the post-war world it would have been difficult to have acted otherwise, for neither the British nor the Indian army was likely to have to fight in France again, but the process did not seem to cause him any heart-burning. When, with the advancing years, men like Montgomery-Massingberd, who had been his Chief-of-Staff at Fourth Army, and Deverell, who was a successful corps commander, achieved the heights of CIGS they remained men of 1918.

To Monash this would have been as unthinkable as the reversion to pick and shovel engineering after having had the use of compressed-air and mechanical tools. His colleagues would more naturally have been the Swintons and the Trenchards, men of the same mechanical bent as himself, and a place would certainly have been found for the redoubtable 'Boney' Fuller. He had himself written that the Mark V tank was as different from the earlier models as the magazine rifle from the Brown Bess and, with the introduction of the Mark VIII, a better tank than any with which the British army went to war in 1939, a doctrine of armoured warfare in which the tank would have become the new queen of the battlefield would certainly have emerged during the winter of waiting. The anachronistic cavalry corps, with its enormous demands for forage, would have disappeared in short order and the men so released would have found their hoof-picks beaten into spanners. From the practical point of view and ignoring all considerations of politics, nationality or seniority, it is difficult to see any general who could have been considered equally well equipped to lead such an army. But it never happened; whether in the long run the world was better off with the events as they occurred or whether a spring blitzkreig which would have killed any legend about an undefeated army having been stabbed in the back might have led to happier times than we have known is an interesting but profitless thought.

Certainly Monash was lucky in that he held no great command at the beginning. His dictum about the desirability of 'Feeding your troops on victory' has much to commend it but it would have sounded rather hollow to Sir John French or Sir Ian Hamilton. He came to his high office as Montgomery came to the Eighth Army, at a time when it really was an army with adequacies of men and equipment which enabled the commander to achieve the victories they deserved. In spite of his Hamel assertion that once a plan has been made no departure from it can be permitted, he demonstrated a flexibility of mind that takes him out of the ordinary ruck of good, sound men. Péronne, which defied all his own principles, was probably his best battle. He had neither tanks nor heavy artillery and his men were tired; he did not know how or where he was going to get his divisions across the Somme but he did know that time was not his friend. Every hour he allowed to the German would have to be paid for with lives when the attack eventually went in against an enemy that much stronger, fresher and better prepared to receive it. Speed and surprise were the only factors in his favour and, as Lord Fisher had said of his battle-cruisers, 'Speed is armour'. His decision to attack as he did with such a delegation of executive authority was in all probability based more on instinct than analytical reasoning; but the instinct was sound and a great battle was won.

His judgments of men are interesting, for in them one can see Monash's view of himself. Rosenthal is 'an egregious optimist, incapable of recognizing the possibility of failure. That is why he invariably succeeded in all that he undertook'; Maclagan, on the other hand, 'was pessimistic. But that was not because he looked for difficulties, but because he preferred to recognize and face all the difficulties there were.' Gellibrand was 'a man of interesting personality, more a philosopher and student than a man of action.

His great personal bravery and his high sense of duty compensated in a great measure for some tendency to uncertainty in executive action.' Talbot Hobbs 'succeeded fully as the commander of a division by his sound common sense and his sane attitude towards every problem that confronted him'. Blamey gets an unqualified confidential report. 'A man of inexhaustible industry . . . nothing was ever too much trouble . . . I was able to lean on him in times of trouble, stress and difficulty, to a degree that was an inexpressible comfort to me.' For good measure, '[He was] a staff college graduate, but not on that account a pedant.' But Rosenthal was the man he most admired.

The greatest contribution to his corp's victories was undoubtedly made before the battles began. Whenever the whistle blew and the Diggers moved out into the open they always found it comforting to know that, no matter what might lie ahead, things behind would be properly done. Hot food would reach them except on very rare occasions, a man's need for water would not be forgotten and, when out of the line, everything that could be done to make life decent and tolerable would be done. The crime rate in the 3rd Division had always been far lower than in the others and this can hardly have been accidental.

Britain and the Britains across the seas have produced many generals of many different characteristics. Never, before or since, has a man emerged whose tenure of high command lasted for no more than four months and whose battles extended over no more than sixty miles but who has left a name of such power. Australia has wisely petrified it for future generations. In 1950 a fine statue of the general, mounted and accoutred, was placed in the Domain Gardens of his beloved city of Melbourne and, twelve years later, his name was given to the new university at Clayton. His country, by an accident of history that cannot be called unhappy, has no great names of founding fathers. In the terrible years of the second decade of this century Australia grew into the full strength of independent manhood: John Monash can fairly claim to have been one of the godfathers.

# NOTES ON SOURCES

The early history of the Monash family in Poland is examined in an article by Rabbi Brasch in the *Journal of the Royal Australian Historical Society* for 1959. This also contains the text of the letter on p. 189. The same *Journal* in its March, 1970, number publishes an excellent article on the general by Dr A. D. Spaull, Lecturer in History at Monash University. Two articles by Major E. W. O. Perry entitled respectively 'Monash: The Biographer's Dilemma' (*The Australian Quarterly*, March, 1961) and 'The Military Life of Sir John Monash' are also essential reading.

Amongst the most important papers are 'The Inaugural Monash Memorial Oration' by his son-in-law, Dr Gershom Bennett, reported in the *Australian Jewish Herald* for 11 October, 1936. The contents are much criticized by Major Perry. Sir George Pearce's speech on the general's death is reported in Hansard for 14 October, 1931. The comments of Sir Robert Menzies are contained in the speech which he delivered on 11 April, 1965, at the unveiling of Sir John's statue in Melbourne and which he has kindly placed at my disposal. The paper on 'The Digger Tradition' to which reference is made appears under that name in *Meanjin*, V, 24, 1965, under the authorship of Dr. G Serle, also of Monash University. There is much that remains well worth reading in *Aussie*, the Australian soldiers' newspaper and comments on the Digger also appear from time to time in *Stars and Stripes*, which performed the same office for the Americans. The English periodicals, including *Punch*, have regrettably little to say, except for a short poem about the Digger, written during the Gallipoli campaign and based on a casual remark by an unknown British officer, entitled 'The Bravest Thing God Ever Made'.

The number of books which are relevant and helpful is small but includes the following.

*The Official History of Australia in the War of 1914–1918.* 12 vols. edited (and largely written) by Dr C. E. W. Bean. Angus & Robertson, Sydney.

*The War Letters of General Monash* (ed. F. M. Cutlack). Angus & Robertson, 1935.

*The Australian Victories in France.* Monash. Angus & Robertson, 1936.

## NOTE ON SOURCES

*The Australians: Their Final Campaign.* Cutlack. Angus & Robertson.
*Canada's Hundred Days.* J. F. B. Livesay. Thomas Allen, Toronto, 1919.
*To Seize the Victory.* John Swettenham. Ryerson Press, Toronto, 1965.
*The Story of the 27th Division.* O'Ryan. New York, 1921.
*The Story of the Fourth Army.* Montgomery. Hodder & Stoughton, 1922.
*Gallipoli.* Alan Moorhead. Hamish Hamilton, 1956.
*Suvla.* Robert Rhodes James.
*Gallipoli Diary.* Sir Ian Hamilton. Arnold, 1920.
*Gallipoli Memories.* Compton MacKenzie. Cassell, 1929.
*The Uncensored Dardanelles.* E. Ashmead-Bartlett. Hutchinson, 1928.
*The World Crisis.* W. S. Churchill. Odhams Press, 1939.
*Douglas Haig. The Educated Soldier.* John Terraine. Cassell, 1965.
*Amiens 1918.* Gregory Blaxland. Muller, 1969.
*Soldier From the Wars Returning.* C. E. Carrington. 1969.

There are a number of books of personal experience by returned Diggers but, while all are interesting, I have found none that add anything useful. A short biography by Mr Vernon E. Northwood was published by the State Electricity Commission originally as a magazine article in 1950 and in more permanent form in 1961.

# INDEX

Abdel Rahman Bair, 115 et seq.
Aghyl Dere, 110 et seq.
Alexander, Rabbi (ancestor), 15
Albert, HRH Prince (HM King George VI), 277
Allanson, Major C. J. L., 118 et seq.
Allenby of Megiddo, F. M., Viscount 156
Amade, General Albert D', 65–71
Anderson Street Bridge, 24, 56
Anthoine, General, 169
Anzac Cove, 81
Aspinall, Colonel Cecil (later Brig.-Gen. C. Aspinall-Oglander), 121

Balfour, Lord ('A. J. B.'), 288
Baldwin, Brig.-Gen. A. H., 125
Barlett, Ellis Ashmead, 100
Bean, Dr C. E. W., 53, 87, 118, 124, 143, 170, 197, 201, 203, 223, 257, 270, 272
Beaurevoir Line, 269
Bertangles, Chateau de, 223, 237
Birdwood, F. M., Viscount, 53, 57, 59, 63, 72, 80, 83, 87, 89, 94, 98, 101, 103, 105, 107, 110, 131, 135, 142, 144, 151, 156, 185, 189, 190, 200–1, 206, 208, 223, 253, 260, 276
Blamey, F. M., Sir Thomas, 45, 208, 210, 212–3, 230
Botha, General Louis, 45, 279
Boully, Princesse, 156
Braithwaite, Lieut.-Gen. Sir Walter, 162, 258
Braund, Lieut Col. G. F., 82, et seq.
Breslau, 15
Bridges, General Sir William, 32, 33, 41, 45, 75, 94, 101–3
Broodseinde, 170, 173 et seq.
Brooke, Rupert, 39 (mtd.), 67

Bullecourt, 162, 209
Buller, General Sir Redvers, 108, 115
Burnage, Lieut-Col, 91–2
Butler, General Sir Richard, 172, 228, 233
Byng of Vimy, General Viscount, 108, 191, 237

Cannan, Brig.-Gen., J. H., 117, 192
Carden, Vice-Adml Sir Sackville, 58
Carrington, Capt. C. E., 176
Casey, Major R. G. (later Lord Casey), 45, 103
Cerisy, 227
Charlton, Air Cdre. L. E. O., 238
Charteris, Brig.-Gen. John, 178
Chauvel, General Sir Harry, 103, 142, 148, 185, 201, 230, 285
Chichester, Maj.-Gen., 156
Chipilly, 194, 227–8, 233, 252
Chunuk Bair, 110 et seq.
Chuignes, battle of, 243–4
Churchill, Sir Winston, 57, 87, 129 140, 237, 253
Clemenceau, Georges, 220, 238
Concert parties, 186 et seq.
Congreve, Lieut-Gen. Sir Walter, V.C., 191, 193 et seq., 208
Connaught, HRH Prince Arthur of, 163
Cook, Sir Joseph, 38
Courage, Brig.-Gen., 212–16
Courtney's Post, 81 et seq.
Cox, Maj.-Gen., E. W., 112, 123, 136, 141, 157, 243
Cummings, Brig.-Gen., 192–3
Currie, Lieut.Gen. Sir Arthur, 200–201, 223, 225, 226–8, 240, 248, 272
Cussen, Sir Leo, 22

Deakin, Alfred, 30–1
Debeney, General, 203, 213, 223, 241
Dering, Major Sir Henry, 153, 161
Dixon, Douglas, 74
Djemal Pasha, 50–1, 93
Douglas of Kirtleside, AM, Lord, 239
Doullens, 191–2
Doyle, Sir Arthur Conan, 253
Duntroon Military College, 32, 45

Electricity Commission, Victoria State, 286 et seq.
Elles, Gen. Sir Hugh, 238
Elliott, Maj.-Gen. H. E., 250
Enver Pasha, 57
Esperey, Marshal Franchet D', 267
Essad Pasha, 78
Eureka Stockade, 29
Ewart, Lieut-Gen. Sir Spencer, 108
Essad Pasha, 78
Ewart, Lieut-Gen. Sir Spencer, 108

Farmar, Col, 171
Fisher, Sir Andrew, 134
Fisher, Adml of the Fleet Lord, 128
Foch, Marshal Ferdinand, 191, 222, 237, 239, 241
Forrest, Sir John, 38
French, FM Sir John, 33, 108, 139, 148
Fromelles, 124, 148, 150, 152
Furphy, Mr, 47

Gellibrand, Maj.-Gen. Sir John, 34, 134, 212, 249, 257, 269
George, Lloyd, see Lloyd George
Gibson, John, 105
Glasfurd, Maj.-Gen. Sir Douglas, 34
Glasgow, Maj.-Gen. Sir Thomas, 34, 242–3
Godley, General Sir Alexander, 40, 53–6, 59, 81–3, 89, 99, 101, 110, 116, 123, 142, 156, 174, 185, 190, 238, 253
Goering, Reichsmarshall Hermann, 239
Goldstein, Major, 20

Gough, General Sir Hubert, 148, 162, 167, 169, 178, 188, 190, 200, 245
Gowrie, Lord, VC, 286

Haig, FM Earl, 141, 145–6, 148, 152, 155, 156, 167, 169, 177, 190–1, 200–1, 235–7, 252, 267
Haking, Lieut-Gen. Sir R., 151
Haldane, R. B. (later Lord Haldane of Cloan), 30
Haldane, Lieut-Gen. Sir A., 204
Hamel, battle of, 212
Hamilton, General Sir Ian, 63–7, 69–71, 78–80, 85, 100–1, 108, 110, 120–1, 125, 128, 130, 280
Hammersley, Maj.-Gen. F., 114, 121
Hankey, Lord, 254
Hare, Brig.-Gen., 72–4
Hargicourt, battle of, 261
Harington, General Sir Charles, 163–6, 174
Harrison, Major Roger, 263
'Hay, Ian' (Maj.-Gen. J. H. Beith), 144
Herbert, Lieut-Col. Hon. Aubrey, 98 et seq.
Hindenburg Line, 221, 252
Hobbs, Maj.-Gen. Sir Talbot, 157, 201, 249, 269
Holmes, Maj.-Gen. W., 157
Horne, General Sir Robert, 191
Hughes, Sir Sam, 39, 226
Hughes, W. M., 30, 134, 183, 211, 215, 255–6, 260, 276, 277
Hunter-Weston, General Sir Aylmer, 72, 81, 102, 204, 206
Hutton, General Sir Edward, 41, 203

Jacob, FM Sir Claude, 204
Jellicoe, Adml. of the Fleet Lord, 177
Jerilderie, NSW, 17
Jess, Colonel Carl, 46, 191

Kavanagh, Lieut-Gen. Sir C., 238
Kelly, Ned, 16
Kemal, Mustafa, 69, 79, 83, 86, 93
Kiggell, Lieut.-Gen. Sir Lancelot, 172, 228

# INDEX

King George V, HM, 154, 220, 239, 275–9
Kipling, Rudyard, 279
Kitchener of Khartum, FM Earl, 30–1, 57, 59, 63–4, 70, 108, 122, 129, 137, 142
Kressenstein, Oberst Kress von, 51–52
Kronstadt, 58
Krotoschin, 15, 27

La Grange, Baronne Ernest de, 156
Lambert, Maj.-Gen. T. S., 242–3, 257
Laurier, Sir Wilfred, 37
Lawrence, Lieut-Gen. Sir Herbert, 136, 216, 237
Legge, Lieut-Gen. J. G., 103–4, 148, 157
Lewis, Maj.-Gen. E. M., 264
Lihons, battle of, 236
Limpus, Adml, A. H., 58
L'Isle, General Sir Beauvoir de, 263
Lithgow factory, 35
Lloyd George, Earl, 57, 128, 170, 178
Lotbiniere, Col Joly de, 95–6
Loutit, Lieut-Col N. M., 79
Ludendorff, General Erich von, 221
Lyle, Sir Thomas, 286

M'Cay, Maj.-Gen. Hon. J. W., 25, 44, 84, 101, 104, 136, 141, 148, 152, 157, 200
McGlinn, Col J. P., 46
Mackenzie, Sir Compton, 67, 98
Maclagan, Maj.-Gen. Sir E. G. Sinclair, 44, 65, 75, 212, 233, 264
Maclaurin, Col H. L., 44, 84–5
Mahon, Lieut-Gen. Sir Brian, 108
Malone, Col W. G., 96, 106, 128
Martin & Monasch, 16
Mary, HM Queen, 279–80
Melba, Dame Nellie, 24
Melbourne Harbour Trust, 22
Menzies, Rt Hon. Sir Robert, 22, 224, 287
Merris, 143
Messines, battle of, 165 et seq.
Meyer, Dr Felix, 158
Millen, Senator, 38

Mitchell, David, 24
Monasch, Bar-Lobel (grandfather), 15, 27
Monasch, Bertha (nee Manasse, mother), 16
Monash, Bertha (daughter), 22, 26
Monasch, Louis (father), 15 et seq
Monash, Louise (sister), 16
Monash, Mathilde (sister), 16
Monash, General Sir John: ancestry in Poland, 15; birth at Melbourne, June 1865, 16; early life and education, 17–18; extra-mural activities and interests, 19; begins career as an engineer and joins the Militia, 19–21; marriage and birth of daughter, 21–2; enters private practice as civil engineer, 22–4, tours Europe in 1910, 26; promoted Colonel and given command of infantry brigade, 27; appointed Chief Censor, 45; assumes command of 4 Brigade and embarks for Egypt, 46–9, in Egypt, 50–5; sails for Gallipoli, 66; lands at Anzac Cove, 81; experiences in the peninsula, 83–112; promoted Brig.-Gen., 104; the attack on Sari Bair, 123–6; the evacuation, 130–1; in Egypt Jan–May 1916, 133–42; sails for France and commands brigade near Armentieres, 143–8; takes command of 3rd Div. at Larkhill, July 1916, 148; Royal review, 154–5; meets Haig, 155; on psychology, 158; his meticulous habits, 159–60; meeting with Plumer and battle of Messines, 163–6; at Windmill Ridge and Broodseinde, 169–77; Passchendaele, 179–80; his views on battle, 180–2; KCB, 187; writes of hopes of State governorship, 188; with 3rd Division in March retreat, Villers–Bretonneux, 206; his attitude contrasted with Birdwood, 207; succeeds Birdwood in command of Australian Corps, 31 May 1918, 208; attempts to

Monash, General Sir John:—*cont.*
have him removed, 211–12; battle of Hamel, 212–9; his position secured and prepares for battle of Amiens, 222–32; Australian Corps part in battle, 233–6; conference with Haig, Foch, Clemenceau *et al.* Villers–Bretonneux, 237–8; knighted by King, 239; battle of Chuignes, 243–4; circumvents Rawlinson's prohibition of further attacks, 245; Australian Corps storms Mont St Quentin and takes Peronne, 246–51; perfects machine-gun barrage, 255; battle of Hargicourt, 261; Australians and Americans penetrate Hindenburg Line, 263–9; his qualities assessed, 273–274; Director-General of Repatriation, 277; at Buckingham Palace, 277–80; returns home and death of Lady Monash, 284; his work with electricity, coal, etc., 287–8; his death on 9 October 1931, 289

Monash, Victoria, 87, 127, 155, 172, 177, 186, 277, 284
Monier Pipe Co., 24
Monro, General Sir Charles, 129
Montbrehain, battle of, 270
Mont St Quentin, battle of, 247 et seq.
Moore, Sir John (mtd.), 130, 248
Morland, Lieut-Gen. Sir Thomas, 192
Mouquet Farm, battle, 157
Munro, David & Co., 19
Murdoch, Sir Keith, 189, 202–3
Murray, Lieut-Col. Harry, 255
Murray, General Sir Archibald, 139–40

Nicholas, Grand Duke of Russia, 57
Nicholson, Lord, 128
Nivelle, General Robert, 162, 166
Nobel, Alfred, 58

O'Ryan, Maj.-Gen. J. F., 263–6, 270
Overton, Major P. J., 110, 116

Park, Air Chief Marshal Sir Keith, 239
Passchendaele, 178 et seq.
Pearce, Sir George, 25, 30, 134
Peronne, 242, 244, et seq.
Pershing, General of the Army, John J., 197, 215, 220
Petain, Marshal Philippe, 177, 230
Plugge's Plateau, 83 et seq.
Plumer of Messines, FM Viscount, 145–6, 163–9, 174, 185, 191
Poincare, President Raymond, 191
Polygon Wood, 170
Pope, Col H., 91, 118, 137
Pope's Hill, 81 et seq.
Pozieres, 152

Quinn's Post, 81 et seq., 105

Rawlinson of Trent, General Lord, 108, 146, 185, 191, 200, 214, 215, 220, 222–8, 235, 237, 238, 242, 245, 249, 250, 266, 286
Read, Maj.-Gen. G. W., 215, 270
Reed, Brig.-Gen. H. L., VC, 109
Richtofen, Rittmeister Manfred von, 205
Robeck, Vice-Admiral Sir John de, 121
Robertson, FM Lord, 34, 140
Romani, battle of (mtd.), 53
Roosevelt, Theodore (mtd.), 26
Rosenhain, Dr, 155
Rosenthal, Maj.-Gen. Sir Charles, 83–4, 87, 195, 206, 249, 250, 253
Russell's Top, 81 et seq.

St Quentin, 258
Sanders, General Liman von, 65, 69, 78, 83, 98
Sari Bair, 107, 120, 125–6
Sarikamish, battle of, 57
Scotch College, 18
Sherriff, R. C., 233
Slim, FM Viscount, 123, 140, 149
Smyth, Brig.-Gen., 157
Stettin, 16, 27
Stevenson, R. L., 43
Stopford, Lieut-Gen. Hon. Sir Frederick, 108, 113–4, 120–1

# INDEX

Tanks, 198, 209, 273
Thursby, Vice-Adml, 80
Tilney, Lieut-Col L. E., 92
Trotman, Gen. Sir C., R.M.L.I., 94

University, Melbourne, 18
University, Monash, 293

Vaire Wood, 217 et seq.
Varley, Lieut, 167
Vaughan, Maj.-Gen. John, 193
Venizelos, Eleutherios (mtd.), 63
Villers-Bretonneux, 195, 206
Vimy Ridge, 162-3

Wales, HRH The Prince of (King Edward VIII), 137, 141, 277, 280
Walker, Maj.-Gen. Sir H. B., 83, 104, 157, 174, 201
Wanliss, Lieut-Col D. S., 147
Wavell, FM Earl, 50, 52, 56
Wellington, FM Arthur, Duke of (mtd.), 158, 207, 251, 271
Wet, Christian de, 45
White, General Sir C. B. B., 33-6, 130, 135, 148, 151, 152, 169, 201-3, 208, 212, 276
Willmer, Major, 114, 122
Wilson, FM Sir Henry, 34, 40-1, 237, 257, 279
Wilson, President Woodrow, 278
Winant, J. G., 239
Windmill Ridge, 167-9
Wolfe-Murray, General Sir James, 140
'Wozzer', First battle of the, 60
Wylie, Col Doughty, VC, 74
Wytschaete, 165

Ypres, 169 et seq.
Ypres, Earl of, *see* French, Sir John

Zonnebeke, 176, 182

ARMIES, BRITISH
First, 235, 252, 267
Second, 18, 145, 146, 163, 167, 170, 176, 212, 219, 223, 267
Third, 146, 156, 191-193, 196, 237, 252, 267
Fourth, 146, 233, 235, 236, 250, 262, 267
Fifth, 162, 167, 169, 190-4, 196, 200
Army, Belgian, 267

ARMIES, FRENCH
First, 169, 203, 212-13, 223, 242
Third, 192
Tenth, 220

ARMIES, GERMAN
Second, 192

ARMY CORPS
I Anzac, 70, 139, 140, 142, 145, 152, 162, 165, 169
II Anzac, 139, 142, 157, 163, 169, 173, 174, 179, 185
Australian Army Corps, 12, 13, 190, 206-9, 211, 234, 242, 243, 257, 258, 260, 271, 273

*British*
Cavalry Corps, 238
IInd, 204
IIIrd, 224, 228, 233, 238, 244, 257, 264-5
VIth, 204
VIIth, 151, 191, 195
VIIIth, 204
IXth, 258
Xth, 192
XXIInd, 190
Canadian Corps, 163, 183, 200, 223, 238, 272

*French*
XXXIst, 223, 229
Portuguese Corps, 191

*United States*
IInd, 214, 264, 271

DIVISIONS
*Australian*
1st: 49, 54, 55, 78, 83, 103, 104, 139,

144, 152, 170, 174, 190, 196, 223, 226, 242, 244, 252, 258, 260, 261
2nd: 53, 104–5, 139, 144, 146, 152, 157, 170, 174, 190, 212, 216, 231, 249–50, 262, 269, 271
3rd: 12, 136, 147–8, 150, 153–5, 157–158, 161, 164, 167, 174, 176, 177–9, 180–1, 185, 190, 191–5, 204, 207, 210, 212, 216, 231, 246, 249, 250, 256, 257, 262, 270
4th: 136, 139, 141–3, 152, 157, 163, 170, 173, 190–1, 194–5, 212, 220, 231, 232, 258, 260–1
5th: 136, 139, 142, 151, 157, 170, 173, 190, 201, 231, 232, 249, 250, 257, 262, 270
New Zealand Division, 53, 134, 173, 174, 176, 180–2, 190

*British*
Royal Naval, 57, 70, 85
1st Cavalry, 192
4th, 174
5th, 175
7th, 174, 177, 204, 275
8th, 206
9th (Scottish), 192, 195
11th (Irish), 108, 114, 174
13th, 110–1
18th (Eastern), 228
29th, 59, 63, 64, 70, 75, 85, 140, 162, 174, 263
31st, 140
32nd, 242–4, 248, 257–8, 270
35th (Bantam), 141, 192, 194–5
37th, 175
42nd (East Lancashire), 59, 72, 101, 140
46th (North Midland), 269, 275
48th (South Midland), 174
50th (Northumbrian), 271
54th (East Anglian), 126
58th (London), 228
61st (South Midland), 151, 195
62nd (West Riding), 162
66th, 180
74th (Yeomanry), 256

*United States*
27th (New York), 263–4, 267, 271
30th (Tennessee), 263, 271
33rd (Illinois), 214

*German*
3rd and 4th Bavarian, 165
13th, 195

*Turkish*
5th, 69
7th, 69, 83
9th, 78
10th, 52
19th, 59, 78
25th, 52

BRIGADES
*Australian*
Light Horse Bde, 41
1st, 44, 78, 84
2nd, 44, 78, 84
3rd, 44, 65, 75, 78, 84, 101
4th, 46–7, 52–4, 66, 81, 83–4, 89, 92, 119–20, 122–6, 131, 137, 146
5th, 134
6th, 257
7th, 250
9th, 195, 206
10th, 283
12th, 134
13th, 27, 134
14th, 250
15th, 250

*British*
14th, 257
38th, 125
39th, 123
137th, 268
4th Tank, 233
5th Tank, 213, 271

*Indian*
29th, 110 et seq, 116–7, 123

*New Zealand*
N.Z. Mounted Rifles Bde, 112, 115
N.Z. Infantry Bde, 83, 112
*South African Brigade*, 192

# INDEX

REGIMENTS, BATTALIONS AND CORPS
*Australian*
Victorian Rifles, 19, 25
North Melbourne Battery, 20, 23
3rd Victorian Coy, Garrison Artillery, 25
Intelligence Corps, 25, 27
Psychology Corps, 159
AIF Infantry Battlions:
10th, 79
11th, 84
12th, 84, 87
13th, 82, 84, 90-2
14th, 84-7
15th, 81-4, 90, 92, 117
16th, 81, 90-3, 117
36th, 195
37th, 166
41st, 234

*British*
Royal Marine Light Infantry:
Portsmouth Bn, 92
Plymouth Bn, 71-3
Chatham Bn, 86-7
Deal Bn, 86-7, 92
Nelson Bn, RND, 86-7, 89, 92

REGIMENTS IN THE ORDER IN WHICH THEY APPEAR IN THE TEXT
King's Own Scottish Borderers, 71, 73
Royal Dublin Fusiliers, 72-3
Munster Fusiliers, 72-3
Hampshire Regiment, 72
Royal Inniskilling Fusiliers, 73
Border Regiment, 73
South Wales Borderers, 73
XX The Lancashire Fusiliers, 74
Worcestershire Regiment, 74
Essex Regiment, 74, 162
Royal Warwickshire Regiment, 122, 176
Gloucestershire Regiment, 122
King's Own Regiment (Lancaster), 123
Royal East Kent Yeomanry, 153
Gordon Highlanders, 177
Royal Flying Corps, 179, 193
Royal Air Force, 205, 216, 218, 241
Tank Corps, 198, 210, 213, 218, 241, 273
Royal Artillery—Ubique

*New Zealand Regiments*
Otago Bn, 89-93
Canterbury Bn, 91

*Canadian Regiment*
The Newfoundland Bn, 162

*United States Regiments*
Marine Corps, 197
106th Infantry, 266
131st Infantry, 233
301st (Tank) Bn, 263

*German Regiments*
Kaiser Franz, Kaiser Alexander and Kaiserin Augusta Regts, 250